# HOW TO MAKE MONEY WITH YOUR MICRO

Paradox 7/31/93

# HOW TO MAKE MONEY WITH YOUR MICRO

Herman Holtz

JOHN WILEY & SONS
New York • Chichester • Brisbane • Toronto • Singapore

*Library of Congress Cataloging in Publication Data:*

Holtz, Herman.
   How to make money with your micro.

   Bibliography: p.
   Includes index.
   1. Small business—Data processing.  2. Microcomputers
—Programming.   I. Title.

HF5548.2.H5925   1984      001.64       84-3589
ISBN 0-471-88455-3 (pbk.)

Printed in the United States of America

10 9 8 7 6 5 4 3 2 1

# Preface

*Plus ça change, plus c'est la même chose*
(The more things change, the more they remain the same)

Many modern philosophers and historians have lately become convinced that we are now in the vanguard of another epochal change—an advance—in world civilization, a kind of Industrial Revolution based on the computer. A few American philosopher/economists have advanced the idea that the economic role of the United States is beginning to undergo a critical change from that of leader in heavy industries to that of leader in information industries.

Whatever the outcome, it is abundantly evident that world society is undergoing a fundamental and significant change: fundamental and significant in global terms because the change affects our civilization in both social and economic/industrial aspects. The computer has, indeed, brought about a revolution in commerce and industry, in science, in government, in education, and finally, in the home and family.

Ironically, the Industrial Revolution brought an end (at least a virtual end) to the cottage industries, and the Information Revolution (if I may presume to anticipate history and so title this era) is already beginning to bring cottage industries back, since microelectronics has placed powerful computers within the reach of virtually every individual who wishes to own and operate one.

Before the Industrial Revolution a great many people survived by working in their homes, usually on a piecework basis. A "factory," especially in the textile industries, often consisted of a roster of such workers producing the goods for the industrialist, who had the means of distribution—marketing the products, that is. The Industrial Revolution brought that to an end through the development of steam-powered engines, which were far more efficient than human labor, thus making the cottage-industry scheme of production no longer viable. People began to work in centrally located factories, where the idea of mass production was not yet truly developed, but the seeds were being planted for its emergence.

It is not likely that we shall return to an economy based on cottage industries. Yet there has emerged a somewhat similar situation in which employers have begun to authorize employees to work in their own homes while linked to the employer's central place of business by the worker's own microcomputer and telephone. In effect, the worker's home has become a remote work location, functionally part of the employer's facility during work hours. The worker in this arrangement is neither an independent contractor nor a self-employed freelancer, but a salaried employee, who includes use of the home space and microcomputer as part of the working arrangement with the employer.

How widespread this practice will become remains to be seen. For the moment, it is viable and applicable to certain special cases where the employee works in a computer or data-processing capacity. Whether it will become more widespread as computers become as ubiquitous as typewriters and telephones remains to be seen.

On the other hand, the use of a microcomputer as the focus of and main instrumentality for a home-based business enterprise is expanding rapidly. Many owners of microcomputers are entrepreneurs who have home-based businesses for which a microcomputer is a decided asset. However, there are increasing numbers of microcomputer owners who use their micros specifically as the basis for earning extra income—moonlighting or part-time undertakings.

There has never been a time when individuals did not strike out on their own as independent entrepreneurs of one sort or another. Some simply rebelled at working for others, at what they considered to be regimentation and limited opportunity. Some had visions of becoming successful merchants or industrialists and could not resist taking the risk and venturing forth into enterprises of their own. Some saw or thought they saw a special opportunity that others, perhaps their employers, did not or could not see and were impelled to exploit it.

Not everyone who ventures forth into an enterprise builds a large company or even intends to; many want simply to be independent and self-employed. Some want to supplement regular income from jobs (their own or a spouse's); others want to build a full-time business, although not aiming at building a large company. Most prefer to work from their homes and minimize overhead and investment. This not only keeps their business operations simple but provides them the advantage of keeping their prices down and being highly competitive. This is a boon to marketing, of course.

There are three bases for such ventures. The entrepreneur can base a venture on some personal skill or talent (e.g., carpentry, music, writing, TV repair), on acting as merchant or trader (selling goods or services not requiring special talents), or brokering (acting as middleman to broker services or goods to be supplied by a third party).

The microcomputer will not change this. Quite the contrary, the microcomputer enhances, contributes to, and expands the field of such activities, making its own contributions to entrepreneurship on the small scale as well as on the large one.

The enterprises based on micros range widely. Some are peculiar to computers: for example, the development and marketing of computer games and other software. Many of those who have the creative capabilities for such development have made a great deal of money. Others have devised money-making plans made possible by the computer. Some home-based typists, for example, now offer word processing with its many benefits and advantages over ordinary typing.

These are obvious ideas as are a great many others. That does not make them valueless; many individuals are doing well with enterprises based on these or similar concepts. However, there are many other possibilities, and resourceful entrepreneurs are constantly developing ingenious ideas for new enterprises. In fact, two acknowledged pioneers of the microcomputer revolution were the two youngsters who created what came to be known as the Apple Computer. They were not truly computer engineers. They were computer enthusiasts, one showing a brilliant talent for innovative design ideas, the other an equally brilliant ability to turn dreams into reality. Their achievement was based on two concepts—or, perhaps more accurately, two *visions*.

1.   They perceived that with the new microprocessor and other microminiaturized components—chips—design simplification was possible. It was time for a revolutionary new idea: all the circuitry on a single board.

2.   The market for big computers and what was known as the *mini- computer* (a less expensive computer suitable for medium-sized com- panies that could not afford the big mainframe computers) was so brisk that no one had yet given serious thought to the market potential of a really small and inexpensive computer, a microcomputer. There was a distinct gap in the market waiting to be filled.

They succeeded brilliantly. Their vision was true. There was such a gap in the market, and the public responded with enthusiasm and almost instant acceptance of the personal or home computer. Small businesses also grasped eagerly at something long overdue: the truly small (desktop) business computer.

The opportunities for industrialists were immediately obvious, and many manufacturers leaped on the bandwagon. There are already per- haps 200 different makes and models of microcomputers. Some of the new manufacturers were large companies; some were small ones. Some were companies already established in other lines; some were newly formed to produce and market microcomputers. Some of those already in business were in allied fields such as big computers, electronic type- writers, calculators, and other electronics; some were in totally unre- lated fields. Some turned on R&D (research and development) efforts and produced creative contributions to the microcomputer art; some simply bought off-the-shelf standard components and assembled lack- luster workaday microcomputers.

Very much the same kind of revolution took place in the support industries, those companies that manufactured printers, tape and disk drives, CRT (cathode ray tube) monitors, modems, and other peripheral and support hardware. There rapidly appeared hordes of new suppliers and new makes and models of such equipment.

And again the revolution exhibited itself in the software-support area— those who produce the programs used in the microcomputers. Here there was a pronounced trend toward a large number of smaller entrepreneurs because it is easy to start a software-production business on virtually no investment and even in one's own home. The development work is almost entirely cerebral, the "manufacturing" or production can be in an easily and inexpensively reproduced form such as disks or cassette tapes, and the marketing can be easily conducted from a home base.

But software development and production is not the only new home-business opportunity made possible by the microcomputer. In this book we look over a great many microcomputer-based business ideas. They fall into those same three categories already named: combining one's own special skills and talents, selling ordinary goods and services that do not require special skills or talents, and brokering goods and services sold by others. Some of the ideas are new and ingenious. Some are inventive and innovative, devised by resourceful and imaginative creators. Some are adaptations of sound, older ideas, modified to fit into a microcomputer environment or to take advantage of what the computer can do. Some can serve as the seeds of important new businesses, even make their hard-working users wealthy, whereas others just furnish welcome extra income. The difference between those that grow into large enterprises has little or nothing to do with the basic nature of the enterprise but has to do primarily with the nature of the entrepreneur, what he or she sets out to do and persists in doing. All, however, are sound business plans for anyone who wishes to put them to work.

All are offered as second-income ideas, not as full-time businesses, although there is nothing to prevent the ambitious entrepreneur from turning any of these ideas to account as the basis for a full-time enterprise. One thing that all the plans here have in common is that none require much in the way of capital investment (front-end money). All can be launched on little capital other than that needed for the microcomputer and required software. Presumably you already have the microcomputer, and perhaps the software as well.

In writing this book, the assumption was made that the reader has no business experience. Whether true or not, no harm can result from offering some general business counsel, as these pages do. For although all the basic business ideas are viable ones, any business venture requires that the entrepreneur exercise reasoned business judgment in setting prices, controlling overhead and other expenses, and managing accounts, especially accounts receivable. Although doing enough business at a profitable rate (i.e., at a *gross* profit,) is the key to a successful venture, it is also necessary to exercise such controls that result in the timely collection of all monies due you and to control expenditures so that there are *net* profits. (Some of the largest and most successful corporations occasionally lose sight of these fundamental truths and lose great amounts of money as a result.) You will, therefore, find a generally conservative tone to all recommendations here which reflects much of my own experience in several enterprises, and the sometimes painful and costly lessons learned.

HERMAN HOLTZ

*Silver Spring, Maryland*
*March 1984*

# Contents

# HOW TO MAKE MONEY WITH YOUR MICRO

# Chapter One

---

# The Micro
# Is Not a Toy

There are few works of man less well understood by the lay public
than the computer. The computer is neither a super-calculator
(it's far more than that) nor a giant brain (it's far less than that).
And the microcomputer does the same things its big brothers do.

## LET'S FIRST GET A FEW FACTS STRAIGHT

Microcomputers, whether bought as "personal" or "home" computers,
or for serious business purposes, are not toys, even though some are
used as toys—to play games with. There are a few low-priced machines
that have severely limited functions and can do little except play games.
But they are relatively few in number. Even the Timex/Sinclair ZX81,
listing under $100, has been on sale for as little as $40, and it, too, is
a "serious" computer, despite its size and price. Its limitations are its
small memory (although that is expandable) and its membrane-type
"keyboard." On the other hand, it has remarkable computing power for
such a small and inexpensive model.

The fact is that even the makers of computers originally designed

**1**

principally to play games, such as Atari, have upgraded their computers in various ways, including preparing programs for them and identifying compatible peripheral units that permit the machines to be used for serious computer purposes.

The confusion apparently arises from the fact that what most of us refer to as a computer or microcomputer is a general-purpose computer, which means that it can be programmed to perform many different kinds of things. There are both special-purpose computers and dedicated computers also, and without a clear understanding of what these are—and what they are not, as well—confusion is almost inevitable.

What we refer to as special-purpose computers are computers with fixed programs, programs built permanently into the design. They are, for example, the computers built into electronic cash registers, supermarket checkout scanners that read the codes printed on packages, computers built into the dashboards of many modern automobiles, and other such devices. They are usually part of some larger system, and cannot be modified or reprogrammed without physical design changes, which are usually impractical alternatives.

Dedicated computers are another matter. A dedicated computer is a general-purpose computer that has been assigned for exclusive use in some given application such as word processing or accounting if the word *dedicated* is used in its most literal sense. However, in common usage, a dedicated computer is a general-purpose computer that was designed to excel at some given usage. It can handle other applications, given other programs, but usually at less efficiency than it handles the one for which it was designed to be dedicated.

However, there are certain specific differences between the low-cost home or personal computers and those listed at much higher prices and often used by professional and business people in serious business applications. One major difference is in the way the two classes of computer are physically designed and constructed. One is designed and built for short duty cycles: to be used intermittently, usually for a few hours at a time. The other is designed for long duty cycles: usually for at least eight hours a day, in continuous use. The difference is similar to the difference between the washer-dryer in your home and the one in the corner laundromat; the latter is a heavy-duty model because it gets many times the hours of use the home model does. It must be built to stand up to that kind of use.

Still, computers are by their very nature relatively free of breakdown with the possible exception of the peripherals which have moving parts (such as printers and disk drives). The computer itself, even the less-costly one, is rather reliable, and will tolerate quite a lot of usage.

The point is that, with only rare exceptions, home or personal computers—which are microcomputers—can do everything that any more expensive computer can do, within the limitations of their memories, external storage, and other peripherals. Certainly, most of them can support a small business adequately. Most are more powerful than was the ENIAC (Electronic Numerical Integrator and Calculator) built during World War II at the University of Pennsylvania in Philadelphia, primarily to calculate firing tables for artillery. ENIAC had some 18,000 glowing tubes, blew a few every time it was turned on, and was impracticably ponderous and sprawling. But it lighted the way, and its progeny soon demonstrated that the name *computer* was a shortsighted one, for this machine could do far more than compute. In fact, computation soon became one of its lesser achievements and certainly one of its lesser responsibilities, but the name *computer* has stuck, nevertheless, and we are stuck with it.

## SOME OF THE THINGS COMPUTERS DO

It's quite difficult to sum up in a brief sentence or even a brief paragraph all the things a general-purpose computer can do. It can do all that its common name suggests: it can calculate and perform an almost endless variety of computations, in just about every mathematical discipline known. It can even manage to generate mathematical functions and results that are inherently analogue functions, rather than digital functions, such as sine waves. (However, probing how computers do such things is well beyond the scope of this book.) It can and does do a great many things that have nothing to do with numbers or calculations of any kind, things that bear absolutely no relationship to the literal meaning of the word *computer*. Here are a few of those things.

## Library Systems

Computers are well suited to organize information into data banks and easily accessible indexes and retrieval services. For example, ERIC, the Educational Research Information Clearinghouse, is a computer system in which are stored names and information about most of the research studies and reports concerning education. Inquirers have ready access to the entire library of such documents by enlisting the aid of ERIC in discovering what is in the files and retrieving it. The National Library of Medicine, in Bethesda, Maryland, has an analogous system, MEDLARS, in which is stored a vast library of medical data, readily available for retrieval. There are many, many other systems of this nature in existence, essentially registers of data classified for reference.

## Communications Systems

Using a device called a *modem* (for *modulator–demo*dulator) computers can "talk" to other computers over telephone lines, given compatibility of languages and programs. Thus one computer can "ring up" another computer and request information transfer by telephone. In this manner, the enormous store of information housed in one system, say MEDLARS, that uses one of the big computers can be made available to a microcomputer. A physician can have a microcomputer in his or her office and call on MEDLARS for information. Such systems can also communicate news, stock market reports, and a host of other information, and this application of computers is growing rapidly.

## Business Systems

A huge variety of business systems is managed by computers, from such obvious applications as accounting and payroll to inventory management to progress reporting. Semi-technical functions such as the PERT and CPM (Program Evaluation and Review Technique and Critical Path Method) charting, used widely by engineers, architects, and construction contractors, can be handled by computers, too. The more modern computers and their programs generate a wide variety of plots and charts, and in color as well.

## Word Processing

Word processing is one of the most popular applications of microcomputers and minicomputers, probably because it has such widespread, nearly universal, application. Almost every business firm, other than perhaps the small retail business, can use word processing to turn out correspondence, reports, and an assortment of other such material. Publishers find word processing especially useful for turning out magazines and newsletters, and it's a rare newspaper of any size today that has not taken the reporters' typewriters away and replaced them with word-processing terminals. Many individuals also use word processors in their own homes, especially writers and others who generate a great deal of copy of one kind or another.

## Engineering Applications

A great many modern systems are designed today with the aid of, if not exactly "by," computers. Computer assistance in engineering design of space vehicles and related equipment was commonplace, and probably made much of the space program possible, or at least cut many years off the development time. The Watergate complex in Washington, DC, was an outstanding example of computer design of buildings.

## Scientific Applications

Computers are widely used by scientists today, although admittedly a great deal of this kind of work is mathematical; scientists, especially those engaged in basic research, do a great deal of quantitative analysis, which means calculations of many kinds. Had Albert Einstein had a modern computer available for his calculations he would probably have produced his theories of relativity at a much earlier time, and might have produced a great many other fundamental breakthrough revelations.

## Experimental Applications

There are some applications that have not proved thoroughly practical (at least, not so far) and must, therefore, be considered to be still experimental. One of these is language translation. Much has been done in programming computers to translate from one language to another, but not all the problems have been overcome as yet. Computers still cannot handle idiomatic expressions very well, even if they have complete lexicons of both languages in memory. They generally make literal translations, so that in one frequently cited example a computer spelled out the translation "water goat," which appeared as a totally irrelevant and irrational term. Painstaking investigations revealed that the computer had thus translated the original term *hydraulic ram*. Of course, our familiar idiom "so long" translated literally into another language would never come up as "goodbye" in that other language. The German idiom for "he was at his wit's end" would translate (literally) into English as "then was advice expensive." Therefore, language translation is something that can be computerized on only a limited scale because it involves many judgmental factors, and that—exercising judgment—is beyond the computer's capability.

That is the main key to understanding what a computer can do and cannot do. It cannot do more than its program permits. Its program permits it to "make decisions" only insofar as the human programmer has *anticipated* all the situations and provided preconceived decisions and sets of rules for selecting one of the preconceived decisions. In the case of the translation problems, for example, it might be feasible enough to instruct the computer that when *hydraulic* and *ram* are used together, as in *hydraulic ram*, look up the term, instead of the two words, to find the translation. But how can you instruct the computer to recognize "how are you" as a greeting, rather than as a question?

Do not assume, therefore, that a computer can "do anything," as some naive individuals believe. The computer is extremely versatile, can do *almost* anything that a resourceful human can conceive and plan for, but it still has its limitations. Happily, the limitations are shrinking steadily as the capabilities of the computer expand, and the expansion of computer capabilities is due largely to the chip, that is, to the ultraminiaturization that has been made possible by the chip. Some of the research and development work under way now is likely to produce still greater miniaturization, which is bound to result in further expansion of computer capabilities as computer memories and control circuits expand further. (Memory and control are the two keys to what computers can and cannot do, with memory the usual limiting factor, but control needs expanding exponentially as memory increases.)

## BUT WHAT *IS* A COMPUTER?

We established earlier some things that a computer is and is not in terms of its functions and capabilities: what it does and can do. It is also necessary to come to an understanding of what a computer is in physical terms, in terms of hardware, for example. Here again, the term *computer* is ambiguous and somewhat evasive as a definition of anything. The problem is that it has more than one meaning.

In an earlier time, during the infancy of computers, the term referred to both the entire system and the central unit. That is, there was (as today) a central processing unit, which was a rather large subsystem that was itself sometimes referred to as the *central computer* because it included the *arithmetic* unit that did the actual calculations and mathematical manipulations. This was usually a separately housed unit and it was surrounded by other units of equipment that served it and were served by it, peripheral units. These included printers, card readers, card punches, paper tape (punched tape) units, input/output typewriters, tape drives, and (later) magnetic drums, disk drives, and sometimes even other peripheral machines.

That apparatus referred to as the *central processing unit* or *central computer* was not useful by itself for humans could not communicate with it directly, could neither instruct it and provide input information to it, nor read output information from it without those peripheral devices. That is what those devices were for. In short, a computer was a *system* of devices, central and peripheral, and it is still so today, even when all the devices, central and peripheral, are housed together in a single, integrated configuration within a cabinet of some sort.

Why is it important to understand this and bear it in mind as we progress through these pages? Because even when the computer (system) is not dedicated, its capabilities are defined by the system configuration and by the peripheral units, as well as by the central computer. What you can do with your computer depends on what the system includes. If you want to do word processing, you will certainly have to have a printer of some sort. Even that is not enough, for the type of printer you need will depend on the purpose for which the output is to be used. To put that in another and perhaps more significant way, the ability of your system to generate income for you will depend on what kind of output you can produce.

Even that is not all. The capacity of your system is important. It is not likely that you can handle word processing effectively without a disk drive or two (probably two as a minimum). The effectiveness and efficiency of your word-processing system will depend on the quality of your software. However, the software you can use will depend on the hardware capability. So you can—must—look at this entire situation in two ways:

1.  If you have not yet bought your computer system, you would be wise to consider exactly what you plan to do with it before making your final purchase decisions.
2.  If you already have a system and cannot or do not wish to add to it in any way, you need to confine your income-producing plans to what the system can do as presently constituted.

As we discuss various income-producing plans, this consideration will come up again and again, and its importance will become clearer and clearer. The old saw that "it takes money to make money" is not an absolute truth. It's probably a fact that it's a bit easier to get a money-making enterprise going with substantial front-end capital for investment than it is when there is little or no money for initial investment. But American entrepreneurs have demonstrated many times that enterprising and determined individuals can start with almost nothing and lift themselves by their bootstraps to entrepreneurial success. There is no question but that it is possible. However, there is another way to look at this. You can launch your enterprise in phases, and the first phase may very well be one in which you've no capital for investment, so the objectives of the first phase are to make a beginning, to start acquiring some capital for a second phase. That may mean that you improvise during the first phase until you have the capital to do things properly so you will not have to improvise. It may also mean that you start by doing something other than that which you really want to do, solely for the purpose of developing and accumulating a bit of capital, after which you will abandon the original enterprise and go on to what you've really decided you wish to do. Or you may choose to operate on a most limited scale initially, offering a most limited array of goods or services with the goal of expanding the list later.

In light of all that, regard the various enterprises offered in these pages from that aspect: that if the enterprise that really appeals to you is not within your immediate reach or is not a practical plan for you now, you need not abandon it as a goal, but only postpone your beginning. Look, instead, for something else that will serve you as something to start with. It's a simple fact that many of the most successful enterprises wound up as something far different than their founders originally envisioned. Milton Hershey never started out to become the king of chocolate candy, and Tom Watson certainly did not envision the computer when he founded IBM. The founder of the Greyhound bus company started his career as an automobile dealer, and Elisha Otis was into several ventures before he founded his elevator company. Keep an open mind as you begin, and be prepared to spot and take advantage of opportunities that happen along.

## SOME FUNDAMENTAL FACTS YOU NEED TO RECOGNIZE

When those early behemoths of computing power first appeared on the market, they cost vast sums of money, prices that only the federal government could afford to pay, and for a while it was only the federal government who bought the big computers. They bought them for modern defense systems such as the DEW (Distant Early Warning) line, the offshore radar stations, and the SAGE (Semi-Automatic Ground Environment) system, space programs, missile programs, and other such huge projects. Even as private corporations began to buy computers, only the largest could afford them for many years; the smaller companies turned to something called *service bureaus* to have their payrolls run and to gain other benefits of computers. Service bureaus were organizations that bought or leased computers and provided to smaller companies the services of computers, charging the companies for the time spent on the computer and other costs, but far less than the cost of leasing or buying a computer.

Today, it's only the tiniest of businesses that cannot afford a small microcomputer, but yet not everyone in business wants to own even a small microcomputer despite the benefits. Take the local dentist or doctor, for example. Each can probably use a computer in many ways, but neither wants to take the time to learn how to use it or to run it, and probably most professional people now utilize a service-bureau type of service to handle their small payroll, if they have one, and certainly their billings and follow-up notices on slow-paying accounts as well as a few other services that a computer can provide.

Those who probably do not utilize such a service, but could certainly benefit from one, are the small retail merchants: the druggist, the shoe store, the hardware store, and others. In fact, almost anyone who is self-employed in a profession or business of any kind can benefit from computer services, but not everyone will take the trouble to buy and use a microcomputer. This field alone—the microcomputer service bureau—is largely untapped and is itself a major potential market we'll have a look at.

This and many other ideas you'll read about here are strictly services you can sell with the aid of your micro. There are also products you can sell, that is, products you can yourself create and sell, and we'll have a hard look at these, too. We'll also look at the basic difference between service-based and product-based enterprises. Simply put, they are these. The service-based enterprise is generally easier to launch, requiring less capital and less marketing effort to get off the ground and running. On the other hand, it is usually more limited in its earning potential. Conversely, the product-based enterprise may or may not cost more to launch (will not, in the case of those to be considered here), is usually harder to market, but has much greater profit potential ultimately. These are only general truths and there are many exceptions to them, but they are likely to be significant truths for our purposes here.

## THE VERITIES OF BUSINESS

There are numerous verities in business enterprises, no matter how small the enterprises are, and you should be aware of these. Even the service business, as a foundation, must be divided into those service businesses that require special skills, talents, or training (e.g., writing skills, knowledge of investments and stocks, and musical training) and those that do not require special skills or talent but may be provided by any intelligent individual who is properly equipped and motivated (e.g., billing services, maintaining appointment memoranda, and printing out a shoppers' guide). However, to some extent the computer has modified some of these verities. For example, if you have an accounting program that runs on your computer and happens to satisfy the needs of a number of clients, you do not have to be an accountant to provide accounting services. The computer and, especially, the software program provide the expert knowledge and skill you would otherwise need to handle such work. Therefore, you must bear in mind that for some services (probably for many services, in fact) you do not have to be an expert at anything but running programs on your own computer.

That itself becomes the key to many micro-moonlighting possibilities: find the programs that will run on your system (if you already have the system) and will fill needs that you perceive exist and are business opportunities for you. Or, if you do not yet have your system or plan to expand it, decide what the needs are, find the programs that are right for your purposes, and then buy the system that will run the programs.

One of the oldest pieces of business advice handed out so freely that it has become a platitude is "find a need and fill it." That, supposedly, is a bit of wisdom that will guarantee success. The problem with it is that by itself it is about as helpful as the sardonic advice offered by the late financier, Bernard Baruch, when he was harrassed by eager amateurs who wanted the gain the Rosetta Stone to the stock market. Baruch imparted this bit of eternal wisdom to such aspirants as the key to making money in the stock market: "Buy low and sell high."

The problem with "finding a need," much less "filling" it, is that no one really knows what a need is, let alone how to find one. Everyone needs an automobile today, but relatively few people needed one in 1900. No one needed a Pet Rock until they appeared on the market, but within 90 days enough people discovered such a need to make Pet Rock seller Gary Dahl very successful indeed.

A need is whatever customers decide they want, and the need is itself created by the appearance of something new in the way of a product or service. Even "new" is an evasive term here, for it does not necessarily mean that the item or service has never been available anywhere before; it may mean simply that it has not been readily available before—available within the means of many people or available locally, for example. The average student did not buy one of the new electronic calculators when they first appeared on the market at prices on the order of $300. Today, at prices running below $10, grade-school children have pocket calculators.

Thus when and if you go in quest of needs to be filled as the basis for your enterprise, keep your mind wide open as to the meanings of such words as *need, fill, new, want, available,* and many others. For entrepreneurial purposes, each of these words has more than one meaning.

## TRUE NEEDS

Before leaving the subject, let us probe a bit more deeply into what that word *need* means, for we have not yet exhausted the discussion, and a deeper understanding will be helpful in recognizing business opportunities.

The simple fact is that needs never change: *basic* needs, which are the true needs, have always been the same and, presumably, will always remain the same. Let us consider a few of the needs of years past.

Our grandparents often amused themselves in their homes with a *stereoscope*. This was a device with a pair of lenses and a bracket on which to mount a pair of photographs, called a "stereo pair," which appeared to be identical, but which actually had minute differences in the angle at which they were taken. This, with the lenses that merged the two photos into one, produced a 3-D (three-dimensional) effect, just as 3-D movies do today. You can find these devices in museums and occasionally in an antique shop.

A bit later there was the primitive phonograph or "talking machine," which Tom Edison had invented, and many of these appeared in people's homes, playing the scratchy 78 rpm records.

Still later, radio appeared in the home, with all the great radio shows of the thirties and forties.

Finally, TV became a universal fixture in people's homes, and most people today have more than one TV set. The companion to TV, appearing in more and more homes, is the VCR, videocassette recorder.

Each of these may have been considered to have filled a need: a need for stereoscopes, a need for radio, a need for TV, but all actually filled the same need, a need for home entertainment. And—mark this, for it is the key to the whole thing—each was and is a *better way* to satisfy the need. "Better," that is, in that most people accept it as better, and it tends to eclipse and make obsolete whatever was the previous better way. No one uses stereoscopes today, except perhaps children, who use a special version sold to them as toys. The old-fashioned wind-up phonograph has long since been outmoded by an entire series of improvements including tape recorders and players. (Is anyone aware that wire recorders appeared first and would have been the favored method had not tape recording appeared so soon after and proved superior technically to the original wire recorders?) Leaping to today, a great many people have been all but abandoning both movie houses and broadcast TV and spending more time and money with their treasured VCRs. The latter is obviously a "better" way for a great many people.

New *needs* are, therefore, almost invariably better ways of satisfying basic needs: less costly, more easily available, more satisfying, more intriguing, more convenient, more certain, or more or less of something. Looking for needs to fill means first of all understanding the basic needs of people: needs for love, security, ego gratification, physical comfort, food, and other most basic emotional and physical requirements. Satisfying these needs is what all of us spend all our lives and all our energies at, even when we do not recognize that we are doing so.

There is another level at which to identify these needs, and these identifiers are also the keys to motivating buyers. For example, there is a need for convenience, but that is itself a buying motivator. People patronize "convenience" stores because they can thus avoid the long lines at checkout counters, the long walk from a parking lot to the store, the long trek up and down aisles in cavernous stores, and other *inconveniences*. Astute developers of the new stores obviously recognized these by calling them *convenience stores,* and in so doing also furthered their marketing by reminding customers that convenience was the basic purpose of these stores. It is, in fact, almost a cliché in the sales profession that convenience is a motivator in all things, no matter what you are selling. Therefore, the able salesperson makes it as easy and as convenient as possible for a customer to consummate the order: credit cards, just sign your name, just mail in the postage-paid form, simply call this toll-free number, and so on. The principle is that the easier it is for the customer to place the order, the more likely it is that the customer will place, or agree to, the order. (The latter is still another technique, as in the case of the book clubs where the customer is assumed by the salesperson to have placed the order and must take a positive action to stop the order from being written up and executed.)

Later, we will return to this subject from the viewpoint of how to sell the services or products you have decided to offer, but for now think seriously about these matters as you scan the local horizon for whatever you believe are the most promising needs for you to fill with your micro.

## HOW TO BEGIN "FINDING NEEDS"

The first time I wrote a book for publication by a major publisher it was almost by accident. I was a professional writer, but it had never occurred to me to bend my writing talents to books. After that first book, I began to think about doing it again, and possibly again and again. I struggled with finding an idea for a second book (my first one was about the very field in which I specialized, which was writing proposals for government contracts) for a long time before I came up with a second idea. The third one came a little bit easier and the fourth one easier than that. Today, I have far more ideas for books than I have time in which to write them all. Why? Simply because I began to expose myself to opportunities to get ideas and, probably far more significant, I conditioned my conscious and unconscious mind to be always alert for book ideas.

To find needs you ought to do very much the same thing. You must begin to train yourself to be always alert to possibilities, while at the same time you must expose yourself to information that creates input for your mind to be alert to. You must read, get yourself on many mailing lists, correspond with people, and otherwise keep ideas flowing across your vision and your consciousness. For example, I recently read in one of the popular computer periodicals to which I subscribe (and which I always make time to read) about John Dick, who had created a directory of computer consultants. I wrote to the gentleman and expressed interest in knowing more about his directory (I have also written a successful book about consulting). In his response he included a letter from one of his employees who had useful information for me and whose enterprise is reported later in this book. The results were two valuable inputs for this book, one of them also useful as an input for another book, all because I took the time to read that periodical and write that letter.

I happen to be on many mailing lists and I get á great deal of what many people call "junk mail." I throw a great deal of it away, but I never throw it away before at least glancing at it. If I recognize it as something I already have seen, I may discard it immediately. I also save and read much of it, not because it is of direct interest to me in what it offers, but because it is potentially useful as information or as the seed of an idea for a book or article. Much of this mail is pure advertising, of course, but it also includes many news releases, some of them quite useful. I also receive many sample copies of magazines and newsletters, including some complimentary subscriptions, special bulletins, memoranda, and a variety of other materials. I find it important to take the time to at least make a quick scan of all of this, and keep some of it for more concentrated study.

If you want to get ideas, you can do the same. Here are some ways to get started.

1.   Read, especially periodicals related to your interests. As you read take note of coupons and other offers of information, samples, or other follow-ups to what you have been reading.

2.   Send in coupons and requests for more information, samples, and whatever is offered. Much of it will be disappointing, but every once in a while you will mine pure gold. In the meanwhile you'll be getting on mailing lists. Do not neglect those reader-response cards printed in many publications. Also read the classified advertisements.

3.   Write to people. They don't have to be long, chatty letters, but do stay in touch with those you know and get acquainted, by mail and/ or telephone, with others. You will make lots of friends and get lots of new ideas.

4.   Join organizations: computer clubs, trade associations, professional societies, or whatever is appropriate to what you do and plan to do.

5.    Attend conventions, conferences, and seminars, whatever events you can find that expand your circle of acquaintances and expose you to information and ideas.

6.    Think consciously and deliberately about finding needs, as you do all this. Before long it won't require conscious effort; you'll be doing it unconsciously and you'll soon have more ideas than you can use. Then your problem will change: it will no longer be identifying needs, but of choosing among the many ideas you have to find the ones that appeal most to you and appear to have the greatest chances for success as the basis for part- or full-time business enterprises.

7.    Make yourself familiar with the greatest possible variety of goods and services offered the public in and by all the means and media used for communications. Study catalogues, products on shelves and on display in stores, advertisements in newspapers, and anywhere else you can learn about products and services offered (especially new ones) and determine what the product or service is intended to *do* for the buyer (what *need* it fills), *who* is the selected prospective buyer, *how* the product or service will fill the need, and what *other* and, especially, *better* ways you might be able to think of.

8.    Do not stop when you have finally identified the idea or ideas on which you will base your enterprise, but make this mental set and search a permanent one. Most businesses tend to obsolescence within a few years today—in as little as five years, in fact—and it is essential to keep up with changes if you are to be successful over the long term. It's not even as clear-cut a proposition as the classic one of buggy whips and horseshoes being outdated today because today changes come about more rapidly than ever, and even relatively small changes can make what you are doing as out of date as the Mom-and-Pop corner store or the mechanical adding machine.

9.    Be creative. That, too, is easy to say, as long as one does not have to explain how to be creative. Here are some suggestions that will help you to be creative:

*Courage.*    Don't be afraid to be different, and never mind asking anyone else what they think about your idea. They may ridicule it and so discourage you. Do your research or sounding out of people for their reactions without revealing exactly what your idea is.

*Think Functionally.*   Identify the need in the most precise and objective terms possible, examine all the possible ways to fill that need without regard to how it is now being filled (don't allow yourself to become biased or prejudiced by "how it's always been done"), and try to choose the best way—*best* in terms of advantages to the buyer, that is.

*Think Intensively.*   Consider the problem for as long as you can. Then forget it and go on to other things. Allow the matter to incubate in your subconscious. Eventually, your subconscious will pop up with something. (Inventors and other creative individuals are almost unanimous in reporting this phenomenon as the basic process underlying their creative efforts.)

The biggest barriers to creative thinking are clichés such as "how it's always been done," "it's a known fact," and "they say." If you allow yourself to be influenced by such things, you will always be an imitator and never an innovator. Begin with the conviction that there is *always* a better way possible, for that is a fundamental truth. The transistor was a better way than the vacuum tube in electronics, but the "chip" or *microcircuit* is still better, and one day science will improve on that and make it as obsolete as the vacuum tube has become.

Bear in mind, too, that the best way is almost always the simplest way. Almost anyone can devise a complex solution to a problem or a complex way of filling a need; the genius lies in finding a simple way to do it. Perhaps the greatest invention of the ages, in some ways, is the ordinary paper clip because it is so simple that no one has yet been able to improve upon it or dislodge it from its place over all the years of its existence. Perhaps that contradicts my assertion that there is always a better way, but I am convinced that one day someone will manage to improve even upon the paper clip. Simple solutions that are effective are extremely difficult to improve upon. One way to seek a new business idea is to study products or services that are successful in winning customers but are somewhat complicated. If you can simplify one of these, there is an excellent chance that you have the basis for a successful enterprise. That gentleman who publishes the directory of computer consultants has solved the problem of maintaining a large and expensive inventory by utilizing a fast and effective printing method, laser printing, which enables him to print copies rapidly and in small quantity. This is almost ideal for a directory because it also enables him to keep it up to date by revising it as often as necessary.

Bear this in mind when making offers to prospects, too, or when you are devising services. Your customers do not want their lives complicated further; they want to have their lives simplified. Even if the product or service is somewhat complicated for you, make it simple for the buyer to use and to order. The Quill Corporation, a successful Chicago-area office supplies firm, makes it extremely simple to do business with them by mail. Instead of the typical lengthy credit application most firms ask new customers to make out if they want to open accounts, Quill asks only that a new buyer furnish the name of his or her bank and account number. As soon as that is verified, the account is opened, and Quill ships whatever the customer has ordered, following with an invoice. It apparently works well because the company continues to grow and to prosper. And there is no doubt that customers appreciate the other simplifications Quill offers, such as the ease with which an unwanted shipment may be returned without any requirement for explanations.

Hang the sign over your desk or, at least, on your mental bulletin board:

### KEEP IT SIMPLE

# Chapter Two

---

# Some Ways
# Owners Are
# Making Their
# Micros Pay

Despite the newness of microcomputers and microcomputer-
based enterprises, the oldest and most conservative business
principles—especially those of sales and marketing—are still
dependable guides.

## IT'S STILL A MATTER OF FILLING NEEDS

The rapid growth of home businesses based on micros reflects the
traditional resourcefulness and ingenuity we have long associated with
Americans. A great many of the new micro-based entrepreneurs are in
fairly obvious enterprises: writing and selling software, trading in used
computers, doing contract word processing, and otherwise satisfying

needs in direct and traditional ways. Many have shown even greater creative imagination and have devised more sophisticated business bases, or have been alert to unexpected opportunities and quick to take advantage of them.

One retired Navy man was a model-airplane hobbyist. In the pursuit of his hobby, he began to catalogue model airplane kits and blueprints and before long he had such an extensive listing that a startled friend urged him to market his information. In the meanwhile, the model airplane enthusiast had bought a Commodore PET and taught himself to program it. He managed to develop the software he needed to get his catalogue into computer storage. He keeps the catalogue up to date, has a local printer duplicate his periodic update printouts, and sells copies by mail. His only problem is that he started without a disk drive, and now struggles with a superabundance of tape cassettes on which his data is now stored. He also uses his PET for conventional business purposes to manage his business and keep track of things.

Another man conceived the idea of using the multilevel sales plan to sell micros. (This is the sales method used by Shaklee, Amway, and other such distributors.) He made a deal with Texas Instruments and started work in his garage. In less than three years he has grown into an organization that markets through 20,000 distributors, selling many thousands of computers.

A woman who created a home-based word-processing service made the trials and tribulations of learning how to operate successfully pay off. Once she had the bugs ironed out of her enterprise and it was running successfully, she created a tape-cassette training package, a how-to-do-it course in word processing as a home-based business, revealing all the most minute details. She has marketed the tapes with the same success with which she marketed her original service.

A spare-time magician uses his micro to help dramatize his presentations and give them a distinctive flavor. For example, when he asks someone from the audience to pick a card, he doesn't simply turn up the card or announce what card the individual picked. He causes it to appear on the CRT monitor of his computer, which he has had wheeled on stage!

J. Norman Goode, publisher of the *Micro Moonlighter*, calls his readers' attention to the existence and opportunities represented by a role some call a "system integrator." That's a kind of specialty in which an individual who is already generally expert in computer technology (both hardware and software) researches the needs of a given industry. The integrator develops a design for a carefully integrated system of hardware and software that will best serve the needs of that industry, and then goes about making arrangements with manufacturers and/or other suppliers of the various hardware and software components necessary to make up the system to implement the design.

That makes the integrator an OEM, Original Equipment Manufacturer, although "manufacturing" actually consists of assembling purchased units. However, the assemblage of units is now a computer system of the integrator's own design (i.e., system design) and, in fact, the integrator may sell the system as his own computer under his own trade name. (In fact, this describes what many small computer manufacturers actually do, but the idea is not peculiar to computers.)

In a sense, this is acting as a self-appointed consultant to an entire industry and offering the industry the result as a physical entity. For example, one might design a system for hotel reservations and offer it to the hotel/motel industry, although it might also fit well into other industries in which handling reservations is important such as restaurants and airlines. That is, one need not integrate a system for an industry per se, but might integrate a system for a function widely used in one or more industries.

What makes this a viable idea is that the very complexity of the computer industry in both hardware and software makes it nearly impossible for a buyer to learn enough in ordinary shopping to make a wise purchase. On the other hand, even the retention and expense of a consultant does not ensure a wise purchase. However, if an integrator can assemble a system and build for it a reputation of excellence—or offer an ironclad guarantee of satisfaction—purchasers can be encouraged to pursue this route to buying the right system for their needs.

One man, Eric Balkan, created a newsletter (*The Computer Consultant*), wrote a book (*The Directory of Computer Consultants*), and occasional other items while also writing articles for several publications. He expanded and updated his self-published directory and sold the manuscript to a major book publisher, sold the newsletter, and advised me recently that he is maintaining two databases, continuing to contribute to periodicals, and is working on another book. He is not enthusiastic about self-publishing as an enterprise (although some newsletters and other self-published products have been highly successful) because that was not one of his most successful ventures.

A probable reason for his limited success was the limited effort he put into his self-publishing because he has so many interests. Success depends largely on total dedication to an effort, and the dilution of effort by being involved in several ventures simultaneously is a severe handicap. Your chances for success are generally far better if you select a single enterprise and keep your head turned resolutely away from distractions that would weaken your concentration on the venture. Rarely does any enterprise continue to run successfully by itself, no matter how much of an initial push it gets.

A woman in San Francisco operates what might be called an information brokerage. She does research for clients, seeking out online databases that can provide the desired information as a primary source, but turning also to other information sources when necessary. She makes the observation that one major problem is the difficulty of selling to customers what most of us in the United States have come to think of as free, access to information. Our extensive free public library system, our free TV broadcasts, our many free government services, and other such resources have made the public skeptical that information must be bought. Later discussions of marketing and sales will shed light on how to solve this problem and others like it. Essentially, however, the solution depends on remembering at all times that every successful business enterprise is based on satisfying a need. As a corollary to that, every successful sales and marketing program depends on helping the customer recognize and acknowledge the need.

## WHOSE NEEDS ARE TO BE SATISFIED?

There are many ways to sort and classify entrepreneurial ventures (businesses) and in planning a venture it is usually necessary to sort out and classify the venture or proposed venture along more than one line. One early definition to be established is this. Who are your customers or clients to be?

There are two general classes of customer: individual consumers, buying as individuals to satisfy individual needs, and businesses, buying as business enterprises to satisfy business needs. These may or may not be mutually exclusive, depending on what you offer, but it is essential that you think about this early in your planning. Here, for example, are three kinds of venture, one of which is most suitable if directed to individuals, another most likely to succeed if sold to businesses, and a third which probably would enjoy a market in both areas:

REGISTER of local food markets, public libraries, and other community facilities likely to be of direct interest to newcomers to the community as "welcome wagon" types of services.

REGISTER of consultants and similar specialists available in emergencies to help complete a project or perform other services to business.

REGISTER of speakers and entertainers who can perform at social events and business meetings.

Some of the services you provide as personal needs may be subscribed to by businesspeople for their personal purposes. If you offer a service in which you keep a master file of important dates for each client such as birthdays, anniversaries, appointments, and others, some of your clients may wish you to send their reminders to them at their offices. However, it would be a rare occasion when someone would ask you to provide information on food shopping to their office addresses. Yet for someone with a great deal of creative imagination, this is not necessarily true. Perhaps there is a way to interest businesses, large companies, in such a service. Consider that large companies, especially those dealing in contract services, often find it necessary to launch major hiring (recruitment) campaigns, and this often means recruiting in other cities and persuading prospects to relocate. In such circumstances, companies try to offer as many inducements as possible, and welcome-wagon types of services are among those large companies often provide new employees in such circumstances when the new employee is relocating from another place. Therefore, it is entirely appropriate in some circumstances to approach companies with such services. Nor is it always new hires who are being relocated. Frequently, large companies must relocate their employees to satisfy the requirements of business and in such circumstances are even more helpful in providing many kinds of relocation assistance. In fact, many large corporations have entire "real estate" departments or close ties (contracts) with major real estate firms to help employees sell their old homes and buy new ones or find apartments. Thus the "welcome wagon" service might well be extended to cover lists of apartments for rent and real estate for sale: homes, condominiums, town houses, and other residential property.

This is a special class of service to keep in mind as a possibility when you are trying to find a need to fill. Whereas most products and services are purchased by the consumer who will utilize them and benefit from them directly, there are situations such as the one just described where there is a third party involved who is to gain the benefits, although the third party is not the purchaser. Of course, the purchaser does gain some benefit, or he or she would not be a purchaser, but the direct benefit of the item is not to the purchaser in these cases. The same situation applies when you sell goods or services by means of another party, a dealer or retailer. The dealer is not motivated to buy by what the product or service does for him or her, but by the presumed salability of the item and the profit potential. In marketing, you must bear that in mind. If you sell something through another party who acts as an agent or dealer of some kind, you have two motivations to consider: the motivation of the ultimate buyer (consumer) and that of the agent or dealer through whom you sell.

Consider this as we look over a few other ideas and give some thought to the many applications of some of these systems and their potential buyers. Bear in mind also that a great many people's personal needs parallel business needs, and computer applications for business have analogous applications for personal use. Individuals must file tax returns, as do businesses, and both can use computer assistance. There are also personal applications for computer communication systems, for library systems, for word processing, and for a wide variety of other computer uses. Following is a small sampling of some products and services practicable for most microcomputer systems that serve the needs of individuals and businesses.

## Register/Referral Systems of Consultant/Contract/Part-Time Labor

| | |
|---|---|
| Writers, editors | Window washers |
| Day maids | Handymen |
| Photographers | Illustrators, commercial artists |
| Plumbers | Models |
| Typists | Baby sitters |
| Couriers, messengers | Charter pilots |
| Actors, entertainers | Engineers |
| Nurses | Speakers |
| Bartenders | Gardeners |
| Cooks | Interior decorators |
| Designers | Hairdressers |
| Dressmakers, tailors | Drivers |

## Registration Systems To Establish Readily Accessible Records

| | |
|---|---|
| Credit card numbers | Serial numbers of autos, appliances |
| Jewelry cataloguing | Important dates, milestones |
| Membership lists | Appointments |
| Cataloguing of personal library | Cataloguing of important documents |
| Real estate listings | Customer files |
| Inventory lists | |

Louann Chaudier operates Nichol Publications in Deerfield, Illinois, using a TRS-80 II as her word processor. Recently, she produced a new publication, *The Chicago Area Day Care Guide 1983–84* (see Figure 2.1). She evidently found a need that many people agree wants filling for she reports that "every major Chicago area bookstore agreed to stock the book."

Publisher Chaudier appears to have been fearful that book buyers would find the typewriter-like composition of her word-processor system objectionable, and she is relieved that they have so far raised no objections. Nor is it likely that they will. Even before word processors came into vogue, this kind of typeface and composition, produced by electric typewriters (principally IBM), was widely accepted. In fact, word processing has improved on that composition in its ability to furnish boldface characters and, if desired, provide justified copy (i.e., copy in which the right-hand ends of the lines of type are aligned, as are the left-hand ends). As time goes on, word-processing hardware and software is becoming more sophisticated and will eventually rival formal typesetting for quality and versatility. In the meanwhile, have no fears; a great many successful books have been set with such composition as this and even with less impressive typesetting. Understand this: it is not paper and ink that you are selling here, anyway; it's information. In years of selling many self-published reports, manuals, and similar publications, all "set" by electric typewriter, not once did I get any complaints about the quality of the composition (although there were complaints about typos resulting from my poor proofreading!).

In fact, it is hard to miss with a good directory. These are the "where-to" books that complement the many "how-to" books that are published steadily, and as our society grows more and more complex, it becomes harder to find things. Printing a directory is a simple matter. What is complex and difficult is compiling it: searching out all the individual items, sorting them out to eliminate duplicates (which inevitably creep in and become a problem in compiling a directory), verifying each entry for accuracy, and organizing them into some reasonable pattern based on how users will want to look things up.

The microcomputer can relieve you of most of the drudgery of

**CONCORDIA COLLEGE**
7400 Augusta St.
River Forest, IL 60305
771-8300, Ext. 339

**DIRECTOR:** Shirley K. Morgenthaler, Ph.D., Dept. of Ed. Assoc. Prof.
**CENTER HOURS:** 7 a.m. - 6 p.m.
**YEARS IN BUSINESS:** 8 **STAFF:** 12
**ENROLLMENT:** 55 **MINIMUM AGE:** 2 1/2 Yrs.

| HOURS | COST |
|---|---|
| 7 a.m. - 6 p.m. (Max. 9 Hrs.) | $80/Week |
| Any Five Hours | $50/Week |
| 2 Mornings or 2 Afternoons (September-May) | $425/Annually |
| 9 - 11:30 a.m. (M,W,F) | $635/Annually |
| 5 Aft./Week (Kndg.) | $1107/Annually |

**EXTRA COSTS:** $25 Registration Fee **DISCOUNTS:** 10% For 2 Or More Children; For Low Income Students **ON-SITE KNDG:** Yes For An Extra Charge **NURSE ON DUTY:** Mornings **SPECIAL PROGRAMS:** Summer Outdoor Program **FOOD:** Catered Lunch; Snacks Prepared On Site **SAMPLE LUNCH:** Spaghetti, Carrot & Zucchini Sticks, Ice Cream, Milk **SAMPLE SNACK:** Apple, Peanut Butter, Juice **CLASSROOMS:** 2 1/2 - 5 Yr. Olds **COMBINED AGES:** Two Rms., One For 2 1/2 - 4 Yr. Olds (12 In Rm.), One For 3 - 5 Yr. Olds (18 In Rm.); For Children Enrolled In 2 & 3 Mornings/Week Program Ages 3-5 Are Combined; For The 5 Day Afternoon Schedule Ages 4-6 Are Combined **TEACHER/CHILD RATIO:** 1/8, 1/10 **MAXIMUM PER ROOM:** 18, 12 **PARENTS PROVIDE:** Blanket, Pillow **MISC:** At The Present Time Only Part-Time Hours Are Available, However The Full Day Care Program Is Scheduled To Begin In February, 1984; Expansion Plans Are Set For September Also; Developmental Playground, College Campus Setting, Christian Environment

**CRICKET'S DAY CARE**
209 E. 79th
Chicago, IL 60619
994-7941

**DIRECTOR:** Jean Willis, B.A. Early Childhood
**YEARS IN BUSINESS:** 6 **STAFF:** 7
**ENROLLMENT:** 69 **MINIMUM AGE:** 2 Yrs.

| HOURS | COST |
|---|---|
| 6:30 a.m. - 6 p.m. | $40/Week |
| 6:30 a.m. - 12 p.m. | $20/Week |
| 12 - 6 p.m. | $20/Week |
| After School | $20/Week |
| By The Hour | $5 |

**EXTRA COSTS:** $20 Registration; $5 Extra Per Week For Non Toilet Trained; Some Special Activities Fees **DISCOUNTS:** 20% Annual Payment; 10% For 2 Or More Children **SPECIAL PROGRAMS:** Ballet, Foreign Language, Summer Camp **FOOD:** Prepared On-Site; Snacks Twice Per Day **SAMPLE LUNCH:** Broiled Liver, Mashed Potatoes W/Gravy, Green Beans, Jello, Bread/Butter, Milk **SAMPLE SNACK:** Oranges W/Milk **CLASSROOMS:** Toddlers-5 Yr. Olds **TEACHER/CHILD RATIO:** 1/6 **MAXIMUM PER ROOM:** 12 **PARENTS PROVIDE:** Blankets **MISC:** Excellent Curriculum & Staff

Figure 2.1. Example of privately published directory/register of day care centers.

verifying, screening out duplicates, sorting, merging, organizing, and other such chores. It cannot do the original research; you must do that. It cannot design the final format; you must do that, too, of course. Here are some tips on how to design any directory or guidebook.

The organization of any directory or guide, like the directory of a library system, is only useful if it is geared to how a user will use it. Typically, in a library system, for example, the keywords (words which are the search terms or the words by which a user looks things up) are titles, author's names, and subject. This permits a searcher to look up all the books of a given author, a specific book by title, or all the books on a given subject. The premise on which the system is based is that there will be searchers using each of these approaches, so the system will satisfy the needs of all.

A directory of day care centers would presumably be addressed to those who wish to utilize their services, working mothers, and simple reason suggests that a user would want to find a center close to home if it is to be useful. Therefore, it would seem most reasonable to organize a directory of day care centers by geography, perhaps by zip code numbers.

Perhaps users are interested in other factors such as cost, hours of operation, ability to handle emergencies (such as a mother who is detained and cannot pick up the child at the regular time), and other such matters. There are specific ways to handle this:

1.    If the list for each geographical area is relatively short, it is practicable to simply list all these factors under each heading. The user can then simply scan all the listings under the geographical heading of interest and select the most satisfactory one.

2.    If the listing is a long one, perhaps too long for scanning each item to be a practical method, each list is subdivided by classes: classes of cost, classes of emergency services available, or whatever the other subordinate categories might be.

If you have any doubt in organizing a directory as to how users might want to begin, think out what their goals are and what their beginning information is. A marketer using a directory begins with the knowledge of what he or she wants to sell. The most useful directory listing for him or her is usually one organized by types of items bought. However, since most salespeople have specific territories, that is a consideration too, and geographical subdivisions might be a subordinate search term or keyword. Some salespeople are commissioned to handle certain types of accounts and might prefer a directory organized by kinds of customers. For such reasons, it is often necessary to cross-index directories so that a user can go from one kind of search to another. Here, again, the computer is an invaluable aid in creating the cross-index.

As a rule, directories have a life of their own; that is, they get old and obsolete because things change. Therefore, a directory is generally a periodical, reissued every year or two. Here, again, is where the computer is invaluable: it retains the original directory in magnetic memory (on disks, usually) and lends itself willingly, even eagerly, to updating as new information becomes available to bring the database up to date and print out a new directory.

## SOME SPECIAL DIRECTORIES

Many large organizations have a need for internal directories. The federal government, for example, publishes many telephone directories, usually one for each major agency. Some of them are as large as the telephone directory of a sizable community, the Pentagon telephone directory, for example. These are subject to even more rapid change than are commercial telephone books, and government telephone directories are so notoriously inaccurate that a private publisher in Washington, DC, publishes a government telephone directory that is recognized as being far superior to the government's own directories. In fact, the federal agencies are among this publisher's best customers! Nor is this the only case of a private-sector entrepreneur selling federal agencies a product that improves on the government's own product. There are several Washington-area publishers of federal-job opportunities that are superior to the government's own system of announcing its job openings and, again, the federal agencies are among the most enthusiastic subscribers to the services.

All of these are directory-type publications, produced by computer/ word-processor systems. Aside from the fact that they are directories, by the nature of their organization and purpose there is a more significant aspect to their success: they are *information* and we are more and more an information society. Information is becoming the real coin of civilization and, if we agree with some modern prophets who predict the decline of "smokestack industries," the rise of information industries is becoming the future of America. True or not, there is little doubt that there is a great hunger and a recognized need for information in an increasingly more complex society which threatens to drown those who cannot keep up with the dam-bursting torrent of information. Whether computers are the cause or the consequence of this hunger is moot, but there is no doubt that we are a computer society already and will become more so, until anyone who wishes to even survive, let alone prosper, as a member of our modern society must somehow keep abreast of the flood.

The computer is equal to the task. But the computer is a mindless machine, despite much modern misunderstanding by the lay public and sometimes even by the scientist who ought to know better. Without human resourcefulness, human ability to discriminate and to make judgments, human ability to understand, and human ability to sort and classify, the computer is helpless. It is here that anyone with a micro can deliver valuable goods and services, especially services.

Many housewives, especially in these days of runaway prices, study supermarket advertising, take the coupon values into account, and go on a wide-ranging circuit of several supermarkets to take advantage of all sales, special offers, coupon discounts, and other methods for making their dollars stretch as far as human resourcefulness can make them stretch. Unfortunately, not every housewife has the patience, forbearance, or even plain ability to do this. A Washington-area housewife who was up to this weekly chore recognized this fundamental truth when she launched a weekly shoppers' guide which she produces on her word-processor system. What she does is simply to do what was just described, but document it for others who cannot or are unwilling to do all the study and mental gymnastics necessary to take advantage of

all the special offers. Carol Stegmaier turns out her weekly *Shoppers'*
*Guide* on her word processor every Friday morning after studying all
the Thursday advertising and visiting all the stores that are running the
"unadvertised specials." She then reports to all the other housewives in
her *Guide*, which is sold by subscription to readers.

Many individuals turn out guidebooks of a different kind: guides to
local restaurants, theaters and other entertainment, guides for sightseeing if they happen to live in that kind of place (e.g., New York, Washington, San Francisco), local-history booklets, and other publications
that are addressed to tourists and visitors primarily, but are also useful
to local residents who may not know about many of the restaurants and
local entertainment or sightseeing opportunities. One woman, who
lived in Santa Rosa, California, for example, developed a guidebook to
the Mendocino coast area that was successful enough to be reissued
each year with whatever changes or updates were appropriate. She
managed to get a number of local merchants to be sponsors with $100
contributions, "distributed" (sold) the book through local bookstores,
museums, novelty shops, and by direct mail. She sold out a 5,000-
copy printing of the first edition and ordered 10,000 copies of the
second edition the following year.

A gentleman in the Washington/Maryland area publishes a weekly,
*The Want-Ad*. It primarily lists things people want to sell privately such
as a bed, a vacuum cleaner, an automobile, or a typewriter. The advertiser does not pay for the ad, but pays 10% of whatever he or she gets
for the item. The publisher also publishes a few advertisements by local
businesses for which he charges an advertising rate, but the bulk of his
advertising is on the commission basis. Thus, in a sense, he is not
really in the publishing business, except incidentally, but is a commission broker, since that is how he is paid for providing the "showroom"
and the customer-prospects through distributing his periodical in a
variety of retail stores and newsstands in the local area. In fact, he
started about 20 years ago in the Washington/Maryland area with a
simple, mimeographed sheet that grew into the approximately 200-page
weekly he now publishes, and has expanded his operations to include
editions in Baltimore and several other cities. He has some difficulty in

collecting his commissions in some cases (he operates on the honor system, which includes some hazards), but he obviously manages to operate profitably nevertheless.

There are some other such publications that specialize (he doesn't) by confining their offerings to some individual kind of item such as automobiles or computers offered by their owners for sale. To succeed, such a publication must have a wide enough range of prospects. That is not a problem with any item that has a great many hobbyists or enthusiasts such as is the case with automobiles, microcomputers, and cameras. Some use the same system of working on a commission basis, acting as middlemen-brokers or agents rather than as publishers, whereas others simply charge an insertion fee for the advertisement. Note, however, that even when the publisher works on commission, he or she does not actually handle either the merchandise or the transaction itself, but only brings seller and buyer together. There are pros and cons to each of these ways of operating "want-ad"-type enterprises, which we discuss in greater detail later in these pages.

The secret of success in this kind of enterprise is no great mystery. The publication must attract a large number of readers so that the service is a useful one. Advertisers get results from their WANTED TO BUY and FOR SALE notices. But readers must also find a great enough diversity of offerings to make reading the publication worthwhile.

There are many fields in which such a publication is likely to succeed. In the case of household goods and other items that are bulky and usually sell for relatively small sums, it is impractical to offer the publication outside the local area; most people will not travel hundreds of miles to buy or sell a radio or bicycle.. Automobiles, computers, and some other items are another matter. A buyer might travel hundreds of miles to get a good buy on an automobile that represents an investment of several thousand dollars and perhaps a saving of a thousand dollars or more. Computer equipment sells for high enough prices to be worth shipping charges, and since a seller can identify for-sale items by make and model number, it is possible to transact such sales by mail, telephone, and shipping services.

In some cases it is easy to handle certain transactions entirely by mail. Suppose one of your own hobbies is philately. You might create a barter newsletter or a guide of some sort for your fellow stamp collectors. The product is easy to send by mail, as are also coins and many other collector's items. Any kind of service to hobbyists is likely to be well received if the hobby is a popular one (one with a great many aficionados) and the service you offer is directly linked to the hobby itself. That is, if it is a collector's hobby, the publication ought to be aimed at buying, selling, and trading the item that is collected, although it might also benefit from some text coverage of related subjects. If it is a craft hobby such as lapidary (cutting and polishing precious and semi-precious gem stones), enthusiasts would be interested in stones, tools, methods, books, and perhaps even related services.

## PRODUCT OR SERVICE?

One well-entrenched school of thought in the advertising and marketing professions holds that every business is a service business, no matter what it sells the customer. The rationale for this is that customers don't buy anything for what it is; they buy it for what it does. For example, the seller of automobiles sells the service of transportation. It's a practical approach to marketing and advertising in many ways, not the least of which is that it helps the seller understand buyer psychology. (Of course, transportation is an oversimplification of what the automobile buyer is buying, for automobile buyers are also motivated by appearance, what they think the car will do for their image, the convenience of luxury features, and many other factors that go well beyond the completely practical one of "transportation.") Whether you agree or not that everyone is in a service business, try to agree with the basic premise that everyone who buys anything is motivated by what the purchase is likely to do for him or her. It will be a helpful orientation for getting your enterprise going successfully.

If you should publish a register or directory of available help for different kinds of needs as just suggested, you will offer the buyers a physical product: the printed directory. However, it is not the paper and ink the buyers want or have bought. They have bought a portion of your labor in compiling that directory. They have bought a portion of the risk you have taken in investing your time and money in creating the directory, in advertising it, in printing it, and in whatever other expense you have incurred in placing the directory in the buyer's hands. It is that, not the paper and ink, that you must be paid for.

Again and again, beginners in business make the mistake of reasoning that since the paper and ink costs about 15 cents, and there is perhaps another 15 cents worth of overhead expense, for a total cost of 30 cents, 50 cents is a reasonable price for the item, with a handsome 20-cent profit.

This is nonsense. It is not the way to calculate costs and arrive at a fair selling price. It is the way to fail rapidly in your enterprise.

## SETTING FAIR SELLING PRICES

The problem just presented of selling an item at 50 cents because it apparently costs you 30 cents is fallacious for more than one reason, chief of which is that it is the paper and ink that costs 30 cents, not the directory. We have already established that it is the service that the directory represents, not the paper and ink, that you are selling. You have an *investment* in that directory, and a successful enterprise is one that recovers the entire investment, plus a reasonable return on that investment—a profit.

Suppose you spent 200 hours of your time developing that directory: collecting the information, verifying it, sorting it out, organizing it, and classifying it. Further suppose that you calculate that your time is worth at least $15 per hour. You have an investment of $3000 in your time alone.

Suppose that you have used 80 hours of computer time, and you set the value of your computer time at $20 per hour. (You should charge for the time of the computer; your investment includes whatever the computer has cost you, prorated to cover the time spent in developing this directory.) That's another $1600.

Add to that whatever other incidentals you have had to buy or spend money for (perhaps another $400) and you now have an initial investment of $5000. That has to be prorated somehow into the total costs of your directory.

One way to do that, and perhaps the only really practical way to do it, is to make a reasonable estimate of how many copies of that directory you are likely to be able to sell. You should make that estimate as conservative, as small, as possible. Don't permit yourself to be carried away with enthusiasm and guesstimate sales in hundreds of thousands of copies. It probably won't happen. It is more likely that you'll do well to sell 1000 copies. Even that would represent an investment of $5 per copy in development costs alone. Therefore, your cost is now a more realistic $5.30 per copy. Even that is not all because there are marketing costs. You are not going to sell those 1000 copies without spending some money to make the sales. If you want to be properly conservative about that, increase your original cost figures by about one-half so that your total cost is now about $7.95. Now add a profit figure of perhaps 20 percent, or $1.59, for a total selling price of $9.54.

If you had offered that directory at 50 cents, you would have had to sell over 10,000 copies just to recover your original investment, even if it cost you nothing to sell the 10,000 copies.

Of course, if you can sell more than 1000 copies, you can reduce the selling price proportionately because the per-copy development cost is reduced proportionately. If you can sell these through a network of dealers, you will have to decide on a wholesale price with minimal marketing costs, other than shipping copies to dealers and the bookkeeping involved. For example, you set a list price of $10, and sell it to dealers at sliding discount sales based on the number of copies the dealer buys but the lowest price still returning your investment (based on whatever you assume will be the maximum number of copies sold) with a profit. If you estimate that you can sell 2000 copies in this manner, your per-copy cost is $2.80, giving you a profit if you set the discount schedule at 40, 50, and 60 percent, and reducing your risks because you are not putting much cash into marketing.

Bear that latter in mind in setting prices and profit margins, too. As in gambling—and business ventures are gambles—the payoff ratios should be in proportion to the odds, to the risk, that is. You can afford to work for a smaller profit on low-risk ventures than you can on high-risk ventures.

## ANOTHER KIND OF COMPUTER-BASED SERVICE

We have been looking at several ways of providing a computer-based service through a product such as a guidebook or a buyers and sellers exchange. There are several other ways to use your computer to provide services to individuals and to organizations. For all operations, even the biggest corporations must vend work out, at least occasionally. There are at least three situations in which an organization will vend or contract out some of its work:

1.   All organizations encounter valleys and peaks of activity, times when they are hard-pressed to keep their employees all usefully employed and times when they are so overloaded with work that they cannot really keep up with the workload requirements.
2.   No organization, no matter how big, does everything, and most organizations necessarily contract out some kinds of work.
3.   No organization does everything well or wishes to do everything themselves, and will contract out work if they have an acceptable source of help.

Take the average publications group, for example. A large group keeps typists or word-processor operators busy. When they get too busy, it is impractical to hire additional typists or operators even if they have the spare machines, so they tend then to contract out the overloads if they know of someone who is reliable and does good work. They are generally willing to pay well for such help.

Sometimes the organization is in a schedule bind. It's Thursday, the job is due for delivery Monday, and they realize it won't get done without weekend work. However, they prefer not to pay the heavy overtime burdens or they can't persuade the staff to work that weekend, and contracting out is the only practical solution. If you are always ready to help them out of such binds, you win their gratitude. More importantly, you win their trust and recognition of you as a dependable contractor and they will turn to you for help more and more often.

Sometimes the organization does not normally do a certain kind of work or perhaps cannot do it. Perhaps, for example, you are equipped to print out a variety of graphics (charts, plots, graphs, etc.) and the client is not so equipped. That wins you the work. (Or perhaps the client is equipped, but the operators are still pretty green and not sure they know how to handle special printouts.)

Once you become a known quantity and the client knows that you do quality work, are dependable, and deliver promptly, there are many occasions when the client simply prefers to turn the work over to you as being the easiest way to get the job done at the least possible risk of problems.

Many small enterprises exist almost solely on the overloads that larger organizations turn over to them. The Government Printing Office, for example, vends out to private-sector printers about 70 percent of its work, rather than expand its operations and plant capacity. (GPO now operates five major printing centers, and still contracts out the bulk of the work.)

## GETTING WORK BY REFERRAL

It is not only doctors, dentists, and lawyers who refer clients to others, or to specialists of one kind or another; it's a practice in many businesses to do so. For example, although large print shops often have composition capabilities, few of the smaller shops do. You can usually make arrangements with local printers to refer suitable composition work to you if you are equipped with a suitable printer. You make whatever arrangements you wish: perhaps the printer will want a commission, or perhaps will settle for a mutual exchange in which you refer customers to the print shop as a reciprocal arrangement. As an alternative to this, you might give the printer a price list (the rates you will charge the printer) and perhaps even suggest list prices to be charged the ultimate customer, although it is usually better to let the printer decide about the final, retail price.

It is not only printers with whom you can make such arrangements. One woman in Washington specializes in resumé work, and even there she tends to resumés for law students (of whom there are many in Washington, DC, universities). Consequently, although she gets some of her patronage from advertising in journals read by law students, she gets much of her work by referrals from the university counselors and administrators.

Another resumé specialist gets a good bit of his work by referrals from employment agencies and temporary-help services. He has an "arrangement" with most of them so that both benefit.

Resumés are not the only item that students buy, however. Students will turn to word-processing assistance for term papers, theses, dissertations, and many other documents they are called upon to prepare. Word processing is particularly valuable for theses and dissertations prepared for master's degrees and doctorates. The reason is that almost invariably the graduate student must revise the original submission, and the theses and dissertations are quite long, book-length in many cases. The advantages of having the original stored on a magnetic disk and the subsequent relative ease of revision are argument enough for word processing in preparing these papers.

These have been just a few of the hundreds of specific ways you can put your micro to work profitably: examples of how a few others have done so, essentially. Now let us take a closer look at exactly what to do and how to do it in launching a microcomputer-based enterprise.

# Chapter Three

---

# Word Processing
# As a Business

*Word processing is not a business in itself, but is an excellent base and medium for a business enterprise—for being successfully self-employed, that is.*

## PERHAPS THE MOST POPULAR USE OF MICROS

There is no doubt that word processing is one of the brightest success stories of the modern microcomputer industry. WP, word processing, is one of the most popular uses of micros today. Freelance writers are taking to such systems in increasing numbers despite the almost instinctive fear of the electronic animal, newspapers have about given up their rattling typewriters, and all but the tiniest offices are taking word processing to their breasts. If that were the only use made of the micro it would justify a substantial industry.

Still, despite the popularity of word processing, there are many, many individuals and organizations who do not yet have word-processing systems of their own, but have uses (applications) for word process-

41

ing or at least the items that can be produced most efficiently by word processing. These are among the prospective customers for the home-based word-processing service. These services can be provided to satisfy the needs of both individuals as individual consumers and entrepreneurs as small businesses. This is in addition to handling the overload word-processing work of the organizations, large and small, who have their own word-processing systems but often need to summon outside help or "contract out," as many in the trade put it. There are several ways to classify and organize word-processing services and products: by type of product, by type of service, by type of customer, and/or by type of marketing approach required to sell the product or service successfully. Nor are these considerations isolated from each other; there are interrelationships among them. For example, the kind of service or product you wish to sell with your word-processor capabilities may dictate the kind of customer and kind of marketing or sales effort you need for success. Conversely, the kind of customers you can reach and/or the kind of marketing or sales methods you are comfortable with or think yourself capable of may dictate what you can offer.

For example, if you wish to avoid all face-to-face selling (and some individuals do shrink from direct, personal selling) you may choose services and products you can sell by mail, telephone, through dealers or brokers, or by other impersonal means. That could include guidebooks, directories, resumé services, manuscript typing, and several other things. However, if you wish to go after the larger projects such as helping busy companies out with their overloads of word-processing requirements, it is difficult to land those contracts without face-to-face selling, at least in winning the first contract. (With a good enough job done on your first contract, you may never have to actually sell that client again, but just accept their orders as they have need for help.)

In short, in surveying the kinds of things you can do using a good word-processing system as your base, you can start from either the marketing or sales considerations or from the product or service considerations. That is, you may start by laying out what the marketing prospects and your marketing preferences are, or from what you wish to offer or feel best qualified to offer. Let us discuss each of those separately, for each is as important to success as is the other.

# THE MARKETS FOR WORD-PROCESSING SERVICES OR PRODUCTS

We have already touched on some of the products and services for which the word-processing technology is especially useful, and some of these mentions have themselves indicated the markets. But markets are not marketing, for the most bullish and profitable market is of no use to you if you cannot reach it and sell in it successfully. For example, take that market of supporting companies in handling some of their overload work. If you are located in a place many, many hundreds of miles from any company who needs help with overloads, you cannot do this work; by its nature, this service requires proximity to the client.

On the other hand, there are some kinds of word processing that do not require that proximity. Therefore, the accident of where you happen to be physically located, your access to certain markets and the nature of the markets to which you can gain access, may dictate your direction. Here are some of the several factors you should consider (must consider, actually) in reaching decisions.

1.   Your personal preferences: the work you prefer to do or feel yourself most qualified to do (e.g., special skills and talents you have), the kinds of customers you want to do business with (e.g., individuals versus companies), the kind of selling that is required or possible (e.g., face-to-face versus by mail or through third party brokers or agents).

2.   The markets available: what kinds of potential customers you have in your local area, problems and/or special advantages you have in reaching them, any special considerations such as a ready-made market of some kind.

3.   Special factors that dictate or strongly guide your initial decisions such as a guarantee of work from a former employer or a contract available immediately from some organization.

Many people launch home-based enterprises on the basis of an offer tendered in advance by a contact, even by an employer, who guarantees work. Approaching a former employer is an excellent and time-honored marketing ploy, especially in initiating an enterprise. If you have been doing word processing for an employer, it is good marketing to approach that employer or former employer with an explanation that you plan to launch or have already launched a word-processing enterprise and solicit that employer's business. Surprisingly often you will be rewarded with a first contract.

## QUICK-RESPONSE CONTRACTS AND SUBCONTRACTS

One situation that compels organizations to seek outside help in doing their work (in contracting out) is schedule pressure. Again and again, organizations find themselves unable to meet an important deadline or promised delivery date unless they get some extra help. In a great many cases, they do not realize this or at least they do not make the decision to contract out until the deadline is difficult for even the outside contractor to meet.

This kind of situation is so common that a name has become attached to the kind of support work needed. It is called "quick-response" or "quick-reaction" service, for obvious reasons. There are firms who specialize in this kind of service and they charge accordingly. When clients are in need of quick-response service, they are often quite desperate and are willing to pay for the premium time (evenings, weekends, and holidays) often necessary to get the job done.

Therefore, if you are in a position to solicit quick-response work in word processing (if there are prospects for such work in your locality) and you are willing to sacrifice what might otherwise be your leisure hours to earn the top prices you can command for such work, you may wish to consider specializing in quick-response word-processing service. If there are enough prospective clients in your area, sometimes all it takes to get this work is a mailing of sales letters and brochures that make your offer of quick-response word processing plain enough. (Of course, that does not mean that you do not also accept normal word-processing work on a normal schedule.)

Typical clients for such work are organizations: companies, associations, and other organizations who do a sizable amount of such work normally. High-technology companies, for example, such as aerospace, electronic, software, and other contractors to the government usually have substantial technical manuals requirements, but they also write many proposals and reports, and they often have deadline and schedule problems. Such companies are prime prospects for such work.

There are also many small to medium size companies in these fields, especially in electronics and electronics-related fields, and these are perhaps the best prospects for such work. For one thing, they usually do not have full-time publications departments because of their size; they are not big enough to have on-going publications requirements that would justify a full-time publications group. Therefore, they generally use some combination of contracting out and in-house help to turn out a proposal, a report, or a manual.

This is not to say that every such company writes proposals and does government contract work, although quite a large percentage of these companies do, and many do almost all their business this way. However, even those who do little or no contract work have occasional needs they can't handle in-house. Even for their purely commercial products they have to write customer instructions, specification sheets, catalogue sheets, and other papers, and they often have need of help in turning out this work.

In pursuing and soliciting such work, bear in mind that even in relatively small companies (and this includes companies with several hundred employees) the departmental and functional division of the company tends to isolate one group from another, and it is important to understand this if you are to sell successfully to these companies.


## TYPICAL COMPANY ORGANIZATION

A typical company is organized into departments or divisions, generally including the following functional organizations in the company, by whatever names they may be known (not necessarily the generic ones suggested here) and not necessarily including all the departments suggested here, since some kinds of companies would not have some of these departments. For example, a software developer would not normally have an engineering department, and a manufacturing company would be likely to have both engineering and production, but many engineering companies do not do production work. You have to determine, for each company you prospect, which of the following are relevant:

Marketing.

Sales.

Engineering.

Production.

Accounting.

Purchasing.

Public Relations.

Advertising.

Publications.

Proposals.

In practice, many companies combine some of these functions. Marketing, for example, might include advertising, public relations, and proposal writing. However, the latter, proposal writing, might be part of the publications department. Whether a company has a purchasing department depends primarily on whether they do enough purchasing to justify a special department (which may be only a single manager with, possibly, a secretary or clerk). If they are a manufacturing firm, for example, they probably do enough buying to require a purchasing manager (also called *purchasing agent* or *buyer*, depending on the company). Otherwise, the company does its buying either by having an administrator who acts as a part-time purchasing agent or by having individual managers do their own buying. (Sometimes, in small companies, the company comptroller wears several hats as comptroller, chief accountant, general administrator, purchasing agent, and general factotum.) In any case, it is not only helpful, but is often absolutely essential to have a general picture of company organization if you are to market effectively to the company. For example, in one company engineering may be responsible for turning out the technical manuals, whereas in another company there is a publications manager (not necessarily a publications department) who sees to all necessary arrangements for getting manuals produced. At the same time, the publications manager may be the wrong person to approach with offers of help in proposal writing, which is most often (but not always) the direct responsibility of the marketing manager, who may or may not have a proposal manager reporting to him or her.

As you can see, it is not a simple matter to draw up a set of rules. However, Figure 3.1 suggests some general guidelines to help you in this respect. As you can see from this figure, the kinds of work you can help with—the kinds of work an organization is most likely to need help with—can fall into different departments or under different managers in different companies. In a few moments, we discuss how to go about finding out what the company organization is and who is responsible for contracting out the kinds of work in which you are interested. Take note that even in companies that have full-time purchasing agents it does not always follow that all contracting is let by means of the purchasing agent, nor that the purchasing agent is even asked to help locate a contractor. In fact, it does not always occur to the people who are responsible for a proposal or manual that they should go seeking outside help, and surprisingly often managers do not even know that there are outside contractors who can gallop to the rescue. (In my own work as a proposal-writing consultant, I run into many clients who do not know that there is such a consultant/contractor, and who have learned of me only through having come across or heard of one of my books.) That illustrates the importance of letting people know of your existence and function.

Figure 3.2 illustrates this from another perspective, that of functional flow of the main functions and phases of work in high-technology contracting organizations. The boxes in the figure drawn with the document symbol identify the outputs of most direct concern to you, those which organizations often need to help with and will contract out often if the contractor makes an attractive enough offer of help.

| Department/Manager | Usual Functions and Responsibilities | Remarks |
|---|---|---|
| Marketing | Proposals, specification sheets, sales literature, catalogues, advertising copy, news releases | May have subordinate managers for some of these areas |
| Engineering | Technical information: manuals, user instructions, maintenance data, inputs to marketing, publications | May or may not have prime responsibility for technical manuals |
| Publications | Manuals, proposals/proposal support, other literature, materials | Usually charged with support in proposals |
| Public Relations | News releases, advertising copy or certain kinds of it, press kits, other materials publicizing the organization, in-house publications such as company newsletters | May work closely with marketing, other departments, and may be second function of marketing or publications |
| Purchasing | Purchase of raw materials, parts and components, various supplies and services | May be used to buy special services or merely to administer such purchases |
| Proposals | Bids and proposals | In companies writing proposals frequently |
| Sales | Actually getting orders, but may include proposal writing | May be part of marketing or may be separate department |
| Production | Manufacturing whatever product of company is; generally does little or no work requiring WP | Mostly blue-collar functions |

**Figure 3.1.** Typical company departments and managers, and their functions.

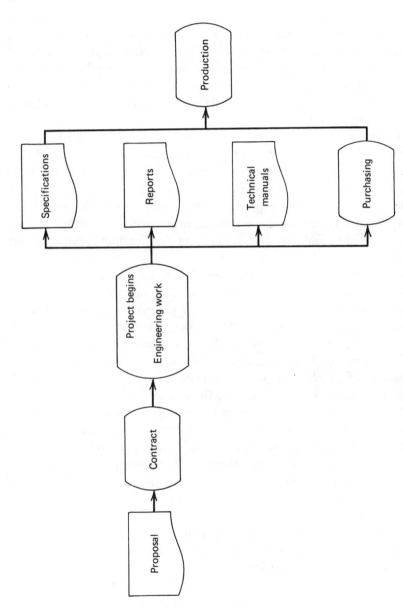

**Figure 3.2.** Typical major functions and phases in technological projects.

The first box is the proposal-writing stage, almost invariably a frantic effort in most companies. That is, it almost always winds up as a frantic, last-minute effort because the time schedule is always a difficult one, and the closer the organization comes to the deadline, the more apparent it becomes that they do not have enough time to do what has to be done. Most companies are likely to be receptive to offers of help in such situations.

The contract award that follows the submittal of a successful proposal is the start of a project that often involves initial engineering, design work, resulting in a set of specifications. This can be a voluminous document, listing the many parts, raw materials, and components required, as well as special parts, machine tools, assembly procedures, maintenance requirements, and many other items. All of this must be documented formally, and often produces a rather thick, bound volume of its own. Much of this is input to the purchasing function since it lists the parts and materials that must be bought to start production.

In the meanwhile engineering generally must produce a series of reports, including a final report, which probably includes that set of specifications. At some point, after engineering work is complete, technical manuals have to be produced for the customer.

Therefore, as the figure suggests, there are at least four places in this sequence of events and phases of work at which a company might welcome outside help to produce written materials.

Of course, not all the companies and other business organizations that are suitable prospects for your word-processing services are engineering and manufacturing firms, and so do not correspond even roughly with the figure. For example, there are engineering firms who do no manufacturing, but produce prototypes or models for the customer, who undertakes to have manufacturing done elsewhere. However, along with the model or prototype, the company produces and delivers all the paper shown, specifications, manuals, and reports (as well as drawings, which have not been mentioned because they do not normally concern those engaged in word processing).

Sometimes there is no engineering work involved, but only manufacturing to an existing set of drawings and specifications. In such case, there is probably only the proposal itself as a business prospect for the word-processing service, but that happens to be the best prospect for the service because that is the place customers most often are in trouble and need help desperately.

There are also companies who handle no hardware or engineering at all, but do studies of various kinds. These companies must write proposals if they are after contract work, and their projects generally require reports, sometimes manuals. These are usually consulting firms of some kind, often describing themselves as management consultants.

There are, in fact, a great many firms whose work entails only "soft goods"—reports, manuals, drawings, computer programs, training programs, and other such items—and who are, therefore, not truly "industrial" firms, but who nevertheless are good prospects for you because they do write proposals, manuals, reports, and other papers. Together, if there is a population of such organizations in your area, they constitute an excellent market for you.

However, do not confine your attention to for-profit companies only, for there are often nonprofit organizations who make excellent customers. These would include: various associations, professional societies, and business organizations; colleges and universities; federal, state, and local government bureaus and agencies; labor unions; sundry other groups. In fact, some of these groups such as unions, universities, and business associations undertake contract work also as a means of producing revenue and constitute the same kind of business prospects for you as do the for-profit companies.


## HOW TO DISCOVER WHAT THE LOCAL MARKET INCLUDES

A first problem for you is research, finding out what companies and other organizations of interest—potential clients—are in the local area. Depending on several factors, there are different ways of going about compiling a list of prospective customers. Here are several of the ways of going about the research in your own locality.

## Local Yellow Pages

The Yellow Pages may be of some help, especially if your local Yellow Pages directory is small enough to enable you to research it thoroughly. This would be impractical in many locations, however, and is suggested only where it is not impracticably difficult to do.

## Local Chamber of Commerce

In many localities, especially those so busy and large that the Yellow Pages is too thick to survey, the local chamber of commerce will either have its own compilation of local industries or can direct you to one or more sources.

## Local Business Clubs

The local chapters of the Lions' Club, Rotary, or other business club may be able to help you find all the local industries and suitable organizations.

## State Chamber of Commerce

Where local governments do not have industrial directories, state governments often do. Hunt up suitable state agencies in your telephone directory such as a chamber of commerce, and see what they can do to help you.

## Local Library

Consult your local librarian. Librarians are usually quite knowledgeable about what is in their stacks, and usually helpful in directing you to or finding for you exactly what you need.

## Biggest Local Bookstore

The exact information you want may be on the bookstore shelves. Check, but check with the biggest bookstore.

## Databases

If you subscribe to a database such as The Source, check with this too for possible input.

## Mailing List Brokers

You may be able to rent a mailing list from one of the brokers listing the kinds of organizations that interest you in the locations that interest you.

## Help-Wanted Advertising

Scan the help-wanted advertisements, both in the local newspapers and in several other large newspapers that companies tend to use for the purpose (*New York Times, Wall Street Journal, Washington Post,* and major newspapers of several other major cities, such as Philadelphia, Los Angeles, Chicago, and San Francisco). You'll learn about the existence of many local organizations this way.

## Local Colleges and Universities

Local universities tend to be familiar with most local employers, especially since most have services to help students find jobs.

## The Financial Pages

Read the financial pages of the newspapers previously cited as well as their help-wanted advertising, and you will find some of the local organizations.

Among all these sources, you will identify most, if not all, suitable prospects in your service area, and you will learn, in most cases, approximately what their major business activities are and with whom they do business, to whom they sell their goods or services. From this you can infer a great deal about how they are organized and what kinds of work they do, relevant to your own interests.

There is at least one special source of information on those organizations that do contract work with federal agencies. It's a government publication, the *Commerce Business Daily*, which the government publishes five days a week (every normal business day of the year), and it lists government requirements, contract opportunities, and contract awards. It's fairly expensive ($100 a year, at this writing), although it is possible to get a six-month trial subscription. If you are interested in pursuing government contracts which are a possible source of business, the *CBD*, as it is commonly referred to, is a must. If you want it only to check the awards section to identify government contractors in your own area, it is not necessary to subscribe. You can usually see copies at local government offices (e.g., those of the Small Business Administration, Commerce Department, or General Services Administration) and often at well-stocked public libraries. However, the federal government is a rich source of potential business and merits some special discussion. Overall, it is a market that spends over $150 billion annually for goods and services in the private sector.

## THE FEDERAL GOVERNMENT MARKET

The Government of the United States consists today of roughly 75 departments and other bureaus and agencies, plus a large number of special commissions and boards. Many of these agencies of the government have regional offices (usually 10) situated in each of the federal government's officially designated 10 federal regions. Some, such as the Small Business Administration and the Department of Commerce, have many offices, 100 or more each; and some, such as the Department of Agriculture, have many bureaus, each of which has its own network of offices scattered throughout the United States and its possessions, and even in many foreign locations.

The net result is an enormous number of federal office locations and other facilities such as military bases, veterans hospitals, and supply centers that amount to many thousands of purchasing offices. (There are, in fact, over 130,000 federal employees dedicated full-time to purchasing activities, although there are probably as many more who request the purchases that keep the 130,000 busy and who must be consulted frequently in connection with the purchases.) There is even a special training institute dedicated to training procurement specialists, in addition to the long-standing training courses of the Office of Personnel Management (formerly the Civil Service Commission) who have long trained clerical and support personnel in procurement functions.

It should come as no great surprise, then, that these agencies make literally millions of purchases of supplies, equipment, and services each year, and they buy these things from huge super-corporations, from ordinary corporations, from small and medium size businesses, and even from freelancing, one-person entrepreneurs. You can sell to the federal government if you wish to, for there are hardly any goods or services you can think of that some federal agency does not buy, and there is virtually no limit, upper or lower, to the size of the purchases federal agencies make, from a few dollars to billions of dollars. Whatever you do, and in whatever volume or quantity you are capable of doing it, you can find at least a few federal government customers for it.


## THE PROS AND CONS OF FEDERAL GOVERNMENT BUSINESS

There are those who will not do business with our government, sometimes for excellent reasons, sometimes for the poorest of reasons. Frequently, those poorest of reasons are a belief in myths, stories about the government that are simply untrue. That is, they are usually 99 percent untrue, for a myth is almost always a gross distortion of a truth, pure hyperbole, all too often. For example, one hears a horror story about someone selling to the government and having a great deal of trouble getting paid. Without ascertaining the cause of the problem (and it may be the seller's own fault and often is, when there are problems in getting paid) protesters begin to shriek that the government *never* pays promptly, and that it is always a struggle to get paid by a government agency. Frankly, as one who has done much government business, I admit that there are a few problems, but many respectable major corporations have been far slower in paying me than have government agencies. In fact, only once did I have real difficulty in getting paid by the government, but that is because I did more than grouse when the government did not pay me promptly: I took suitable follow-up measures, which got me paid shortly thereafter. I will admit, however, that I did have to take those special measures more often than I should have had to.

The government agencies are usually difficult to deal with. Not because it is the government per se, but because it is a bureaucracy. Sometimes private-sector corporations are just as bad.

However, it is usually pretty impersonal, dealing with a government agency, and you can complain, yell, scream, and harrass them into action without arousing personal resentment or getting yourself "black-balled" from further work, whereas it is difficult to do that with a private-sector customer.

If you are handling small jobs under $10,000, as a rule you can do business rather informally (by simple purchase order) and you can get a decent price for your work. It is possible, if you are alert and handle yourself well, to persuade the agency personnel to approve prices that compensate you for the extra trouble that dealing with bureaucracy puts you to.

There is some red tape, paperwork, but it's really not nearly as bad as the mythology makes it out to be, especially if you are a small business, which exempts you from much of the worst paperwork problems. Moreover, you can get at least some help from the Small Business Administration.

You can get progress payments. You don't have to wait until the job is finished to start billing and getting paid for your work. As a small business, you have a legal statutory right to progress payments, and a contracting officer will not object to monthly billings and even to biweekly billings, on a long-term job.

There are, in general, statutory considerations: Federal bureaucrats can't arbitrarily give the job to whomever they please, but must abide by the rules laid down in the procurement regulations, which have the force of federal law, are federal law, in fact.

The only way to arrive at a sensible decision about doing government work is to try it and see if you like it. That's the best test. Some quarter-million companies in the United States do business regularly with the federal government, and many do little or no business elsewhere. Like it or not, it's too big to ignore.

## HOW GOVERNMENT PROCUREMENT WORKS

Space here does not permit a complete description of how the government's procurement system works, and it has been thoroughly documented elsewhere (see Reference Data, Chapter 14). This is a brief review to give you the general idea.

Government agencies buy by two basic methods: "advertised" procurement and "negotiated" procurement. Both are competitive, as the law requires (although a large proportion of federal procurement is by means of noncompetitive negotiated methods, authorized as exceptions to the law), but *advertised* procurement is price competitive and *negotiated* procurement is basically competitive in a totally different sense.

In advertised procurement, bidders submit prices as sealed bids, which are opened publicly, read aloud, and contracts awarded to the low bidders. Negotiated procurement requires that bidders submit proposals, and the government reviews and evaluates them to decide which is the best proposal, with price a factor but not usually the most important factor. The government then selects a winner and awards a contract. However, the government may select several of the best proposals and conduct negotiations with the authors of all the best proposals until they reach a decision and make an award.

The difference is simple, in principle. When buying some commodity that can be specified in great detail, which will not differ significantly, no matter who provides the goods or service, price is the only important difference, and so the advertised method is used to buy shoes, canned goods, nuts and bolts, trash removal, construction, and numerous other things. However, when the government wants a training program written, a new airplane designed, a study made, or some other work or product that must be custom designed and cannot be specified in detail, the qualifications and plans of the bidder must be considered, and so proposals are requested under the statutes governing negotiated procurement, and a study of the bidders' qualifications is made.

In this, each bidder is generally evaluated for the following general things:

1. Understanding of the requirement and quality of the proposed project.
2. Estimated probability of success using the proposed project.
3. Proposer's experience, facilities, and resources as an organization or enterprise.
4. Qualifications of proposer's staff, as individual(s).
5. Price.

This is based on what the proposer says in his or her proposal, which the proposer swears is factual as far as reporting qualifications and resources. (There are penalties for making false statements deliberately in a proposal.) That is, the award is made largely on the basis of what the proposal says, although there is also some follow-up investigation such as checking references, sometimes visiting the proposer's facility to verify the resources and capability to do the job (an office in a private home is perfectly acceptable, as long as the capability to do the job there is demonstrated).

To demonstrate that it is a fact that an individual can win government contracts, I can cite at least 40 to 50 that I have personally won as an individual to write various things for government agencies and to deliver a few seminars as well.

There is a government Standard Form 129 which you can get from any government contracting office in person or by mail, that will place your name on a bidders list. In that form you describe what you offer to do, and you mail out a copy of it to each government office by which you want to be listed. They will then send you invitations to bid and write proposals as they have requirements that match what you offer to provide. In fact, you make up a single copy of this one-page form, make a generous supply of copies, and send one to each government contracting office as you learn of the ones you believe will have work for you from time to time.

You should subscribe to that *CBD* mentioned earlier, and scan it daily for opportunities. Whenever you spot a government office with a suitable requirement—they synopsize the requirements with a general description (see Figure 3.3 for examples) —you call or write for a copy

T--**MAILING SERVICES FOR ALASKA**—Contractor will be rquired to maintain various mailing lists from a total population of 750-1000 names, mail publications on periodic basis, and provide pick-up and delivery service to the Deputy Federal Inspector (Alaska) in Anchorage, Alaska. Solicitation OFI-81-0009 is planned to be issued on or about October 1, 1981. Requests must be in writing. (259)
    **Office of the Federal Inspector for the Alaska Natural Gas Transportation System, Contracts Management Division - Attn: T. Griggs, 2302 Martin Drive, 1st Floor, Irvine, CA 92715**

★ T--**MAILING SERVICES**, Modification to Contract No. 53-3A94-1-03. Negotiations conducted with the D.C. Association for Retarded Citizens, Washington, DC 20011 to continue providing services for fiscal year 1982. Sol. FSIS-6-W-81 See note 46. (274)
    **USDA, Food Safety and Inspection Service, Administrative Services Division, Room 0136, South Building, 12th and Independence Avenue, Southwest, Washington, DC 20250**

U--**CONDUCT COURSES ON DIGITAL EQUIPMENT** at NCBC Port Hueme, CA and Gulfport, MS, on PDP-1123 Minilomputers and peripherals—Deliver to Port Hueneme, CA—Schedule No. N00123-82-R-0289—Code CDB-30C. (299)
    **Bid Desk, Naval Regional Contracting office, Bldg 53, Terminal Island, Long Beach, CA 90822 213/547-6410**

T--**TO PERFORM PAGE MAKE-UP FOR PUBLICATION BY USING COMPUTER PRINTOUTS.** Page make-ups shall be IAW NRC specifications. Performance shall be from date of award through 30 Sep 82. All interested firms should submit their written requests to U.S. Nuclear Regulatory Commission, Division of Contracts, Attn: Lynne Martin, IFB No. ADM-82-365, Washington, DC 20555. Telephonic requests will not be accepted. Copies of the solicitation will be available O/A 30 Oct 81. (299)
    **U.S. Nuclear Regulatory Commission, Division of Contracts, Washington, DC 20555**

★ T--**PREPARATION OF CHANGES TO TECHNICAL MANUALS FOR THE T700-GE-700 ENGINES**—IAW the statement of work (SOW) and DD 1423 contract data requirements list (CDRL) attached to the solicitation, RFQ No. DAAJ09-82-Q-A088, due date 31 Nov 81. This proposed procurement is to be awarded sole source to General Electric Co, Aircraft Engine Group, 1000 Western Ave, Lynn, MA 01910. See notes 27, 40, -46 and 73.
    **US Army Troop Support and Aviation Materiel Readiness Command, 4300 Goodfellow Blvd. St. Louis, MO 63120 314-263-3229**

T--**CORRECTION: WRITING, EDITING, MANUSCRIPT PREPARATION, AND RELATED SUPPORT SERVICES FOR PRODUCTION OF PUBLICAITONS.** DELETE the requirement that bidders must be located within a 20-mile radius from the USDA Forest Service, 12th & Independence Ave., SW, Washington, DC. RFP-85-81. Closing date is September 30, 1981. (257)
    **USDA, Forest Service, AS, Room 707 RP-E P.O. Box 2417, Washington, DC 20013**

**Figure 3.3.** Some typical CBD synopses.

| BIDDER'S MAILING LIST APPLICATION | INITIAL APPLICATION | | FORM APPROVED OMB NO. |
|---|---|---|---|
| | REVISION | | 29–R0069 |

Fill in all spaces. Insert "NA" in blocks not applicable. Type or print all entries. See reverse for instructions.

| TO (*Enter name and address of Federal agency to which form is submitted. Include ZIP Code*) | DATE |
|---|---|
| | |

| 1. APPLICANT'S NAME AND ADDRESS (*Include county and ZIP Code*) | 2. ADDRESS (*Include county and ZIP Code*) TO WHICH SOLICITATIONS ARE TO BE MAILED (*If different from item 1*) |
|---|---|
| | |

| 3. | TYPE OF ORGANIZATION (*Check one*) | | | 4. HOW LONG IN PRESENT BUSINESS |
|---|---|---|---|---|
| | INDIVIDUAL | PARTNERSHIP | NON-PROFIT ORGANIZATION | |
| | CORPORATION, INCORPORATED UNDER THE LAWS OF THE STATE OF | | | |

| 5. | NAMES OF OFFICERS, OWNERS, OR PARTNERS | |
|---|---|---|
| PRESIDENT | VICE PRESIDENT | SECRETARY |
| TREASURER | OWNERS OR PARTNERS | |

6. AFFILIATES OF APPLICANT (*Names, locations and nature of affiliation. See definition on reverse*)

| 7. PERSONS AUTHORIZED TO SIGN BIDS, OFFERS, AND CONTRACTS IN YOUR NAME (*Indicate if agent*) | | |
|---|---|---|
| NAME | OFFICIAL CAPACITY | TEL. NO. (*Incl. area code*) |
| | | |
| | | |
| | | |

8. IDENTIFY EQUIPMENT, SUPPLIES, MATERIALS, AND/OR SERVICES ON WHICH YOU DESIRE TO BID (*See attached Federal agency's supplemental listing and instructions, if any*)

| 9. | TYPE OF OWNERSHIP (*See definitions on reverse*) | |
|---|---|---|
| | MINORITY BUSINESS ENTERPRISE | OTHER THAN MINORITY BUSINESS ENTERPRISE |

| 10. | TYPE OF BUSINESS (*See definitions on reverse*) | |
|---|---|---|
| | MANUFACTURER OR PRODUCER | REGULAR DEALER (*Type 1*) | REGULAR DEALER (*Type 2*) |
| | SERVICE ESTABLISHMENT | CONSTRUCTION CONCERN | RESEARCH AND DEVELOPMENT FIRM |
| | ☐ SURPLUS DEALER (*Check this box if you are also a dealer in surplus goods*) | | |

| 11. | SIZE OF BUSINESS (*See definitions on reverse*) | |
|---|---|---|
| | SMALL BUSINESS CONCERN* | OTHER THAN SMALL BUSINESS CONCERN |
| *If you are a small business concern, fill in (a) and (b): | (a) AVERAGE NUMBER OF EMPLOYEES (*Including affiliates*) FOR FOUR PRECEDING CALENDAR QUARTERS | (b) AVERAGE ANNUAL SALES OR RECEIPTS FOR PRECEDING THREE FISCAL YEARS |

| 12. | FLOOR SPACE (*Square feet*) | 13. | NET WORTH | |
|---|---|---|---|---|
| MANUFACTURING | WAREHOUSE | DATE | AMOUNT | |

| 14. | SECURITY CLEARANCE (*If applicable, check highest clearance authorized*) | | | |
|---|---|---|---|---|
| FOR | TOP SECRET | SECRET | CONFIDENTIAL | NAMES OF AGENCIES WHICH GRANTED SECURITY CLEARANCES (*Include dates*) |
| KEY PERSONNEL | | | | |
| PLANT ONLY | | | | |

| THIS SPACE FOR USE BY THE GOVERNMENT | CERTIFICATION |
|---|---|
| | I certify that information supplied herein (*Including all pages attached*) is correct and that neither the applicant nor any person (*Or concern*) in any connection with the applicant as a principal or officer, so far as is known, is now debarred or otherwise declared ineligible by any agency of the Federal Government from bidding for furnishing materials, supplies, or services to the Government or any agency thereof. |
| | SIGNATURE |
| | NAME AND TITLE OF PERSON AUTHORIZED TO SIGN (*Type or print*) |

129–105

STANDARD FORM 129 (REV. 2–77)
Prescribed by GSA, FPR (41 CFR) 1–16.802

**Figure 3.4.** Government form 129, Bidder's List Application.

of the solicitation, sending them a copy of your 129 in the meanwhile. Even if the notice is not of direct interest to you but the contracting office is, send them a 129 (see Figure 3.4).

Eventually, you will get invitations to bid and requests for proposals on a fairly regular basis, and you will eventually learn how to win also. (See the last chapter for some books that will help you with this.) Government agencies buy a great variety of goods and services, of which word processing is one but certainly not the only one. However, there are many ways in which word processing can be utilized in satisfying government requirements, even when the agencies do not specifically identify word processing as the service they wish to buy.


## HOW TO SELL TO THE GOVERNMENT

If you happen to think that we have already covered this topic, let me point out that how the government buys is not the same topic as how to sell to the government. You must, of course, understand the government's purchasing procedures and regulations, at least in general, but all marketing is a competitive activity. You must assume that you have competition for each and every job or contract you pursue, and "how to sell" includes such things as coping with competition, with beating the competition, that is. There are occasions when you can get work on a noncompetitive basis for one reason or another, but if you allow yourself to get "fat, dumb, and happy," complacent, you will soon start losing out to the competition.

Selling to the government is not different in principle from selling in the private sector, except that the government has a much greater number of procurement regulations and prescribed procedures than do most private-sector organizations. Still, the federal agencies can use the simple purchase-order procedure for procurements under $10,000 ($25,000, currently, in the Department of Defense), rather than the relatively complex and more time-consuming formal contract. That means that you can sell government bureaus spontaneously, "across the counter," as you do private companies.

Some of the advantages of selling to government agencies are these:

Relatively large jobs up to $10,000 regarded as "small purchases"; therefore, government often offers larger jobs to small businesses than private companies do.

No risk; the government is always able to pay its bills.

Many unique requirements; a large market for custom work, rewarding creative imagination.

An abundance of sales opportunities, good times and bad; always lots of work to be done.

Often offers opportunities and justifications for premium prices; can be highly profitable.

All is not sugar and spice, of course; there are also some disadvantages:

Bureaucracy is sometimes highly frustrating to deal with; may strain your patience and sweet disposition.

Some red tape and paperwork; not as bad as commonly reputed, but there is some of this to cope with.

Can be slow pay, mostly because of delays in approving work so invoice can be scheduled for payment (where several approvals are needed).

Government agencies are like private organizations in their needs. They, too, have weekend emergencies, impossible schedules, work overloads, and other occasions requiring outside help, even when they do not customarily contract out. Some agencies do little or no contracting out, whereas others do a great deal of it; therefore, it is wise to be always alert for unexpected business opportunities in government agencies as well as elsewhere. For this reason, once you have identified those government offices you think are business prospects for you, be sure to keep them on your mailing lists for your cards and brochures, as well as for the Forms 129 you filed originally with them.

What has been pointed out here as true for the federal government is also generally true for state and local governments: city, town, township, and county governments. State governments usually have purchasing departments for all or many of their bureaus and agencies (sometimes many of the agencies buy independently), and local governments generally have purchasing agents or offices on a smaller scale but operating on the same basis. Usually the way to learn of their requirements is by registering with them, using a form they supply that is similar to the Form 129, but also watching the classified advertising columns of your local newspapers, where governments advertise frequently under the heading *BIDS & PROPOSALS*.

Be aware, however, that in the case of both the federal and the state governments, there are often special offices or departments in control of much of the purchasing of computer-related services due to the assumption that it is a highly specialized field. This special office or function is used to create standards for computer equipment and services such as programming, and to assist the other agencies of the government in making the right purchases in this field. However, it is not all-encompassing, and probably would not apply to much of the work you might pursue such as word processing and graphics development, nor would it apply ordinarily to typesetting or related composition.

## FINDING GOVERNMENT OFFICES: MARKETING RESEARCH

Government offices in your own area will be listed in the telephone directory under *UNITED STATES, GOVERNMENT OF* (or similar listings for state and local government offices). However, it is not absolutely necessary to be in proximity to government offices to do business with them. It is entirely possible to do business with distant government offices by mail and telephone, and never make a face-to-face contact with the customers. Therefore, you can do business of almost any kind with federal agencies anywhere in the United States, no matter where you are yourself located. (See Figure 3.5 for award notices illustrating this.) In some cases this may be impractical, such as those cases where the schedule makes it impossible to mail materials and yet meet the deadlines. In fact, there are procurements where the contract requires that the contractor be within some specified distance of the customer. In the general case, however, it is not necessary to be in proximity to your government customer. Do not be deceived into believing that most government purchasing is done by Washington, DC, offices, either. In fact, there are more federal employees in the State of California than there are in Washington, DC! There are, in addition, major federal centers in Boston, New York, Atlanta, Chicago, Denver, St. Louis, San Francisco, Dallas–Fort Worth, and Los Angeles, with many other federal facilities scattered throughout the United States.

You should be aware, also, that not everything the government buys is listed in that *CBD*. The law itself requires only that contracts expected to run to at least $5000 must be announced in that publication,

T - - AUDIO-VISUAL SERVICES for Laughlin Air Force Base, TX. Contract F41685-82-C0005 (F41685-81-B0012), $156,084 awarded to D - K Associates, Inc., Suite 9; 932 Hungerford Drive, Rockville, MD 20850.
Contracts Division, Laughlin AFB, TX 78843

T - - COMPOSITION SERVICE, Program 1890-M. Multiple-Award Term Contract, estimated value $28,114. To Anderson Advertising Art, Lakewood, Colorado 80215.
USGPO, P.O. Box 25206 Denver Federal Center Denver, CO 80225

H - - AUDIT SERVICES IN EPA REGION V AREA 1 Contr. 68-01-6332, in the amount of $127,000, to R. H. Ritchey 100 S. Royal St., Alexandria, VA 22324.
Environmental Protection Agency, 401 M Street, SW, Washington, DC 20460

T - - AUDIOVISUAL SERVICES AT WILLIAMS AFB AZ. Contract F0260081C0017 (IFB F0260081B 0013) was awarded 10 Sep 81 to Dwain Fletcher Company (S), RT 5 Box 264, Valdosta, GA, 3161 in the amount of 171,239. Period of performance is 81 Oct 1 through 82 Sep 30.
Services Contracting Branch, Base Contracts Office, Williams AFB AZ 85224

H - - ADP STUDY AND DESIGN SERVICE RFP 101-13-81 for $83,088 Cont. V101(93)P-861 to Applied Research of Cambridge, Inc. 765 Cayuga St. Lewiston, NY 14092.
H - - ADP STUDY AND DESIGN SERVICE RFP 101-15-81 for $79,100. Cont. V101(93)P-862 to Decision Graphics, Inc 11 Main Street Southboro, MA 01772.
Veterans Administration Procurement and Supply (93A) 810 Vermont Avenue, N.W. Washington DC 20420

**Figure 3.5.** Notices of contract awards to awardees distant from customer.

so there are thousands upon thousands of smaller contracts that never appear there. There are also many purchases done spontaneously, and on such a "short fuse" that there is not time to get an announcement in the CBD, sometimes not even time to send out solicitations. In such cases, solicitations can be made by telephone, and verbal bids or quotations accepted. That is one of the reasons it is important to keep sending your local government purchasing offices cards and brochures periodically, to remind them of your existence and availability so they will think of you when the next emergency or other quick-response need arises. That is an especially important consideration for quick-response contracts.

## INDIVIDUALS AND THEIR NEEDS

So far we have been focusing on business-to-business sales: selling to other people in business or government who need help sometimes in getting their own jobs done. There are also individuals who are in much the same position. Here is just one such situation.

For many years the monthly publication, *Writer's Digest*, has carried a section of advertisements by women who did typing at home, offering to type manuscripts for writers using the mails as the medium for the transaction. Today, however, many of the notices offer word processing instead of typing or, in some cases, as an option to typing. For example, the current issue of the publication carries 115 such advertisements, of which 44 offer word processing. The advertisers are in 31 states and the District of Columbia. Not all advertise their prices, but among those who do, the rates range from a low of 85¢ per double-spaced page to a high of $1.50 per double-spaced page, with most at or close to $1 per such page. Most offer a carbon copy, with the typed original, will do some minor corrections, and will do either justified or ragged right columns if they are working with word processors.

One thing not all advertisers do is to point out in their advertising the advantages of disk storage, evidently assuming that readers are well aware of the advantages. Later, in discussing marketing in more detail, we discuss methods for increasing response from advertising without increasing cost, and that is the factor that restrains advertisers from doing as much selling as they would like to do in these small advertisements (which are really announcements, rather than advertisements, unfortunately).

Other individuals who are or ought to be good prospects for word-processing services are other professionals and small-business proprietors, people who are likely to be able to benefit from word-processing services to help them create and maintain speeches, newsletters, sales letters, news releases, catalogue sheets, and all the other kinds of paper that self-employed professionals and small-business owners tend to need more or less regularly.

Many of those services suggested as useful for companies and other organizations in your area are equally useful and perhaps even more sorely needed by self-employed individuals and other small businesses. Many of those self-employed individuals and small businesses are in custom work, contracting, essentially, and like the larger organizations must write bids and proposals to win business. That is likely to be true for many, perhaps all, of the following local professionals and merchants:

| | |
|---|---|
| General contractors | Earth-moving contractors |
| Plumbers | Well diggers |
| Electricians | Dealers in all large equipment |
| Tile setters | Dealers in major appliances |
| Concrete contractors | Wholesalers of all kinds |
| Landscape contractors | Architects |
| Civil engineers | Builders |
| Real estate developers | Major printing companies |
| Real estate agents, brokers | Surveyors |
| Home improvement firms | Heating and air conditioning contractors |
| Consultants | Furniture dealers |

Virtually anyone who seeks business from other businesspeople such as a furniture dealer seeking to sell furniture to a motel, a wholesaler seeking to supply food to a local institution, a real estate broker seeking to handle a major property, and almost all other kinds of merchants who pursue such things, must usually submit bids and proposals for contracts. This can constitute a full-time specialty for you if you have enough prospects of these types in your local area and you choose to specialize in this work. Once getting your foot in the door with such merchants and professionals you are in a good position to solicit other types of work from them if you prefer not to specialize.

Most merchants also have occasions to send out sales literature, sometimes in a small and steady stream, sometimes in a steady and fairly large stream, and sometimes spasmodically in very large mailings. If you are equipped to handle this work, and there are firms who specialize in this work alone, you can probably compete successfully for this kind of work too.

Professionals such as doctors, dentists, lawyers, engineers, architects, educators, and others who belong to professional societies and attend annual conferences and conventions often have need to write professional papers for their societies and sometimes to make speeches. Many can use your help in this, especially since both professional papers and speeches tend to go through numerous drafts and revisions. Your word-processing capability can take a great deal of the pain and expense out of the process for the individuals who have to develop these papers and speeches. (Some are in that "publish or perish" situation, too.)

Much the same can be said for articles many professionals write for their professional journals. Again, such pieces tend to require several cycles of drafting and revision before a final copy can be printed out. The sheer labor of retyping an entire piece after each mark-up and revision has tended to discourage many professionals from taking advantage of the opportunities to be published and the many benefits they would derive from such activity.

There is also a market in the need of both graduate and undergraduate students for dissertations, theses, and term papers of various kinds.

It is a rare case that a graduate student does not have to make revisions to a thesis or dissertation, for example, even before the first submittal, and this is doubly true for such papers already submitted. These tend to be rather voluminous documents also, many of them full book-length manuscripts.

Students, especially graduate students and undergraduate students nearing the end of their last year, are also excellent prospects for resumés, and often are the basis for full-time work in that area alone.

## PUBLICATIONS LORE: SOME USEFUL BACKGROUND

To gain a full understanding of what significance word processing has for many of its applications today, it is helpful to understand the general background of publications work in general: where it once was, where it is today, and how it has gotten to this point. The better you understand this, the more you will be able to help others in this work and the more valuable your own services will be.

We won't go back too far, but only to the days just before and just after World War II, when by far the bulk of all printing was done by raised metal type and duplicating anything in the average office was a matter of using a mimeograph or "ditto," spirit duplicator, machine. Most offices still had manual typewriters, and used this means to cut stencils for those duplicating machines, or sent their typed drafts to the printer, who set the copy in metal type and printed it. It was a time-consuming, laborious, and costly process, to say the least.

The offset system changed it all. Photo-offset lithography was new and revolutionary yet it was based on an old system. Lithography meant using a flat stone as a plate from which to print. Instead of inking a raised surface against which to press paper and so transfer the image from metal to paper, lithography created a greasy image on the stone. Because the image was greasy, it would reject water, while the rest of the surface would accept water. The stone plate was brushed with water, and the image areas rejected the water, while the water clung to the rest of the stone. A greasy ink was then applied to the stone, and the ink clung to the greasy image areas that had rejected the water, but the rest of the stone was wet and rejected the greasy ink. Therefore, when paper was pressed against the stone, only the ink on the image areas was transferred, and so duplicated on the paper the image that was on the stone. Hence the name for prints of paintings, *lithograph*.

Combining photography now with the principles of lithography, it became possible to photograph anything and create from it a metal plate that would act as that stone, with a greasy area that accepted greasy ink, and a remaining area that accepted water and rejected the greasy ink. It was now possible to print anything by these much simpler and much less time-consuming, less laborious, and less costly methods. Anything that could be photographed could be printed in this manner. It was now possible to simply paste up a page of type, photographs, drawings, or combinations of these, and make a printing plate of the page. (The photographs had to have a special process of *screening*, breaking the photograph down into a pattern of dots, before making a plate of it and printing it.)

Over the years, even newer and better methods have evolved, so that now the plates may be made of plastic, foil, and even paper, and may be produced on office copiers or similar machines. It is now possible for anyone to create pages ready to be made into plates, pages now referred to as "mechanicals" and "camera-ready" copy.

The rapid growth of these methods has had close connections with computers in some respects. Since it is no longer necessary to cast raised metal type, most typesetting is done by what is now referred to as "cold type," to distinguish it from that type created by casting molten metal in molds. Some of the earlier machines that were used to do this included typewriter-like devices such as one called a *Varityper*. These kinds of machines and newer ones such as IBM's *Composer* produced what the trade referred to as "strike on" type, to distinguish it from *photo-type*, produced by other systems. Those other systems produced type by photographic means, generally using matrices or stencil-like devices through which light was focused on photo-sensitive paper. This was done under computer control, so that the system was automated and could turn out type for large documents at speeds rivaling those of earlier systems, such as *linotype* machines (see Figure 3.6). In fact, today's phototypesetters resemble word processors quite closely (see Figure 3.7).

Along with these developments, typewriter technology itself advanced steadily, producing today's generation of electric and electronic typewriters and word processors which rival typesetters in many ways. At least, the copy produced by these machines and the printers used with word processors is often entirely acceptable as "camera-ready" copy from which mechanicals can be assembled to be made into printing plates. That is, if you have a printer that produces "letter quality" copy, many customers will accept that as camera-ready from which to print final documents.

As an alternative to this, you may very well be able to tie the output of your word processor, by means of modem and telephone line, to the input to a typesetter–vendor's equipment, and either transmit a copy of your disk or provide direct input to the vendor's typesetter. (You may find it very much to your advantage to investigate local typesetters to see if this is a practical possibility for you.)

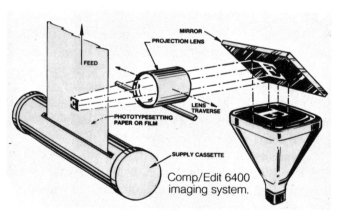

**Figure 3.6.**  Phototypesetting. (Courtesy Varitype)

Figure 3.7.    Phototypesetter. (Courtesy Varitype)

## COPY PREPARATION

Whether you are preparing rough-draft copy or final copy makes a considerable difference in preparation methods, and whether you are preparing camera-ready copy for printing or page make-up or final copy for typesetting/composition elsewhere makes quite a difference too, a difference you need to understand.

First of all, let us take the simplest case. Let us assume that the output of your printer is to be camera-ready and that there are no figures or tables to worry about, but that the entire output will be running text, page after page. In such case, you need merely to be sure that your system produces the copy consistently in the approved format: specified page lengths, leading, margins, page numbering, headlines, and whatever else the customer requires. This is exactly what the printer will print, making printing plates of the pages and going straight to press with them. Now let's add some complications.

Let us suppose that there are some illustrations, figures, and perhaps even a table or two. The tables may not require any special attention if the formats are simple, but may simply print out just as the text does. However, they may require special *rules* (lines) which your printer can't produce and may, therefore, have to have some extra work done on them after printout.

Figures, illustrations, are another problem. If they are graphs or charts that you can do on your system, and the customer is satisfied to have them done that way, you may be able to handle this as part of your routine printout. However, if they are photos or other material that has to be added, you have to make up a "frame page," as exemplified in Figure 3.8. This is simply a blank page on which you have printed out the folio (page number) and legend (figure title and/or other information). Whoever makes up the pages, you or someone else, will paste up the drawing if that is what is to go there, to create the mechanical, the page ready for the platemaker. However, if the illustration is to be a photograph, a somewhat different procedure is necessary. The photo has to be "screened" first. That means that it is made into a "halftone" negative by being photographed through a glass screen that breaks the photo up into a pattern of dots. The screened negative is then mounted on a paper form (called *goldenrod* in the trade) together with the folio and legend which have also been photographed and made into a film negative. The resulting product is called a *composite negative*, and is made into a metal printing plate which prints the photo as a *halftone*.

There are even more complex possibilities. In the one just discussed, it was assumed that the figure would occupy a full page, and so it had no effect on the text, which was printed out as full pages. Suppose the figure is much less than a full page in size. What then?

There are three possibilities in this case, depending on what the customer wishes to do. If the simplest method is to be followed, a full page may be assigned to this figure, despite its size, with the figure centered on the page. Or it may be set in the middle of the top or bottom half of the page, the other half used for text. This is a bit more

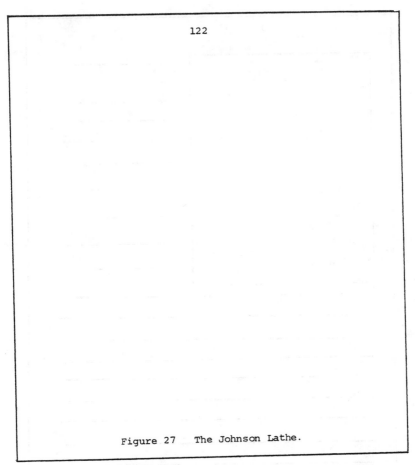

Figure 3.8.   A typical frame page.

complicated, requiring that space be left for the figure, but with the legend entered. Or, as the most sophisticated and professional, but most complex solution, the figure may be printed with *runaround* type, as shown in Figure 3.9. Again, as in the case cited, if the illustration is a line drawing it can be pasted up with the text and the resulting page becomes a mechanical which can be used to make a printing plate.

**Figure 3.9.** Example of figure and runaround type.

However, if the figure is a photograph, the same procedure of making a composite negative on goldenrod is usually followed to create a master for platemaking.

In doing that, if a blank area is left on the page when it is photographed to create the line (text) negative that will be combined with the screened negative, the blank area will be solid black on the negative, and the screened negative will be spliced in; the black square will be cut out with a knife to make room to splice in the screened negative. However, in practice many make-up people prefer to paste up a *mask* in the space that the photograph is to occupy. The mask is of black or dark red paper (the camera sees red as though it were blacker than black) which results in a clear space where the mask was, instead of a black block. Therefore, it is not necessary to actually cut the block out and splice in the screened negative. Instead, the screened negative may simply be mounted on the goldenrod behind the "window" of clear film thus created, and the platemaking takes place through the window. This is far easier than cutting and splicing and so is a preferred method.

There may also be cases where in addition to illustrations and/or tables with special rules and layouts, the copy is to get headlines created by other equipment, such as a *headliner*, a machine that makes large-type headlines by photographic methods on a strip of sensitized paper which is then pasted up on the mechanical in the same manner that other materials such as line drawings are. In fact, it is fairly common to do this and sometimes the pages are composed of various combinations of text, illustrations, tabular data, headlines, and perhaps special text such as footnotes or text of a different size than the regular body copy. In short, a given job may entail a fairly complex paste-up of some or all pages, requiring study and planning to make it all turn out right.

Full-time publishing organizations usually have one or more make-up specialists, people who do this kind of work. The "independent" or self-employed individual, however, has to know how to do a bit of everything, and must do his or her own make-up, paste-up of all the elements to create the mechanicals, that is. It is not really that complex, once the basics are mastered.

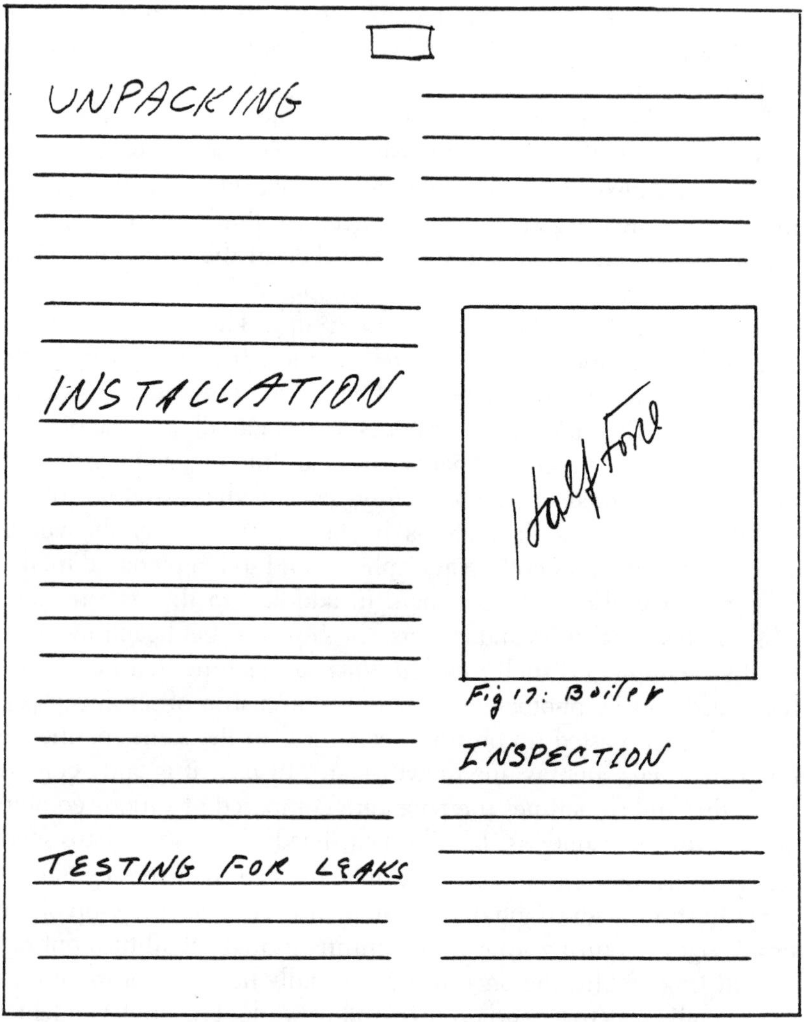

**Figure 3.10.** Comprehensive for a single page.

## LAYOUTS, COMPREHENSIVES, AND PASTE-UPS

To do this work, it is necessary to plan ahead. That means planning each page, but especially those pages that are composites of several elements. The basic plan is called a *layout*, but there are two kinds of layouts: the rough layout and the comprehensive layout, generally referred to by the shorthand *rough* and *comprehensive*. These are simply sketches showing where the various elements fit on the page. The rough is a preliminary sketch showing approximate positions. The comprehensive is more precise, showing exactly what is to fit where. Figure 3.10 illustrates the point in a comprehensive for a simple page. It is thus the guide for the final paste-up of text and other materials that make up the page.

Organizations that regularly publish the same or approximate same kinds of publications often have standard forms on which to paste up the elements, making the job easier and faster. These forms are printed in a light blue shade that the camera cannot see; light blue appears as plain white to the camera lens. Hence, you can make marks on camera-ready copy with sky-blue pencils, but never use any but those.

However, there may be occasional exceptions to that, as some xerographic-type copiers (and, presumably, xerographic platemakers) are not blind to blue, but see yellow as though it were white. In such cases it is necessary to use yellow as the nonreproducing "blue pencil."

## CAMERA-READY: WHAT IT MEANS

The term *camera-ready copy* is used freely in the printing and publications businesses and yet may be misunderstood. *Mechanicals*, those pasted-up pages ready to be used for plate-making, are always camera-ready copy, but camera-ready copy is not always ready for plate-making. The terms *mechanicals, reproducibles*, and *masters* all refer to camera-ready pages. However, *camera-ready* refers generically to copy that needs only to be pasted up. For example, a rough sketch is not camera-ready because it needs to be made into a final, finished drawing to become camera-ready. A final, finished drawing is camera-ready, which simply means that it is in a condition to be pasted up or photographed preparatory to plate-making. Therefore, when someone asks you to deliver camera-ready copy, you have to inquire as to whether that means mechanicals or just copy that can now be pasted up into mechanicals, for the term can mean either.

## A FEW MARKETING HINTS

Later in these pages we get into serious discussion of marketing, which is of course a most important part of any business venture. It is appropriate at this point, however, to relate some of what we have just discussed to marketing your word-processing services.

Word processing is itself a specialty, and you may have decided to confine your venture entirely to word processing. However, it is also possible to specialize within word processing itself without overdoing the act or restricting yourself unnecessarily because word processing is itself so versatile a function. There are, of course, pros and cons to specializing, as there are to almost everything. There are also different ways or different areas in which to specialize.

First of all, you may choose to specialize in quick-response work as suggested earlier, if you are in a position to do so and wish to do so. That is specializing in the kind of service you offer, rather than in the kind of work you do. It has the distinct advantage that it is something not everyone is willing to do and, therefore, requires less effort to sell the service. It has the advantage also that it pays quite well, can be made to pay quite well, that is. It has the disadvantage that it is burdensome work, makes it difficult to plan ahead, even your personal life, and perhaps gets you a reputation for being high priced, which can be disadvantageous at times.

You can also specialize in the kind of work you do, proposals only, for example, or perhaps technical manuals only. Specializing in this way enables you to become more and more expert in the work, develop special methods and perhaps special equipment and other facilities, and thus become more and more efficient. In fact, some entrepreneurs become so well developed in some specialized work that they are soon dominant in their field and enjoy the reputation of being the best at what they do.

Somewhat analogous to this is specializing in the type of industry or client you work with: electronics engineering firms, real estate, medical sciences, or other such specialized field. Here, again, you can develop special methods and capabilities, and dominate the field.

The obvious overall advantage to specializing is that you develop a reputation in that specialized field and you also develop special capabilities. At the same time, however, you tend to shut out other opportunities. Customers tend to view you as a specialist, even when you do not specialize, and if you are a generalist and wish to do any and all kinds of word processing, you have to work steadily and unceasingly at reminding prospects that you do any and all kinds of word processing.

However you orient yourself and your venture, the latter admonition—to remind your prospects constantly of what you offer to do for them and of your continued presence and eagerness to serve them—is the key to entrepreneurial success for most people who venture into business. The typical prospect does not remember you unless you have been doing business with him or her frequently, and will generally turn to whomever has been most visible most recently. In fact, on at least one occasion, a federal government agency seeking a writer turned to the local Yellow Pages directory to find one. One self-employed TV serviceman built a flourishing business primarily by distributing 4 × 6-inch advertising cards that began with the prominent headline: SAVE THIS CARD—YOU'LL NEED IT SOMEDAY.

That's why many vendors prefer to distribute calendars, memo pads, and other advertising novelties that keep their names before the prospects, rather than one-time advertisements. Spending $5000 on a major, one-time advertising splash will probably not produce as much business for you as will spending $2000 over many months for a low-key but continuing campaign.

A main message in all of this is PATIENCE. Only rarely does a new venture become a total success rapidly. (And of those that do, many prove to be flukes and ventures built on sand, rather than rock, and many perish and vanish as rapidly as they sprang up.) Most ventures must have time to take root and grow if they are to develop a solid foundation that can survive the normal business peaks and valleys.

For this reason, because it takes time to build your business, you may find it practical to generalize, in the beginning, and take on any work you can win, leaving it to later to select a specialty. It is sometimes not clear in the beginning what specialty you will want to opt for, or even if you will want to specialize at all. Therefore, you do not have to do so in the beginning, but may defer that to some later time.

# Chapter Four

## Helping People Keep Their Books and Other Business Services

You don't have to be an accountant to help people keep their books. For that matter, "keeping books" is not confined to accounting and bookkeeping.

## YOU DON'T HAVE TO BE A PHI BETA KAPPA

For some reason, the thought of keeping books frightens a great many people who appear to believe that one must have a great deal of advanced or graduate education, an extraordinary IQ, and/or other special attributes to manage a set of books. To some small degree, those who

81

so reason may be right, if they refer to the elaborate and complex accounting systems that many major corporations and other highly diverse enterprises require. However, this complexity does not transfer to the typical small enterprise: the retail store, the local mechanic, the neighborhood butcher. When such small businesses retain professional accountants to establish and maintain their books, they often (usually, in fact) wind up with far more sophisticated and complex systems than they need, systems which the accountant has designed especially for them and which now do, indeed, require the services of the CPA (Certified Public Accountant) to keep for them.

Most often it is overkill. The typical small business does not need a complex accounting system, and certainly does not need a system custom designed. There are, in fact, a great many standard systems available that do the job admirably for the small business, even for fairly large business, in fact, and which will run on any good microcomputer. *List*, a quarterly periodical directory of software programs (see Chapter 14 for more information about *List*) alone lists hundreds of such programs. A great many of these are generalized, suitable for any business; others are specialized and designed for specific businesses and industries. Here are a few program titles and classifications to illustrate this:

| | |
|---|---|
| Computer Systems Accounts Payable | Computer Systems General Ledger |
| Computer Systems Payroll | AACS Accounts Receivable |
| Business Accounting | Sales Analysis |
| Business Bookkeeping System | Entry Management System |
| Cash Register Program | Check Writer |
| Construction Job Costing | Contact Vendor for Information |
| Expense Ledger | Fixed Assets Accounting System |
| Cost Recovery System | Job Cost Accounting |
| Invoicing | Lease Classification |
| Membership Billing | Purchase Control |
| Inventory Control | Financial Decisions |

| | |
|---|---|
| Financial Analysis | Financial Planning |
| Business Analysis | Spreadsheet Analysis |
| ROI Analysis | Ratio Analysis |
| Target Financial Modeling | Statistical Analysis |
| Econometrics | Asset Depreciation |
| Tax Writeup | Amortization Program |
| Depreciation System | Professional Billing |
| Timekeeping System | Offset Printing Cost Estimating |
| Dairy Cattle Recordkeeping | Farm and Agribusiness Management |

The lists go on, and the few programs listed here as examples are in almost every case only one of a large number of similar programs. There are dozens of programs, for example, in inventory management, in accounts payable and accounts receivable, and in other areas of accounting that are common to all or virtually all enterprises. It is not really difficult to select programs that are adaptable to most businesses, and programs that are especially designed for certain kinds of businesses or industries. It is rather hard to imagine that there are many small businesses whose accounting needs could not be fully satisfied from this array of programs. In most cases, the needs could be satisfied by a single general accounting program.

Unfortunately, accountants and financial experts, like most professionals, are extremely protective of their special knowledge and skills, and they tend to mask both behind a cloud of exotic and mystical jargon, and to attempt to combat all efforts to explain the functions in simple English. Nevertheless, although the books of the supercorporation may indeed be difficult to comprehend, perhaps even necessarily so, the basics of accounting or "keeping books" is quite simple, and any intelligent human can grasp them readily.

## WHAT IS "KEEPING BOOKS"?

The most basic and most easily understandable principle of business is this. The venture must return every dollar invested in it and spent in its behalf together with something extra, called *profit*, if the business is to survive. To put it another, and perhaps more understandable, way, there are only two kinds of dollars in business: those that are paid out and those that are received. There must be at least one dollar in for every dollar that goes out for the barest survival, but the business will not prosper and grow unless there is something more than a dollar in for every dollar out—profit, that is—for it is profit that enables a business to grow, to develop some surplus for emergencies, and to become a solid enterprise.

Although all dollars handled in a business are one of these two, dollars in and dollars out, even the simplest business is not quite that uncomplicated. Within each of those two categories of dollars there are subcategories which explain other things about those dollars in and out so that the business can be managed properly. That is another most important and very much misunderstood principle. The main purpose of accounting is to provide proper information to guide the management of the business. Accounting information is management information or it is nothing at all. Accountants and others, the Internal Revenue Service, principally, tend to view accounting as existing for tax purposes only, but that is a distortion. It's true enough that tax requirements do influence the way in which accounting systems are organized and how accounting information is handled (taxes are paid on the basis of what the accounting information reveals) but that is not the purpose of accounting nor should it ever be permitted to obscure the true purpose of accounting.

Bear this in mind as we discuss what accounting is, and you will see how important accounting information is to successful management.

Now to answer, in at least a simplified way, the question of what "keeping books" means. In the literal sense it means keeping records of all the dollars in some organized way that allows you to study what is happening in and to the business, and to judge what things you should do as an owner or manager to keep the business healthy. In fact, it is not really different from accounting per se, although a bookkeeper is not necessarily an accountant, and an accountant does not generally like to be regarded as a "mere" bookkeeper. In the sense professionals use the words, the accountant is someone who designs accounting systems, analyzes records, and makes up reports such as balance sheets, P&L (Profit & Loss) statements, annual reports (for corporations), and other such documents, whereas bookkeepers merely maintain the records, journals and ledgers. The more sophisticated computer programs will generate all these latter reports from the information entered by the bookkeepers or those performing the bookkeeping functions of inputting the data.

Most systems have two kinds of records: journals and ledgers. The journal, sometimes also called *day journal,* is a kind of log or diary in which are entered payments received, invoices, and other transactions as they occur, on a daily basis. Depending on the size of the organization and the accounting system overall, there may be more than one journal: for example, one for receivables and one for payables. (Very large systems may have many journals.) The journals, therefore, establish what might be regarded as a kind of "rough draft" record of everything that needs to be recorded in the system.

Later, perhaps once a week or however the system works, the entries in those journals are transferred to the ledgers, where they become the official entries, organized according to whatever system is used. For example, suppose the journal lists only payables, and the entries recorded are the bills received every day for whatever the company buys. The bills are listed in no particular order in the journal, but they are listed in some order in the ledger. One bill may be for raw materials (for inventory) whereas another may be for electricity (overhead expense) and still another may be for equipment (long-term investment). Each is a different category in the ledger and must go into its proper category.

The reason is simple. Dollars paid out are of several different categories, even in the broadest sense. Some are overhead: light, heat, rent, insurance, labor; some are for depreciable investment such as major equipment or furniture; some for merchandise to use in manufacturing or to resell directly. In the latter two categories, the dollars are not spent in one sense, but are simply converted to another form, to needed equipment or to resalable merchandise. However, whereas the resalable merchandise will be marked up and resold, the equipment or other depreciable investment will be "spent" over several years, as it is depreciated and written off each year. Thus that kind of expenditure is a dollar out and yet is not a dollar out as far as the balance sheet is concerned, for it is an asset that is at least nominally the equal of the dollars paid out for it.

Of course, all of this applies to your own enterprise. Your micro and other equipment that makes up your capital-items list, including furniture and anything else necessary to your daily operation, should be on a depreciation schedule of some kind, representing an annual expense to be written off. For example, if you have a total of $5000 invested in your equipment, furniture, and fixtures, and you have it on a five-year depreciation schedule, your books should show it as a $1000 business expense each year, even though you have paid for it the first year. That does not mean that it is worth nothing the sixth year, but it does mean that you can't take a tax deduction on it after it is fully depreciated. However, any new equipment you buy can be added to your capital-items list and depreciation begun on those. That includes other items such as property improvements. If you build an office in your home, dedicating that office to your business, you can write that off too, on some depreciation schedule.

Items that are not capital items such as a stock of paper, repairs to equipment, gasoline, or office supplies are *expensed*, which means taken as 100-percent cost when they are bought and written off as deductible for tax purposes the year in which they were bought.

Some items fall into a gray area. If you spent money developing a new product that has not returned a cent, you may choose to make it R&D (research and development) and call it *inventory*, which means that it is investment, not expense. Or you may call it expense, and list it under your overhead accounts. If you charge your customers separately for the supplies you use (e.g., the fanfold paper), the paper you bought is inventory and not office supplies. That means you can't deduct it, but must show it as an asset equal in value to the dollars it cost. If you decide that anything that has a useful life of one year or more and costs $250 or more is a capital item, you may have to place some small equipment on a depreciation schedule and wait for five or more years to write it off for tax purposes. If you arbitrarily decide to set the cost for capital items at $500 or more, you can write that small equipment off (expense it) immediately, and get the entire tax deduction that year.

Perhaps you can begin to see now the direct relationship between accounting and general management of your business, between accounting information and management decisions. There is more.

Old inventory, material that has been in your storeroom for a long time, is usually less costly than newer inventory because of the general tendency for prices to rise. How do you value the old inventory? By what it cost you when you bought it or by what it now costs you to replace it? How do you sell it: first-in, first-out or last-in, first-out? There are pros and cons to both methods, and a great many business people find it more profitable to sell *LIFO*, last-in, first-out, because it commands a markup based on the higher acquisition cost.

When do you replace a piece of equipment? Is that an arbitrary judgment, or do you base it on your records which tell you how much it costs to keep the old equipment working?

How much to you charge customers for various services or products? Is that arbitrary, or do you base it on your costs as shown by your records?

All of this applies to you, but it applies equally to your customers, who operate their own businesses. Armed with (1) a basic understanding of accounting principles and (2) the right programs for your customers, you can not only serve their immediate needs for keeping books and records required to operate their business and pay their taxes, but you can help them operate their businesses most effectively.

## SOME FOR-INSTANCES

To illustrate this further, let us look at a few selected programs and see just what they are capable of doing and what they offer you and your prospective clients. First is a program called *B.I.S. General Ledger* (B.I.S. for Business Information Systems). The supplier reports that the program can handle three completely separate sets of books, including the following:

170 General ledger accounts.

3 Profit centers per account.

510 Account profit center combinations.

3,000 Entries per day allowed.

1,095,000 Entries per year allowed.

All entries permanently saved.

14 User-defined journals.

50 Controllable account prompts.

5 Video screen save options.

40 Split entries per transaction.

Tutorial and reference manual.

A program titled *Professional Billing* is designed to keep account records for lawyers, doctors, dentists, and other professionals, and prepare billings. It can handle on each diskette, according to the supplier, the following:

Up to 150 clients.

Up to 350 accounts.

Time and expenses for up to 15 professionals

Also, the system can handle up to 1000 transactions per subaccount or client matter.

AG-*Finance* is a program that is designed for Farm Finance, according to its supplier. Useful for farms and ranches, the program offers the following:

Check register.
Enterprise records.
Overhead accounts.
Prices and quantities.
Multiple checking accounts.
Check writing.
Other management reports.

A program titled *Wholesale/Retail Industry Distribution System* contains three modules, the supplier reports: inventory, order entry/invoicing, and accounts receivable. A daily register provides reports on either a daily basis or on a batch basis for transactions and invoices, as well as sums of transactions and invoices, along with printouts that include other charges such as freight and taxes.

## BOOKKEEPING NEEDS VARY

The list of accounting programs available is a long one including many dozens of program, some of which are rather general accounting programs covering all the needs of small businesses, whereas others are highly specialized and cover such specific needs as those listed a few paragraphs ago. Note, however, that keeping books is far different for one firm than it is for another. This is not merely a function of size such as the difference between the corner gasoline station and the meat packer; it is a function and consequence of the varying natures of different industries, different enterprises within those industries, and different ways of doing business. Let us look at a few examples to see why this is so, and what it means to us in terms of services we can offer.

## The Local Supermarket

Supermarkets are characterized by steady turnover of their inventory (much of which is perishable), must do business on a large-volume/small-markup basis (strictly cash and carry), usually must carry a large and diverse inventory, and must keep close watch on prices, both those they pay and those they must charge. Finally, it's a highly competitive business, and the typical supermarket's marketing and sales campaigns are one of frequent special sales, loss leaders (no-profit items, advertised to bring people into the store), and every kind of promotion one can think of.

The larger supermarkets are now computerized, and are probably not a suitable target for the small computer entrepreneur, but there are many smaller supermarkets who can use help. Although the big stores are strictly cash and carry, small neighborhood stores sometimes permit customers to maintain open accounts and may, therefore, have a collection problem. In general, such businesses do have inventory-management problems, complicated by not only the size and diversity of the inventory, but by the volatile nature of it: part of it is highly perishable, much of it is fast-moving, although some of it is not, and the pricing (both cost and selling prices) is dynamic, almost constantly changing, although rising overall in recent years.

## Professional Services

Professionals such as doctors, lawyers, dentists, architects, consultants, and other such specialists rarely are concerned with inventory. If they carry one, it is a small and simple one, since what they sell is not goods, but services, expert, specialized services. Their charges are for their labor primarily, although in some professions there are substantial cost and profit centers in X-rays, laboratory tests, prosthetic appliances,

and other ancillaries to the central service. Aside from general accounting needs, for many professionals the bookkeeping includes invoicing
patients and clients, sometimes with follow-up statements and even
dunning; scheduling and keeping appointments with patients and clients;
scheduling and keeping appointments to attend professional meetings,
conventions, and conferences; other such needs.

## Manufacturing

Manufacturers tend to have inventory-management problems since most
manufacturing means keeping stocks of raw material and/or parts and
components. If some or all the inventory is of the *long lead* type (the
type that takes a long time to get delivery on and so must be ordered
well ahead of the time it is needed), it is a special and usually difficult
problem in inventory management, requiring careful study of earlier
history and other factors to judge future needs.

## Brokerages

"Catalogue selling," taking orders, usually by mail, from customers to
whom the merchant has mailed catalogues, does not require extensive
inventory if the merchant is having the materials all *drop shipped* or
sent out by the manufacturer or distributor. This is only one example
of brokering or acting as a *middleman* or agent in the selling process.
There are those who broker the goods and services in many industries:
printing, real estate, public speaking, entertainment, and many, many
other kinds of ventures where brokering has become a way of doing
business for one reason or another. For these kinds of enterprises,
bookkeeping has some special needs according to which party pays the
fees or commissions, how billings are made, and what the general
arrangements are. In any case, the broker earns a fee or commission of
some sort, usually from the seller, and must keep books to keep straight
on payables and receivables, which are the chief accounting problems
to be addressed.

## Custom Services

Custom services constitute a wide-ranging set of business ventures which probably need to be subdivided into categories. Even then it is not easy to make all the useful discriminations. For example, one subdivision would be professional services and nonprofessional services such as dentistry and automobile repairs. We have already covered such things as dentistry as a professional service; therefore, we deal here with spontaneous services of a nonprofessional nature such as automobile repair, household repairs, carpentry, and other such services.

## Project Contracting

This is the other kind of services on a custom basis, usually a long-term effort, contracted for as a project such as doing a survey, developing a manual, designing an airplane, or otherwise undertaking a task that will involve a team of people for at least several months.

Both spontaneous custom services and especially long-term custom projects entail special bookkeeping. For one thing, such projects are often *labor intensive*; the chief cost and chief item for which customers are billed is labor, although there are exceptions, projects that entail a great deal of material costs also. A major bookkeeping problem here is keeping track of all labor charged to the project (some organizations have people working on more than one custom project and so must keep track of hours spent on various projects). Overhead is also an item here, so that bookkeeping for a custom project also requires keeping close watch over all costs. To do that, it is necessary to keep good status records: to monitor project progress versus expenditures. This, in fact, is a problem for such enterprises, and business success or failure often depends on how well this reporting is done. This is essentially what a good *MIS* (management information system) provides, and every entrepreneur who is contracting for projects ought properly to have a really effective MIS. And "effective" means accurate, timely, and diagnostic.

## THE "WORRY ITEM"

Every entrepreneur has his or her own special worry items: those items which appear to him or her to be the most critical ones or the most troublesome ones. That is what we have been trying to point out in general terms here, another way to study the market for bookkeeping services which tend to go beyond such traditional bookkeeping as accounting strictly for dollars. Traditional bookkeeping is almost entirely in terms of dollars. Modern bookkeeping recognizes, must recognize, that inventory is also dollars. Labor hours are dollars. Sales campaigns are dollars. Everything done to keep the business moving forward is dollars and is, therefore, something that bookkeeping must consider.

Some entrepreneurs worry most about taxes.

Some worry most about inventory.

Some worry most about overhead.

Some worry most about status reports.

Some worry most about markup.

Some worry most about payables.

Some worry most about receivables.

You get the idea by now. What an entrepreneur—a prospective client—worries about most is what you need to know if you are to market effectively. Obviously, the middleman broker will not be highly enthusiastic about your marvelous inventory-management program because he or she doesn't have an inventory to worry about. However, he or she might be excited at the prospect of a program that *ages* payables properly to maximize cash flow while also maximizing profit through taking advantage of all discounts. Marketing effectiveness—the effectiveness of *your* marketing, that is—is heavily dependent on your understanding of the problems of your prospects (their worry items). Everyone has problems, and the most effective marketing is based on understanding the prospects' problems and offering satisfactory solutions to those problems. (Later, in discussing marketing, we probe more deeply into the meaning of this.) Therefore, you can go at the business of deciding what to offfer in the way of services related to keeping books in either of these possible ways:

1.  Determine what are the main and most common concerns or problems of your prospects and offer solutions.
2.  Decide what services you prefer to offer (or feel in the best position to offer) and seek out the right prospects for those services.

Both approaches work: if you have the range of prospects from which to choose to make the second one work for you. In practice, however, you must first survey the *potential markets available to you*, because that is the range from which you must make your choices. Therefore, as a first step, do the market survey and determine what kinds of enterprises exist in sufficient quantity to constitute a market of adequate size within your chosen service area. That brings up another factor. What is your chosen service area? Your city or town? Your county? Your state? Your region?

## RESEARCHING THE MARKET

Some methods for doing general research of your market area were suggested earlier. These will do to help you get an idea of what kinds of enterprises exist in your service area and how many there are of each kind. As a first step you should collect this kind of information and thus develop a profile of the market area. Then start filling in the profile with some details until the profile begins to approach the coverage illustrated in Figure 4.1, which suggests a format for the profile.

The figure is only a partial listing, and may or may not be appropriate to your own market area even on the partial basis of its coverage. The purpose is to try to determine what kinds of bookkeeping services

| Type Enterprise | Estimated Number | Probable Prospect For: |
|---|---|---|
| Retailers: | | |
| Supermarkets | 7 | |
| Clothing, independent | 12 | |
| Clothing, chain | 3 | |
| Small food markets | 35 | |
| Department stores | 6 | |
| Hardware stores | 23 | |
| Home improvement contractors | 9 | |
| Large construction firms | 2 | |
| Small service firms | 29 | |
| Large service firms | 7 | |
| Manufacturing: | | |
| Heavy, large | 1 | |
| Heavy, small | 3 | |
| Light, large | 13 | |
| Light, small | 19 | |
| Offices/plants of large corporations | 6 | |

**Figure 4.1.**   Suggested format for profile of local market.

would be most useful to this market. In most cases you will probably have far more success with the small, independent stores than you will with the large stores and the chain stores. However, don't accept that as necessarily true. There are enough exceptions to that rule to make it worthwhile to be alert for those exceptions. At the least, let these firms know that you exist and that you offer services. Some of these large stores and chain stores may get overloaded or have special needs that their existing systems do not satisfy. Especially, let them know if you can offer something that is different, better, and/or new, perhaps so new that they have not yet heard of it. (Imagine what would have happened if you could have offered something such as VisiCalc to large companies when it was new and yet unknown!)

## OFFERING NEW, BETTER, DIFFERENT SERVICES IN KEEPING BOOKS

Probably no field of endeavor in the entire world, or even in history for that matter, has been as dynamic and rapidly changing as the micro-computer software field. Its entire history has been far more revolution-ary than evolutionary. Close attention to what is happening in this field is likely to produce the equivalent of getting in early on the "next VisiCalc." If you are going to specialize in offering help to merchants in keeping their books, you would do well, quite well, to study the software market constantly, with a view to becoming so familiar with what is offered that you can quickly spot new trends and new or better software products.

It is not only the new and different program that offers you the opportunity to be better and different than your competitors. (And your "competitor," in any given case, may be only the prospect's existing system.) Better service and greater convenience than a competitive system offers is reason enough to switch to what you offer. Customers will pay for convenience.

One thing that is wrong with many bookkeeping services provided by public accountants is that they provide a report to the customer many weeks, even months, after the event. For example, the merchant may find out only in September how he did in June or July, and perhaps how he has been doing ever since. If he was losing money in June, for example, he wants to know about it immediately so he can take some remedial action. Two or three months later is far too late for the small entrepreneur to discover that his business is a disaster area. Make your prospects aware that your service is spontaneous and reports immedi-ately so that the client knows at all times what is happening.

Select programs that turn out easy-to-read, easy-to-understand re-ports, too. Many accountants, like lawyers, doctors, engineers, and other professionals, speak and write in a jargon that is difficult to fathom if you are not one of them. Explain to your prospects that your reports are in everyday English, easy to read and understand.

Tailor your service to the client's needs and desires. Some clients prefer to do their own journalizing, even do their own postings, but computerizing the system changes all that. They have to be educated, made to understand that they can now relieve themselves of all that, and simply turn over the invoices and other paper to you, and you'll handle it all, you and the system. Make the convenience of the system clear.

Some public accountants do all or much of their work on the client's premises, whereas others take the work to their own premises, or even keep the client's books on their own premises. You can do either if you have a portable system, or a *transportable* one, as some are now calling the portable micro to distinguish it from the pocket or notebook-sized computers. Since some clients for accounting services prefer the work done on their premises, it may pay you to think about this if you plan to offer bookkeeping services.

# Chapter Five

---

# General Data Processing

*The term "data processing" is used in a *most* general sense here, to cover a great many activities of potential profit and growth.*

## AN INTRODUCTORY DEFINITION

General data processing is really not a separate category of computer services, but logically includes all that was covered in the previous chapter. However, in terms of marketing effort, it was useful to segregate keeping books as a service because everyone in even the smallest business recognizes the need to keep books and is, therefore, far more likely to be interested in a computerized service to help them with that task. On the other hand, many small merchants will not so readily agree that they can benefit by turning over some of their management functions to a computer service. In practice you will probably find that those who have begun to use computer services in their accounting or bookkeeping functions and have used the service long enough to begin to appreciate what it does for them are more likely to be receptive to the idea of using computer services for other functions such as purchasing, inventory control, status reporting, and other business management functions.

The kinds of services a business can best use varies according to the nature of the enterprise, just as was the case with bookkeeping needs and services. In fact, Figure 4.1 is just as appropriate to analyzing the market for other data-processing services as it was for identifying best prospects for bookkeeping services. Therefore, what we are really discussing at this point is the rest of the typical uses of computers in supporting enterprises with a broad variety of data-processing services and functions, most of which are just as important and valuable to the small business as they are to the big business.

## GENERAL SERVICE BUREAU

Even today there are many computer service bureaus based on one of the older, big computers. A service bureau, you may recall, is one of those for-profit organizations that originally served the needs of companies who could not justify or afford a computer of their own, but who had need of computer services to run their payroll, print out reports, analyze inventory, and do all the other chores that can be done more efficiently with computer assistance than by any other means.

Microcomputers have made it possible for those organizations to own and operate their own computers if they wish to, although not all do. However, microcomputers have now made it possible to shift the scale of service-bureau operation. Now it is the local merchants, the professionals, and other self-employed or other very small enterprises (those employing fewer than 10 people, for example) who need computer-supported services but who cannot or do not wish to own or operate their own computer.

Thus the situation is tailor-made for the part-time and/or home-based service bureau based on a microcomputer and printer. Among the kinds of computer services needed by small businesses are most of those needed by large businesses, albeit on a smaller scale, a difference of degree, but not of kind. Even small businesses need to manage inventory, do purchasing, keep track of market trends, monitor and report on status of many interests, plan and schedule projects, and carry out a host of functions, including some of the following ones.

## Tax Returns

Even those small businesses who do their own books often prefer to have someone else prepare their tax returns. (I am myself an example of this.) You do not need to be a tax accountant for this because there are many programs you can buy that will do the job. Don't be deceived by the fact that the season is at a peak in the first quarter of the year, because business firms must file all kinds of reports throughout the year.

There are many other kinds of programs offering needed services to businesses, some of them not exactly keeping books, but closely related. Some of these are covered in greater detail in later chapters, but are worthy of at least brief mention here.

## Inventory

For many businesses, inventory is a problem in itself: keeping track of it, managing it, ordering at the right times, depreciating it, and doing whatever else needs to be done to inventory according to the nature of the business. Like accounting in general, there is a quite large array of inventory programs available, and you can almost surely find one that suits your customers' needs.

## Alerting and Calendar Maintenance

Many businesses can use a kind of business "wake up" service, a service that maintains the customer's calendar of events such as trade shows, conventions, sales conferences, and sundry other such occurrences that managers need to be reminded of in time. This may even include a list of appointments for the busy executive, and the service may be one that provides the executive a reminder sheet on weekly, daily, or other basis.

## MIS

Management information systems are not the sole province of the large corporation. Small business can often use such programs to advantage and will contract for them, if they learn that they can have one of their own.

## Scheduling

Scheduling service is along the lines of the alerting/calendar service, except that the service includes scheduling projections, using such programs as spreadsheet programs and charting programs for such things as CPM (Critical Path Method) scheduling.

## Running Client's Own Programs

Some clients have their own programs, perhaps custom made or perhaps proprietary, which they want you to run (assuming, of course, that they will run on your machine). In effect, they are asking simply to rent time on your machine, the charges for which would normally include payment for your own time as machine operator. As an alternative, a client may wish to own the program used for him or her, and will ask you to recommend a suitable program which you may keep on the shelf, but as that client's own property. This is a not unheard of practice in the service-bureau business.

## SOME MISCELLANEOUS SERVICES AND PROGRAMS FOR BUSINESSES

Some of the services you can offer businesses are suggested by the descriptions of available programs being offered by software developers.

Here are just a few ideas and suggestions resulting from a casual reading of *List* entries.

Many businesses have use for charts and graphs of various kinds for sales meetings and for other occasions. Preparing some of these by conventional methods, such as manual collection of numbers and manual plotting to create a rough sketch for a commercial artist or draftsman to transform into a finished, professional drawing, can be quite costly and time-consuming. There are numerous programs that enable you to use your printer as though it were a plotter and generate useful charts and graphs with your system, even with a letter-quality printer. One such program, called *Chart-Master*, illustrates these capabilities with a list of its own, as reported in *List*.

Produces clustered or stacked bars, line, scatter, and pie charts.

Plots up to 24 variables and 600 pieces of information.

Provides on-screen reviewing.

Produces charts on paper, up to 9 charts on same page.

Uses special input data or data from files.

Accompanying text in variety of fonts and styles.

Variety of tones, hatching, or solids.

Operator-selected or automatic X- and Y-axes.

Many small businesses can use mailing services or, at least, such services as are provided by a program titled *Mailing List Maintenance and Label Printing System*. It's one of many such programs that update mailing lists—deleting nixies (undeliverable/invalid addresses) and inserting new entries, printing out mailing labels, and selecting any desired portion of the list—sorting by zip codes, by states, by cities, by alphabet, or by other search-term.

There are also programs designed to help custom-services businesses prepare estimates for such industries as the construction industry. Some of these are industry-specific, whereas others are adaptable to most businesses that provide services on a custom basis, that undertake custom projects, that is. Basic estimating data is maintained in a set of files and new data may be entered by the user or old data updated. Some of the programs include or specialize in scheduling information, using such industry standard methods as CPM, and some graph the CPM charts or the analogous PERT charts.

Earlier you read that although most business firms must handle certain basic functions such as accounting, marketing, buying, and filling orders, large firms have managers and departments to do these things, and small firms often have one individual doing all or several of these functions. However, even for the smallest firm it is difficult and often even impossible for one person to handle all the functions. The only option remaining to the proprietor who can't handle it all alone and can't hire more help to handle it is to vend it, contract out to someone who will handle it on a fee basis of some kind.

It is on this basis that you can handle a customer's accounting and bookkeeping functions and other, related duties. These duties need not be confined to accounting services and word-processing services; many firms contract out sundry other functions rather than hire more help. For example, many firms that require salespersons in the field, traveling and calling on clients, do not have salespeople on their direct payroll, but use contractors or commission people known as "manufacturers' representatives." Others sell through brokers and other kinds of distributors, or through salespeople-dealers, as Fuller Brush, Amway, and Avon do.

One man who obviously understands this need of companies to buy services they cannot or do not wish to handle with employees is David Voracek, of Alexandria, VA, who provides a marketing service through his company, "The Marketing Department." (The significance of the name suggests the idea clearly, does it not?)

For some functions, businesses, even large businesses, subscribe to services such as credit bureaus. Where once the companies asked for credit references and verified the credit references themselves, they now turn the matter of credit approval over to separate firms, who provide a credit-reporting service. Even in the matter of hiring people, many firms utilize "headhunters" to whom they pay fees for recruiting the new hires they want.

The environment and mood are, therefore, right today for many services which are useful to business firms, and which they would find more troublesome or more costly to do themselves (if they even knew how to organize and carry them out) than to have a service firm provide them. Nor do you necessarily have to confine yourself to small-business customer prospects if you believe that you can handle the volume of work that would be necessary to handle large-company accounts. Let us consider some needs that you might be able to satisfy for other businesses.

## Special Referrals

This subject got brief mention earlier in these pages, as a possible service to both individuals and businesses, but without serious discussion of how to go about organizing such a service or how to make it pay. In the services we discussed earlier in this chapter, it was obvious that the services were based on proprietary programs you can buy, and that the customer would be billed directly for the service on some basis or other. The referral idea of bringing together a writer, architect, engineer, draftsman, or other specialist with a client who needs such special services on a short-term basis is not so clear-cut in respect to who pays for the service and how, and this requires some discussion of the twin considerations of who should pay and who will pay, which may prove to be two entirely separate questions.

A case can be made either way since both parties benefit from the arrangement. However, it is most often the seller who pays a fee or commission to whomever makes the sale possible, and in this case it is that specialist or consultant who is the seller. Logically, then, it is the consultant/specialist who should pay a fee for the service. Even with that established in principle, however, the final question of how to arrange for revenues from the service is not settled, but let us defer that for a moment while we consider how you would organize and arrange the service itself.

In principle, the service is based on building and maintaining two registers. The first is a register of available consultants and other specialists who are self-employed and interested in finding assignments or contracts. That register must be subdivided into the various classes of specialists, and perhaps the subcategories need further subdivision. Engineers, consultants, stenographers, writers, illustrators, and others tend to specialize within their professions (are inevitably specialized within their professions, in most cases) and so it is necessary to organize the register accordingly.

It would be useful to develop a second register of users: companies and other organizations who do or are likely to have at least occasional need for some of the specialists. The latter register ought to list the names of executives in each organization who would be interested in each class of specialist, with as much information as possible about that interest and potential need.

The result could be either physical product or specific service, but we are considering the service aspect here, so we discuss that only, assuming that the registers are resident in computer storage (on disk) although you, as the operator-owner, probably print out an up-to-date hard copy whenever either register is revised or updated. However, you guard that hard copy jealously because it is the key to the service. Presumably, it has cost you time and money—and much effort—to compile, and it is now a valuable property. To mass-produce printing copies of the registers as directories for sale would bring in some income, but would probably be far less profitable for you than other approaches. There are several possible ways of using this base as an income-producer:

1.  Charge each specialist for being listed.
2.  Charge each specialist for each placement or contract consummated.
3.  Charge each employer or user for each placement or contract consummated.
4.  Some combination of these.

Probably the most practicable method and the method that would give you the least trouble to administer and enforce would be to combine all these along these lines:

1. Charge each specialist or consultant a fee for being entered in the register.
2. Charge each employer or user a small fee for each inquiry (which you respond to by sending a printout of suitable candidates from the other register).
3. Charge each specialist a fee for successful placement.

To make this work in this manner it is necessary to get the inquirer's agreement to report to you a successful placement so that you can verify the validity of a placement fee due you, but that should not be difficult, especially if the inquirer (the potential user of the specialist's service) is paying only a nominal fee for getting the printout.

A version of this system is being employed successfully in Rockville, MD, right now. An enterprising woman registers specialists whose services are used normally by householders such as electricians, plumbers, TV servicemen, and other such tradesmen, but she admits them to her register only after she has checked out references they have provided and satisfied herself that they are reliable and competent. Her charges are to the tradesmen only; unlike business proprietors, householders resist paying for such services.

## Supply Referrals

A service that is rarely offered, but would be most valuable, would be referrals of the best sources of supply. Strangely enough, a great many businesspeople never think to investigate better (less costly) sources of routine supplies. Getting yourself on a few mailing lists will soon multiply itself, and before long you will be getting numerous catalogues almost daily. From this you can build a register of suppliers, determining what the best sources are for typewriter ribbons, computer disks, paper, calculators, binders, office furniture, file cabinets, and hundreds of other items, including at least the following:

General office supplies        Office furniture and special equipment
Office machines                Printed forms, standard
Raw materials                  Printing, special
General hardware               Electronic parts and components
Machine tools                  Machine shop services
Personnel recruiting           Advertising novelties
Office temporaries             Professional temporaries
Support services, various      Consulting services, various

(For example, ribbons for the most popular electric typewriter tend to be approximately $36 per dozen purchased in local office supply outlets in most localities, but can be bought from several mail-order houses for less than one-half that price. The service can save customers many times its own cost.)

## Local Credit Bureau

If there is no local credit bureau in your area, or even if there is, there is almost surely room for a better service which you can provide. First, you have the merchant send in the applicant's credit application form and verify what's on it, plus making other general inquiries, and you simply report what you have learned. (No rating or judgment, but simply reporting; that's the way to keep yourself out of difficulties.) Little by little, you build files on individuals, and these are enhanced by the credit files your subscribers send you on their customers. In time, you have a resource in your own files, as well as in the information on the application form. (Merchants always request a credit application from a customer prospect, even though they use a credit bureau to check the applicant out.) It's a business that will grow steadily. Remember, however, that there is now a federal law governing the operation of credit reporting services, although its requirements are not especially onerous. You must be careful that you comply with this law.

## Club and Association Listings

Many businesspeople are interested in knowing of all clubs and associations in the area, and you can sell a list of these in some cases, or incorporate the list into another, related service, producing local directories.

## Letter Service

Local businesses often want to send out form letters that are personalized and typed individually so that they do not appear to be form letters. A mail-merge program does this nicely.

## A SPECIAL PROMOTIONAL SERVICE

Perhaps someone you do business with such as your bank, a local restaurant, or someone else has recently given you a free brochure that lists important dates, such as holidays, income-tax time, annual fairs, and other such things that you may like being reminded of. Perhaps one of your local merchants keeps a supply of free almanacs or other such giveaways on counters.

You may have discovered that some of these kinds of items are available in more than one place. Maybe they are also available at local hotels and other business establishments. Further, perhaps in each case the item is identical except for the name imprinted in a box somewhere, the name of the establishment where you were offered your own free copy.

This is itself a profitable business, and is a form of advertising and sales promotion. In fact, in some cases it is a form of cooperative advertising and sales promotion. Here are some of the ways in which it works:

1.  Some establishments will pay a writer—you—to collect information and write the item up, giving the client either a number of printed copies or a camera-ready set of masters for printing, according to whatever arrangements have been made, including the customer's own advertising in the item.
2.  You (the writer) prepare the copy and then get orders from various businesses each of whom will pay some share, based on the advertising space the businessperson has bought and the number of copies delivered.
3.  You (the writer) simply sell advertising space, as many organizations do in their "ad book" fund-raising campaigns, with some number of copies to each advertiser and the advertiser's imprint priced into the package.

What you need to do is to first decide which of these approaches appeals most to you, then decide what kind of brochure or booklet you will assemble, and then go out and get orders. You should have prepared a *dummy* of the thing, however, so the people you talk to can get a fair idea of what the final product will be and how it will be useful to them.

## IDEAS FOR THE PROMOTIONAL GIVEAWAY

Some of the data-processing services already listed can furnish at least part of the basis for the promotional giveaway brochure. If you have collected a list of local associations such as business and social clubs, hobby groups, professional societies, and others, that might be an interesting directory to form the main theme of the giveaway. The names of consultants you have collected (those whose services would be of interest to individuals such as psychologists and interior decorators) would be a candidate item for inclusion or perhaps even the main item. Special sources of supply such as discount houses and mail order sources for rare items or unusually low prices might interest readers.

In any case, the product should have a main theme, although it may have subordinate ones. It can even be an address book with only blank pages for listing addresses and telephone numbers, although it would also have the obligatory calendar and list of holidays and important dates, plus the advertising which is the main objective of the thing in the first place. Here are a few other kinds of items which would be appropriate to such a product:

Local radio, TV stations, and newspapers: addresses, telephones, key people.

Local restaurants, theaters, museums: things to see and do, with hours, prices, credit cards accepted, other useful data.

Names, addresses, telephone numbers, key people in state and local government offices, plus police and fire-department numbers.

Where or how to do such things as get a birth certificate or passport, complain about something, appeal something, ask for help from government office responsible.

Where or how to get various kinds of information such as census data, status of one's Social Security account, various government programs, other.

## IT DOESN'T HAVE TO BE A BOOKLET

A booklet is a desirable item because it can be of almost any size: it's highly flexible, in that respect. It's easy to handle and highly portable, and it's relatively inexpensive to produce. It is possible to do very much the same thing on a large card and still manage some advertising space on it. This card has the one advantage that people tend to keep it more than they do little booklets and will often keep it by their telephone. It does limit itself to a large degree, however, to only one or two sponsors or clients because it has limited space for advertising. It's also generally more expensive to produce. Still, if you wish to seek out single clients for such projects, it's a viable idea that may help you make the sale.

Of course, the card is suitable also to being imprinted with the names of more than one sponsor. If you wish to approach it this way, leave a fixed block of space for each sponsor to accommodate both the sponsor's name and advertisement, so that there is only one advertisement per card.

Whichever you do, card or booklet, or even some other item, such projects as these are not one-shot deals, but can generally be made into annual projects, since the data tends to become more or less obsolete with time, and an updated (revised) edition should be produced every year. This means that you must maintain your database throughout the year, always alert for new information to update the database, and doing so. It is the database that enables you to turn out the product quickly and efficiently, so you must safeguard it as your main asset.

## PROMOTIONAL NEWSLETTERS

Another, more ambitious product some business firms use for promotion is the newsletter. This is most often an $8\frac{1}{2} \times 11$-inch format of two or four pages, although some are larger, usually a multiple of four. Newsletters are published more frequently than are those special promotional brochures or cards. Newsletters are published daily, weekly, biweekly, monthly, and so on. However, when published as a purely promotional device, it is more likely that the publisher will publish less often, possibly monthly or bimonthly, but more likely quarterly.

Most commonly, the publisher of a promotional newsletter is the sole publisher of that newsletter, and shoulders all the costs connected with producing it. Like most rules, this one can have exceptions, although admittedly they are so rare in the case of newsletters that if you offer the exception, it will be something new and innovative, although it has precedents in other publications. For example, you may have seen the free TV guide brochure made available in supermarkets and elsewhere, printed on newsprint as a saddle-stitched (stapled in the center and folded) brochure, carrying advertisements. This is a franchised enterprise, with local publishers (perhaps they are more accurately called *copublishers*) who sell advertising in their own areas, but are furnished guidance and some *boilerplated* material by the franchisor. That local copublisher, in turn, may choose to permit large distributors to have their name imprinted on the thing as its original source.

Another example of this exists in the form of a number of mail-order advertiser publications, where the publisher will have a given number of copies imprinted with the names of his copublishers which they will then distribute as their own publication, selling advertising for it, and sharing in the advertising revenue while running his or her own advertising in each issue.

This idea is adaptable to the promotional newsletter if you design the approach properly. The main prerequisite is that you design the newsletter in such a way that it has equal appeal to the prospective customers of a number of entrepreneurs who are not competitors. For example, if the newsletter covers health and related subjects, you could approach as prospective sponsors (clients) for the project local physicians, dentists, psychologists, psychiatrists, pharmacies, hospital supplies dealers, dealers in prosthetic appliances, and others who are in the health field. You might find that there is no serious problem of having more than one dentist, for example, if there are no advertisements except the imprinted name of the sponsor, because they would not be in head-to-head opposition. You would find it much easier to sell participating sponsorship if you offered exclusivity, however, only one dentist, one internist, one psychiatrist, and the like.

If you pick the field carefully, you will not have any trouble planning in such manner that you have an ample number of prospects to whom to sell sponsorships.

For some kinds of newsletters, you may wish to consider advertising. For a newsletter directed to a professional field such as health or law, however, it is probably inadvisable to consider advertising, because even in today's liberalized climate which permits some professionals to advertise commercially, few do. They still consider it unethical and demeaning to their image. Therefore, the chief "advertising" is the non-advertising or only-implied advertising of the sponsor's name as the source. There is, however, another possible kind of such subtle advertising, which we discuss now in considering how and where to get suitable information for the newsletter.

## GATHERING NEWS AND INFORMATION

When doing a newsletter for clients, especially for professionals, as sponsors, they are themselves a prime source of information. Certainly, they should have the option of offering materials. The kinds of material you want in the typical newsletter vary but, in general, newsletters fall into one of these categories as far as the kinds of material and coverage they supply are concerned:

> In-depth coverage of a rather narrow or specialized subject which most general news media do not cover.
> Investigative reporting, such as the "story behind the news."
> Advisory and counseling services such as stock-market advisors' reports.
> Coverage of some area generally skipped over by other media.

"News" is stretching it, a bit, as far as typical newsletters are concerned. How fresh and up-to-date is news in a monthly or quarterly publication? If it is news, it is news because it is highly specialized so that there is too limited an audience for it for the trade journal or newspaper. Newsletters seek out that small segment of people with that interest. Among the more successful newsletters today is one that covers contests, and another that covers methods for restoring old homes.

You cannot allow the sponsors to dictate the content to you, nor to use the editorial content to promote themselves. They should be welcome to have their names used freely in your pages when they merit the mentions, and even to be permitted to write columns, articles, brief pieces, or anything else—subject to your editorial control. Given bylines for these things, they get some advertising in this manner.

As in the other kinds of cases, each sponsor gets some number of copies, with his or her name imprinted, and even with a one- or two-line ad in the imprint space, where such is appropriate, and mails out or somehow distributes his or her own copies. (Some will mail; those who have enough traffic in their places of business will simply hand them out to customers or leave them where they can be picked up readily.) You should utilize every means you can to distribute even more copies, for the greater the circulation, the more valuable the newsletter is; hence the more revenue it can produce.

According to the type of newsletter you publish, you seek out the relevant sources of news and other information. For the health newsletter hypothesized before, for example, you would search out some of the trade publications that are not too technical such as *Drug Topics* and *Home Health Care Business*, to name two periodicals in that field, and see about subscribing. (Subscriptions to many trade journals that have "controlled circulation"are free to qualified applicants.) In any case, get as many sample copies as you can and read the advertising. Send off some kind of form letter to the marketing/advertising/public relations departments of major advertisers (and even smaller advertisers, for that matter) explaining what you are doing and ask to be put on their distribution list for news releases and other information.

Do the same with federal, state, and local government agencies that relate to health and health care: Public Health Service and Food and Drug Administration, to name two. Do the same with all associations, especially the large ones, in related fields. In this case, for instance, you might try American Health Care Association and Group Health Association of America, to name just two of many associations.

You will soon find your mailbox stuffed with literature of many kinds, especially with news releases. These are a favored and most popular PR (public relations) tool. A large proportion of these will be of little or no value, written as thinly disguised advertising. All news releases should more properly be called *publicity releases* because they are bids for free advertising. However, some do have worthwhile information despite the poor quality of so many others and they, therefore, do serve a useful function for the newsletter publisher.

Figure 5.1 illustrates a more or less typical news release. Note the

ONE PANASONIC WAY · SECAUCUS, NEW JERSEY 07094

FOR IMMEDIATE RELEASE

Justin Camerlengo or Gerry Eramo or Chris Broadwell
(201) 348-7182        (201) 348-7130 (212) 546-2200

PANASONIC INTRODUCES NEW "STEREO TO GO" MINI STEREO CASSETTE RECORDER/PLAYER

TARPON SPRINGS, FLA. -- Panasonic's new addition to its Stereo To Go line, Model
RQ-J36, is an AC/battery powered mini stereo cassette recorder/player with stereo
headphones.  The new unit records in stereo with a built-in stereo microphones or
optional auxiliary microphones.  The new unit comes equipped with lightweight stereo
headphones, and its lockable mic on/pause control lets you hear outside sounds without removing the headset.

The RQ-J36 is compatible with metal and normal tape, with a selector for tone
control, and other convenience features of the new model include full auto-stop
function at the end of each tape, digital tape counter, cue and review controls and
a stereo/mono mode selector.

Recording with the new mini cassette recorder/player is easy with its one-touch
recording control.  Output level can be controlled and the unit has an LED battery
indicator.

Included with Model RQ-J36 is a carrying case with shoulder strap, and the
recorder/player runs on 4 "AA" batteries that are not included.  The suggested
retail price for Model RQ-J36 is $109.95.

-30-

031682mcs

**Figure 5.1.**   Typical news release.

"contact" names. They are people connected with the PR function
(often writers) who can supply more details, perhaps a photograph, if
you want to pursue the lead furnished by the release and try to get "the
story behind the story."

Read widely, with an eye alert for good stories and leads to good
stories. Don't allow your newsletter to degenerate into a mere flack for

the sponsoring clients or a window for all the publicity releases, no matter how bad some of them are. Encourage readers to write, as evidence of the quality and appeal of your newsletter. You will need this to help your newsletter grow.

## BUSINESS ARRANGEMENTS

It is possible that some major organization may want to have you create and produce a newsletter for them exclusively. In such case they will foot the entire bill for your services and all costs, and you will have to decide for yourself what that is worth. (At the minimum, estimate the number of hours you must devote to this and charge on that basis. Later, we discuss fees and pricing in more detail.) It is likely that it will be more practicable and more profitable for you to create a newsletter and provide it to a number of clients as a service, although you may start with only one or two. That is of no consequence; if you continue to market effectively, you will eventually have enough sponsoring clients to make it pay.

If you must start with only one client, although you intend to make this a copublished newsletter, you cannot very well charge that one client for all the labor and expense to which you are put. You must regard that as an investment, and underwrite it yourself; subsidize the newsletter at first, in substance. Charge that first client as you would if he or she were one of perhaps a dozen or more clients.

The base price must include some number of copies of the newsletter for the sponsor to distribute, and you will do well to encourage the sponsors to distribute as many as possible, at least 100 to 200 each. Your base price is for that nominal or minimum number of copies. Let us suppose that that is 100 copies at a price of $100. That doesn't mean $1 per copy; it means that you require that amount from each sponsor to cover costs, labor, and profit. You make additional copies available at some much lower figure because that is to cover the cost of the additional copies plus some little profit for you. You might wish to charge additional copies at $25 per 100, or even less, depending on what they cost you to print and to have imprinted with the sponsor's name.

## SALES APPEALS AND EXTRA PROFITS

Inasmuch as you have the facilities, you may wish to offer your sponsors an additional service, at an extra fee, of course. You may wish to also do their mailings for them. For some, those who must rely on the mails for distribution of most of their copies, this would be a boon, relieving them of just about all labor except writing you a check and furnishing you a mailing list. This makes it a total service, and offers the complete convenience that is, for many, the clinching sales argument.

As in the case of the other promotional publishing ideas, you need some kind of dummy or sample issue to show prospects and sign them up. Explain the benefits, especially stressing exclusivity (no direct competitor will be signed up), the independence of the medium, the prestige and professional image imparted by something with as much "class" as a good newsletter, and any other pluses you can think of. (These will vary with each case.)

Don't neglect the larger businesses, especially the large local corporation, or branch of some corporation. The bigger the company, the better a prospect it is, although there is the downside of this in that large companies may tend to borrow your idea and hire their own direct staff or order someone already on staff to create the newsletter. To combat this, and as another argument to use in selling the idea, talk up the special information sources you have developed (by the time you are ready to go out and sell the idea, you should have gotten some. sources lined up and enough good information to dummy up the sample issue). Even the large company may have to stop and think about starting their own newsletter effort in-house when you point out that you are ready to begin publishing almost immediately, whereas it would take them at least a few months to gear up for their first issue, and even then it might be many more months before they had reached the point where you already are.

## TYPED OR TYPESET?

Although by far the majority of newsletters are done with typewriter composition, prospects you approach are likely to be far more impressed with typeset composition. Moreover, since the newsletter is (presumably) to be only a quarterly, it will probably be a good idea to typeset it. To sell it, you should have a typeset sample issue, perhaps, in fact, a first issue or, at the least, the front page of a sample or first issue.

## PROSPECTING FOR SALES LEADS

If you choose to offer services along the lines of the service bureau or other generalized services on some custom basis, you will want to prepare a brochure or announcement of some kind that suggests a broad variety of services, specifies that you can devise a suitable service to satisfy almost any need, and invite prospects to write or call for a free consultation.

The way to handle all responses to this is to press for a specific appointment to discuss the prospect's needs and the remedies you can offer. In this you must stress that there is no obligation for the initial consultation. (Don't call it a sales appointment. It's a sales appointment as far as you are concerned, but it's a consultation as far as the prospect is concerned.)

Be a good listener when you make the call. Draw the client out about his or her problems, needs, fears, desires, and concerns. Identify one or two of the concerns that appear to you to be the most serious ones and suggest the service you can offer to relieve the problem. In most cases it will be unwise to push for a large sale. This is a foot-in-the-door kind of opportunity, a chance to show the prospect what you can do with little risk. Time enough later, after the client–supplier relationship has been established, to press for expansion of the services.

If you decide to specialize in some way, adapt the approach accordingly. Make your brochure or other announcement such that it discusses the specialized service and stresses the specialization, but show the several (perhaps many) problems that it solves, and proceed to follow up leads established by an offer of free consultation.

A number of other ways to develop and follow up those leads are presented later in the chapter on marketing and sales.


## DP SERVICES FOR INDIVIDUALS

Until now we have been focusing primarily on service-bureau types of data processing and related services, usually of interest only to businesses, small or large. However, there are many DP (data processing) services that are useful to individual consumers who cannot or choose not to own their own microcomputers. If we look at the many programs designed for the use of personal-computer owners for their personal affairs, and consider how many individuals can and would use such services if they did not have to own and operate their own micros, a quite large and diverse market is revealed. All you need do is study the list of such programs, and you can soon see more than a few such opportunities. Here are just a few ideas.

### Education

There is a steadily growing supply of academic programs useful for tutoring students of all ages and school grade levels, but also useful for adults who want to improve their knowledge of math, history, science, or other subjects.

### Training

Training, as the term is used here and generally in industry and the business world, differs from education in that it is not general, but is specific to some industry, trade, skill, craft, or other occupational field. Typical programs train individuals in accounting, automobile repair, electronics, carpentry, salesmanship, real estate, marketing, and other fields. Many of the programs are basic or entry level, but there are also upgrading courses, enabling those already in some field to upgrade, expand, diversify, or update their skills in their chosen fields.

## Investment Analysis

There are numerous programs that help individuals with their investment portfolios through individual and comparative analyses of various stocks and bonds, indications of general market trends, comparisons of different types of securities, and other subjects useful to both the expert and nonexpert alike.

## Bio Charts

For those interested in the biorhythm theory as applied to their personal lives and careers, there are several programs that will do their analyses and report the results to them.

## Special Education

There are programs to teach the user gambling games such as blackjack as practiced in the casinos, and other games where players' skill and judgment are major factors in the outcome. Some of them teach even those games where chance is the major factor (but even learning the various odds may be helpful to players).

## Household Finances

There are programs designed to help the individual function more effectively in managing personal finances generally, perhaps in such matters as making trade-off analyses with regard to when to trade an automobile for best value, whether to upgrade a house through renovation or trade up, and other such matters well beyond the obvious ones of managing day-to-day household finances and filing personal tax returns.

## Retirement Planning

In these times, with more and more individuals covered by retirement and pension or annuity programs, planning for one's retirement is more and more a consideration of individuals in middle age who are approaching retirement. Some of these individuals want to actually begin doing nothing but fishing and enjoying life at their ease, whereas others are looking forward to having a second career. In addition, many far-sighted younger people also wish to study retirement possibilities and plan ahead for their eventual retirement.

## Hobbies

For those who take hobbies most seriously and put serious effort into becoming experts at their hobbies, there are programs in philately, numismatics, gems and gem cutting, and many other hobbies involving extensive knowledge and/or skills.

## Personal Inventory/Record Keeping

There are many kinds of personal records we need as individuals. For example, we need to keep precise data on personal property covered by insurance if we are to enjoy the full benefits of insurance compensation of losses due to fire, theft, or natural disaster. We also need to keep serial numbers of property that has serial numbers to help police recover stolen goods. We need to remember birthdays, anniversaries, and important appointments. There are programs to do all these things and more.

## DESIGNING AND MARKETING RELEVANT SERVICES

There are several things to consider in designing and marketing the services to users that the preceding types of programs and needs suggest.

1.   Some of these services require the customer to work at the micro in an interactive situation. Education and training programs, for example, fall into this category. In some cases, you can run the program, inputting data supplied by the customer, and produce a printout as the result representing the service for which you charge.

2.   If the program required is highly specialized and/or the customer makes frequent or regular use of the program, it may be in your interest to have the customer buy and own the program so that you avoid the risk of investing in a specialized program with no guarantee of recovering your investment and turning a profit. On the other hand, you can and should charge more for use of a program you own—have invested in—so you should try, as far as possible, to use programs that are useful to a great many customers and will, therefore, offer little risk.

3.   If you feel it unwise to invest in a program for which there are several interested users who are also reluctant to invest in the program individually, you may be able to interest them in forming a syndicate or group to buy the program and leave it in your care for their exclusive use. They can, of course, seek and enroll new members of their syndicate, with adequate contributions from the new members. You charge appropriately for the computer time and your own services.

Bear in mind that for any program or need that requires direct and spontaneous interaction between the customer and the computer, there are certain direct and indirect consequences. One of these is that you will not yourself have access to and use of your system when a customer is using it. You may find this unacceptable. If so, you will have to avoid offering services that have this consequence. However, if you do offer such services, there will spring up the inevitable "prime time" and "off-peak time." You will have to scale your prices accordingly, because it is likely that for your purposes prime time will be early evening hours and weekend hours.

Some programs, such as making personal records and biorhythm charts, require only that the customer supply you the input data to be operated on, and you can deliver a printout to satisfy the need and command the charges. You will need to have a printer and, again, you will have the equivalent of prime time and off-peak time in real-time data processing and batch or off-line data processing. If the customer demands results immediately—perhaps on a while-you-wait basis— your charges should reflect this highly personalized, custom service, with a surcharge or premium charge of some kind.

This imposes on you the possibility of another problem. If you do agree to offer services that require the customer to work at your micro and/or do DP in real time, you will have to schedule customers (have an appointment system) and this creates some problems since you cannot always know in advance how long a given appointment will take. That is, you run into the typical problems of appointments that run overlong, keeping the next customer waiting, and the no-shows, who create another kind of problem for you. You must consider these potential problems in deciding what you wish to offer.

Bear in mind, however you decide to structure the services, that all of these are custom services, offered to individual customers on an individual basis. You must structure your rates accordingly. It is not that printed report or record you are selling, but the entire service of preparing that report or record. The entire service includes your investment in equipment, software, and other facilities that make the venture possible and make the service itself possible. You are also selling your own know-how, your personal investment of time and money in learning what you need to know, developing the skills and knowledge that make it possible to provide the service.

All of that is represented by the paper you hand the customer, or even the time you make available to sit at your CRT and press the right keys to go through the training or other program on your micro. Don't sell the paper per se, then. Sell the entire thing, making sure the customer understands that the service is a custom service. Along with that, sell the benefits, such as better grades in school for children tutored by means of your micro; *that* is what fond and/or worried parents really pay for.

# Chapter Six

---

# Computer
# Communications
# Service

*The line between "communication" and "information" is a fine one, and getting finer all the time—almost to the vanishing point.*

## COMMUNICATIONS AND INFORMATION

It is pretty well known by now that anyone with a computer can dial up any of several database/information services (if they have subscribed to the service) and get a variety of information such as news stock reports and newspaper columns. Two of the best-known and most prominent such services are The Source, 1616 Anderson Road, Mc-Lean, VA 22102, and CompuServe Information Service, 5000 Arlington Centre Boulevard, Columbus, OH 43220. Membership costs vary as there are some special deals available, but run generally from about

$25 to $100, and connect charges run from about $5 per hour to about $22 per hour, depending on several variables such as time of day. In addition, there are a few miscellaneous "surcharges" levied for various and sundry reasons.

All in all, then, it isn't exactly inexpensive for the average individual to use these services for personal ends. However, as a resource to support a for-profit enterprise, the costs are far from oppressive.

The information available is impressive in its diversity and scope: you can find sources for aiding youngsters through college, instructions for playing *chemin de fer*, airline flight schedules, newspaper features, and a seemingly endless array of information items, all listed in stepped menus.

The complaints from some users are that it's slow at 300 baud (you can get faster, 1200-baud service, if you're willing to pay the premium prices for it), that it takes forever to get through all the menu levels to find the access codes you need, and that sometimes the information is wordy but not at all detailed or especially helpful. Still, despite drawbacks, overall it's a distinct service with profit potentials in these times when information has become a major commodity of value—when buyers are willing to pay for information, that is. The significance of microcomputer use in communications (telecommunications, to be more precise and more definitive) relates to the commercial value of information services as much as it does to the value of communications services.

## MARKETS FOR COMMUNICATIONS SERVICES

As an industry in itself, communications generally and telecommunications in particular are huge markets. There are few business or industrial activities that do not depend on the services of communications industries. Even as individuals we make extensive use of these services, and of industries and services that themselves depend on communications networks and in many cases owe their very existence to the availability of efficient and rapid communications systems. Until recently, most adults were at best barely conscious of the existence of communications companies other than the operating telephone companies and their parent, AT&T, American Telephone and Telegraph, also known widely as "Ma Bell." Since the breakup of AT&T we have begun to become aware of other business and industrial entities in the communications industries. In that field, serving the needs of telephone and telegraph operating companies (primarily, however, telephone companies), they refer to what they do and the generic field of their industrial activity as *telecommunications*. Some computer specialists state unequivocally that *telecommunications* refers only to computers "talking" to each other. Inasmuch as computers talk to each other, when they do, over telephone lines, using modems to make the translations at each end (from electrical pulses representing binary digits to audible pulses, at the beginning of transmission, and reversing that process at the other end of the transmission), the distinction seems relatively unimportant. Moreover, telephone equipment is using digital (computer-like) equipment more and more, and is dependent on software for the effective operation of modern switching and transmission equipment. Therefore, it appears somewhat doubtful, at least to this writer, whether there is any great advantage, or even a significance, to discriminating between the two definitions of telecommunications. We favor the broader one, which includes any exchange or transmission of information over telephone lines, no matter who is at the two ends.

*Communications* has another, broader definition, and the so-called communications industry includes all of publishing (for the purpose of publishing is to communicate information to an audience of readers) and all of radio and TV, with all the subordinate systems and industries of cable, microwave, community antenna, VCR (videocassette recorders), and other outgrowths of all the media.

The markets for communications, using the term in its broadest sense, are therefore universal and virtually without limits. We have already touched on some of them in earlier chapters, and we touch on them again in later ones. In this chapter, however, we confine ourselves to telecommunications primarily, although touching on how it affects, supports, reinforces, and/or helps make other communications activities possible. That is, we are concerned here only with what computer communications offers you in the way of profit possibilities, either directly or indirectly.

## MARKETS FOR INFORMATION SERVICES

If communications is a broad term ranging widely into almost all human activities, *information* is almost equally broad, almost synonymous with communication. Information has been an identifiable commodity of value for quite a long time, antedating the rise of the microcomputer and even the rise of the earlier, "big" computers. In one sense, information has always had value, at least since it became possible to vend information through the spoken word and the printed word, and later through other media. The importance of information has grown steadily, with an increasingly complex society and increasing complexity and sophistication in our technologies. Today's high school student is more knowledgeable than the learned individuals of only a few centuries ago. Man's total store of knowledge is increasing exponentially, and it is increasingly difficult to be well informed or, at least, to be well informed about a broad range of subjects. In fact, without today's computers, it is most unlikely that we could handle the avalanche of information that has descended on us in the past few decades.

Information, then, like telecommunication, has become a somewhat ambiguous term. The computer industry and the profession of specialists in computer technology long ago appropriated the term for their own use, and to them the word information and several derivations (e.g., *information theory* and *information industry*) have significance only in connection with computer systems and computer technology generally. Again, as in the case of communication, we use the term here in whatever sense it relates to profit possibilities for your microcomputer-linked ventures. As we explore those possibilities, you will find that in most cases it is information that is the commodity you can most easily sell, although the communication capabilities are often the instrumentality that makes the venture possible. In fact, you will soon discover that it is not easily possible to determine whether it is the communication or the information that you are selling, nor does it matter greatly except as it enables you to market it most successfully. The distinction is usually important only as it pertains to motivating prospects to buy the commodity or the service.

Despite the steadily falling prices and steadily increasing user-friendliness of microcomputers and their programs, there are a great many people who do not and will not own their own micros, although they have use for benefits to be derived from the micro's capability for accessing such major databases as those offered by The Source and CompuServe. For example, there are many individuals who would have use for and would be willing to pay for access to the information such as the following few examples.

1.  Investors seeking the latest stock market information from the various stock markets (one's local newspaper rarely carries them all, and those which do are not usually available as rapidly as access to these databases makes the information available).

2.  Writers researching general or specific data on any subject, particularly those under schedule pressures and trying to shorten the research time.

3.  Businesspeople with sudden needs for information and little time (or perhaps little knowledge of how) to ferret it out.

4.  Students with a need to research data for term papers, theses, and dissertations.

5.  Professionals writing professional papers for their societies, and a concomitant need for research data.

6.  Anyone preparing to address a group or attend a meeting or conference, with a need to gather data in preparation.

Obviously, for such needs as these, the customer must pay for the connect time, any surcharges or special fees (certain types of data require such special charges), some fee to cover your overhead costs, and something to cover your profit markup. This may prove to be a relatively expensive service, but when the need is great, customers will pay whatever is required to get the service. However, as in the case cited in Chapter 5, it may be possible to organize a syndicate of individuals who want access to those databases enough to form a pool of money to cover the expenses. They need to have some community of interest to make the syndicate a practical possibility, but for some uses such as late reports on securities, it should not be too difficult to find enough interested individuals to form a syndicate.

Nor is this the only linkage with the coverage of data processing for individuals, as discussed in the previous chapter: there are other coincidences of interest. The individual who wants that program that analyzes securities is most likely to also want those late reports and quotations, and even straight news items of happenings in the business world are likely to be of direct interest. If you have customers for whom you are doing DP such as some of that described, it is quite likely that you have some excellent prospects for the communications/information services you can offer.

The information categories themselves suggest markets and customers. For example, Herb Friedman, writing in *Radio Electronics* magazine on the subject of dial-up software networks, reports accessing the *Washington Post*'s classified advertisements to help his son seek out a suitable used car. He listed the type of car, equipment wanted, and price range in his request, and got back a list of candidate cars that matched his specifications.

There is quite an amazing diversity of information available. Here are brief descriptions of just a few databases now in existence.

U.S. Prices Data Bank contains information compiled by the Bureau of Labor Statistics (a federal agency) on consumer, wholesale, and industrial prices.

The Value Line database can supply information on more than 10,000 American companies.

The CIS Index, a product of Congressional Information Services, has information on hearings, reports, and publications of the two houses of Congress.

The National Library of Medicine (part of the federal Department of

Health and Human Services) operates MEDLARS, a database of medical information.

NTIS, for the federal National Technical Information Service, can cite over one-half million reports and other technical publications reporting on federal and federally funded research and development projects such as technological achievements of NASA, the National Science Foundation, the National Bureau of Standards, and other federal agencies.

ERIC, Education Resources Information Center, is a product of the U.S. Office of Education (now a full government department), with well over a quarter-million education-related reports and publications cited.

The National Library of Medicine also operates TOXLINE, a database on pollutants, other toxic substances, and their effects on humans.

NYTCD is the New York Times Consumer Database, with over two million article abstracts from its own newspaper and others.

These are by no means all the databases available that may be reached by means of your own microcomputer and one of the established services; there are many more and new ones being created frequently. The database and the information service are not identical, however, although the NYTCD cited happens to be. Most of the information services access more than one database; that is, you gain access to the database through the service. Other services to which you can subscribe are listed next, with their addresses so that you can make direct inquiry into their charges and specific services:

Dow Jones News/Retrieval, P.O. Box 300, Princeton, NJ 08540.

New York Times Information Service, 1719 A, Route 10, Parsippany, NJ 07054.

Dialog, 3460 Millview Avenue, Palo Alto, CA 94304.

TEXNET$^{SM}$, c/o The Source$^{SM}$.

The TEXNET Information Service is a special program of The Source, offered by Texas Instruments, and claiming more than 1200 programs and services. Its many files illustrate vividly what such programs offer typically to their subscribers. The following is a general listing of services, as reported by the company. Costs are $1000 as a one-time subscription fee, with user costs of 10 cents per minute for off-peak hours (evenings and weekends), 30 cents per minute for peak hours (during weekday business hours), and approximately 7 cents per minute for service from midnight until 7:00 AM.

| | |
|---|---|
| UPI News Service | Late news stories, with keyword searches for special interest news available |
| Electronic mail | Communicate with other subscribers anywhere in country |
| Electronic travel service | Make your own airline and hotel reservations, using your credit card; also has restaurant rating guide and airline schedules |
| Educational programs | Mostly academic programs for schoolchildren |
| Consumer aids | FYI (for your information) features on reducing energy costs, choosing wines, buying vitamins, list of toll-free numbers, and other such useful data |
| Sports news | Current data on major sports events, records |
| Programming power | Programming languages made available as help in writing programs |
| Financial service | Economics and business news, forecasts, other information from established professionals in appropriate professional fields |

| | |
|---|---|
| Market reports | Quotations for securities, commodities, Treasury bills, foreign-exchange rates, mutual funds, warrants, options, and other such |
| Portfolio management | Help in managing investments in securities |
| International document research | Makes available the services of many research specialists throughout world who will carry out research projects for fees |
| LEGI-SLATE | Tracks bills reported out of Congressional Committees, lists Members of Congress by state, party, committee, and subcommittee; updated weekly; includes ordering service |
| COMP-U-STAR | Enhanced shoppers' program, allows subscribers to shop or buy 30,000 items available at discounts |
| Management Contents Ltd | Keyword search of abstracts from recent issues of 27 leading business journals, with ordering service for reprints |
| Commodity News Service, Inc | Tracks price movements in commodities futures markets and provides market commentary and commodity news with frequent updates while the market is trading |
| Media general | 58 items of historical information on more than 3000 NYSE, Amex, and OTC stocks to enable subscriber to analyze stock portfolios, updated weekly |

The TEXNET service is organized so that the subscriber can dial a local number in any of more than 350 cities, type in a private ID number, and then type in commands in the English language.

TEXNET is a special program of The Source, as already noted, and is, therefore, reached at the address already given for The Source in McLean, VA.

This is a rather broad spread of information and resources, but it is typical of the several general-information databases, as distinct from those such as the Dow Jones and New York Times services which tend to specialize, each in their own special spheres of interest, a not surprising turn. It raises the same question of the directions open to you to go in providing an information/research service, if you opt for this kind of venture at all. It is possible to opt for an information/research service along an entire spectrum of subjects, professional areas, business areas, and industrial areas, as we have just seen. There are virtually no limits to the variety and number of types of information one can seek out.

## GENERALIST OR SPECIALIST?

If you decide to offer customers custom research services by means of your micro and accessible data banks, you will have to decide whether it will be a generalized service, accessing all data banks available to you, or a specialized service, with less scope and more depth. There are pros and cons to both choices. The generalized service offers the broadest possible appeal for your marketing efforts, something for everyone or nearly everyone. But it is also more expensive if you truly want to cover the whole field of information, and also more complicated. The specialized service offers the drawback that it has a narrower range of appeal (hence a smaller total population of prospects), but it is probably more efficient in that you can subscribe to just one service and offer more in-depth coverage. It offers some marketing advantage, too, however, in that the specialized service always has the edge in appeal of appearing to be more comprehensive and more capable within its field; prospects tend to place more faith in the specialist than in the generalist.

## WHO BUYS INFORMATION?

Recognize, first of all, that there are at least two broad markets for the information services we have been discussing here. We have talked largely about the market represented by individuals concerned about managing their securities investments: to those students, professionals, and others having a need to gather data for a paper or a speech; to businesspeople with pressing needs for business information. Matthew Lesko, founder of Washington Researchers, Inc. and author of *Information USA* and other books on information-gathering, has explained that he stumbled into the information-research business by accident when a client asked for his help in finding out something about potato agriculture. To Lesko's dismay (which ultimately turned to delight as he perceived the business opportunities), he discovered an individual in the Department of Agriculture who was probably the world's outstanding expert on potatoes. If he could not direct you to the information you wanted on potatoes, it probably did not exist or was not worth knowing about.

Obviously, you cannot build a business on a specialty as narrow as that. However, it illustrates the existence of information in depth, especially in government agencies. It illustrates, too, the viability of selling information as a business venture and, perhaps more significantly, just how sharply focused the information needs of clients can be. Here are a few typical questions for which business executives have asked information/research services to find answers:

What are the long-range birth-rate projections through the year 2000?

How many new ammonia plants have been built in the United States since 1975?

What was last year's consumption of imported beer?

How many wearers of contact lenses are there in the United States?

What is the profitability of the health club business?

What is the cat population of the United States?

What were the top two songs of 1923, 1933, 1945, 1950, and 1967?

Provide a bibliography of recent books or articles on aphrodisiacs.

What is the total market for fireplace accessories?

List all the experts on potato chips.

What states do not have income tax?

How many new products/inventions are marketed each year? How many succeed?

Find an article from the *New York Times* on automobile gas mileage, especially Mercedes Benz.

How many supermarkets accept credit cards?

List New York's richest men.

What states have the lowest property taxes?

Who designed the L'Eggs™ Pantyhose display rack?

How much oil is needed for one month's electricity generation for New York City?

List names and addresses of four consultants in marketing to the black community.

What percentage of people read books after college?

Who makes nonstationary offshore drilling platforms?


All these questions have been abstracted from a longer list which appears in the book *How to Win With Information or Lose Without It*, by Andrew P. Garvin and Hubert Bermont, published by The Consultant's Library, 815 15th Street, NW, Washington, DC 20005. Garvin is chairman and chief executive officer of FIND/SVP, The Information Clearinghouse, a leading information retrieval service located in New

York City. Hubert Bermont is a consultant, lecturer, and president of Bermont Books, Inc., publishers of The Consultant's Library. The book is itself a useful treatise on the information business and a most helpful reference and guide if you contemplate entering this business.

Overall, the list illustrates, again, typical needs of clients. Study this list, which was selected at random from the longer list. Are these all queries from business executives? Maybe. A manufacturer of disposable diapers was concerned about birth-rate projects for the next two decades, but it could as easily have been a writer seeking data for an article or book. It could have been a student seeking data for a term paper or thesis, or a professional seeking information for a professional paper or an address to his professional society.

Look at the other questions. You could make the same speculations for all of them, could you not? Almost any executive, writer, student, professional, or individual with a speech to prepare, a paper to write, or a commission or board meeting to attend might be the inquirer in every case.

You can see, then, the market potential in this business, if it is the one that most interests you. If you do, and you want to investigate databases and their accessibility more thoroughly, you will find that the book just cited lists some additional sources of information on that subject. You can also order the following directories and/or make inquiry of their publishers:

*Computer-Readable Databases*
American Society for Information Science
1010 16th Street, NW
Washington, DC 20036

*Directory of Online Databases*
Cuadra Associates, Inc.
1523 6th Street, Suite 12
Santa Monica, CA 90401

*Directory of On-Line Information Resources*
CSG Press
6110 Executive Boulevard, Suite 250
Rockville, MD 20852

*Computer Bank Book, The Executive Guide to Computer Data Banks*
FIND/SVP
500 Fifth Avenue
New York, NY 10036

Remember only, in selling this service, that it is neither the research nor the communication that interests the client or for which the client is paying. It is usually not even the information per se. What it is that the client is willing to pay for, as the last few paragraphs should have illustrated, is the answer to his or her question. The answers to questions are worth money.

# Chapter Seven

## "Pen Pal" Services

Traditionally, "ham" radio operators have always been "hackers" in their own field, and have liked nothing better than gabbing with each other as much as possible. Between the pen-pal tradition and the ham radio tradition, computer hackers will inevitably follow suit.

## VIRTUALLY AN INSTITUTION

Even today, despite the many facilities people have for meeting other people, there are many who are basically too shy to seek out friends of either their own or the opposite sex by direct, face-to-face contact. For many years there have been those who "met" friends through their post offices, through correspondence, that is, becoming "pen pals." Even now there are magazines and other periodicals that encourage such contacts. Candidates for such friendships initiate the action by placing small classified advertisements in a magazine or newspaper with a brief self-description (appearance, vital statistics, and interests are common factors covered in such advertisements) and an invitation to respond and exchange letters and photographs. There then follow exchanges of letters and in some cases protracted correspondence. Some people want nothing more than to correspond with others and maintain pen-pal friendships, whereas others want something more and seek to extend the written correspondence into face-to-face meetings and more intimate friendships. Some result in marriages, whether by original design or by spontaneous development.

This is a time-honored practice, also referred to sometimes as a "lonely hearts" club, suggesting that most of those engaged in the activity are really seeking conjugal mates or, at least, girlfriends and boyfriends. Perhaps more women than men traditionally used this method for making contact with those of the other sex because other methods for initiating such contacts were not open to them, whereas men had fewer restraints on their social activities. Even today, when it is accepted that women need not be shrinking violets, as a class women tend to be reluctant to frequent singles bars and engage in other activities that might lead to meeting people and forming friendships. The pen-pal method offers a shield, even anonymity, if the writer prefers. One may shrink from face-to-face contact and even shield one's physical location by using a post office box and/or an unlisted telephone.

## OTHER WAYS PEOPLE BECOME PEN-PALS

The growth of a pen-pal relationship does not always take place through deliberate design, but sometimes grows spontaneously out of a correspondence undertaken for entirely unrelated reasons. For example, those engaged in small mail-order enterprises, particularly those which are small, home-based, and/or part-time, often find that before long they are part of a kind of fraternity of such dealers, sometimes referred to as "the inner circle." Before long one finds oneself writing to others, more or less continually, sometimes having telephone discussions, often doing business together, and becoming quite "close" without ever having met face to face. (It's quite interesting to attend conventions of small mail-order dealers and witness many "old friends" actually meeting for the first time. It's even more interesting to do so yourself, and see how different many people appear from how you imagined they would look.)

You soon discover that you can become quite fond of someone you have never actually met or broken bread with. Such friendships can continue for many years, and continue to grow stronger and stronger, without ever a face-to-face meeting. Some can become so strong that they can lead to serious disagreements, arguments, and survive those too.

Everything changes, and yet things do not change. In the modern world of microcomputers chance acquaintanceships have sprung up through the correspondence of computer exchanges by means of modem and telephone lines, and some of these have bloomed into firm friendships. There is at least one case on record where such a friendship led to marriage between two computer correspondents who were of the opposite sex. They had made the initial exchange as a purely business transaction, had to have several exchanges, and finally began to correspond with each other for personal reasons.

Of course, corresponding with each other by computer has a spontaneity that corresponding by mail does not have because the correspondence takes place in *real time*—spontaneously, with immediate response to each stimulus as in a telephone conversation, or in conversations between *ham* (amateur) radio operators. That is another interesting parallel situation: something quite similar to pen-pal correspondence takes place between short-wave radio hams who talk to each other frequently and get to know each other by their station's call letters, much more than by their personal names.

## MICROCOMPUTER PEN-PAL SERVICES

At present, microcomputer pen-pals are a fairly new phenomenon, confined primarily to chance encounters between owners of microcomputers who then decide to continue and extend the correspondence. That is, there are as yet no organized efforts, no central medium, and no specific instrumentality for initiating such correspondence. One can read letters from others in computer magazines and newsletters and try to make contacts on a hit-or-miss basis, but these are rarely satisfactory because they are hit or miss. They can work only if both parties wish to begin a correspondence, a distinct uncertainty. Only once in a while will such an initiative result in a true pen-pal correspondence.

At the same time, there is definite need there, a definite market. Human nature has not changed. Individuals are still lonely, shy, introverted generally, wanting to form friendships, but so afraid of rejection that they find it necessary to shield their effforts by hiding behind the anonymity of box numbers, unlisted telephone numbers, and indirect contact by means of the written word. Even then, many are reluctant to attempt to initiate a correspondence because in a chance contact what probability is there that the other wants to have such correspondence? Is there not a possibility of rejection shock in this situation, despite a great deal of anonymity?

Because of this, what is needed is an organized program in which it is established in advance that all parties are actively seeking pen-pal correspondence, and in which all state their preferences and give some description of themselves, their interests, and their objectives. Given this, the probability of rejection shrinks dramatically and participants are much less fearful of rejection. This, in fact, is what a great many of those who seek pen-pal friendships want.

The design of the system must be based on several factors and basic decisions. For one thing, there is the matter of the area you will service. Another is how you will undertake the initiation of contacts. Let us consider some of the factors.

## DECIDING ON SERVICE AREAS

Perhaps a first consideration is scope. Given the cost of the telephone lines for long-distance correspondence, it may be advisable to operate, at least in the beginning, entirely within a local area (non-toll calling) extending the service only later after becoming established. It seems likely that success will come easier and sooner under that condition.

As a possible alternative, if you wish to make the service unrestricted by area, you might concentrate on the local area without foreclosing those who wish to subscribe despite being many miles away.

It is not the distance alone that is the problem because if you were based in, say, Denver, your subscribers in Miami could very well limit their own pen-pals to Miami. But it would take a long time, probably, before you had a large enough number of subscribers in each area of the country. Therefore, it is probably wise to take this into account and work only your own local area at first. Moreover, what you learn in that early effort will make your later extension of the service much more efficient. The logical phases would be along the following lines.

## Phase I

Start system on basis of local area only (e.g., your city/town and environs) and use as a prototype in which you learn, while improving it until it works well.

## Phase II

Extend system, based on perfected model of first phase, to cover somewhat broader area, perhaps state-wide or region-wide. Continue to observe, learn, and improve.

## Phase III

Go national now, with a firm foundation established, and begin covering entire nation.

## Option

You may want to operate a number of systems or programs, one for each major region, rather than a single national program. This will depend to some extent on the rest of the design as you will soon see.

## INFORMATION-EXCHANGE MEDIUM

Equally important is deciding how you will bring prospective pen-pals into initial contacts, to enable them to solicit computer correspondence with each other. Bear in mind that not everyone is interested on the one hand, and that you must design this in such a way as to protect your own interest—to give you a viable business venture—at the same time.

The traditional way of enabling individuals to solicit correspondence with others has been classified advertisements such as the following:

> 29-year-old bachelor who appreciates music and painting wishes to correspond with woman of same generation and similar interests. POB _____, Horseyset, VA 22022.

> Mature woman executive wishes to correspond with mature executive or professional who enjoys theatre and literature. Please send photo and personal description, and I will reciprocate. Box _____, Slumbertown, PA 19117.

> Electronics hobbyist wishes to exchange information with other electronics hobbyists. Jerry, 1677 Snowbound Lane, Beastly Weather, MN 55455.

Many of these kinds of notices appeared in general-circulation publications and still do. There were and are other publications that are devoted solely and exclusively to this purpose, and their publishers solicit subscriptions to these publications through advertisements, often classified advertisements. Or the publishers offer something more, as a service for which individuals pay, and the publication is one of the services provided.

Therefore, one of the plans you might consider is advertising in publications likely to reach computer owners, soliciting names and addresses of individuals interested in computer pen-pal correspondence with other computer owners. To get started, you might accept the advertisements of the first to respond at a nominal price, or even free of charge, since the success of your program depends on building a circulation. Your first advertisements might read somewhat along the following lines:

Like to have a computer pen-pal, meet, talk to interesting people? It's free. Send name, address, telephone number to _____ .

Or, if you want to charge, even to get your first listings, offer free information so that you will get responses. Then send out follow-up letters explaining the entire proposition and soliciting advertisements. It will produce far better results than trying to persuade readers of a small classified advertisement to send money. That is called *inquiry advertising*, because it is designed to elicit inquiries from readers, although its purpose is to start building a mailing list of individuals who have shown some interest in what you offer. To induce them to inquire, dangle the essence of what the proposition is about—it's no use drawing inquiries from people who would not be interested in your offer—and offer free information. Then send out the follow-up letter and other parts of the direct-mail package, which we present in more detail in the chapter on marketing.

Presumably, the medium of information exchange (the way prospective pen-pals contact one another) is through learning of each other's existence and interest by reading each other's advertisements in the journal you publish, and for which you make a charge, perhaps nominal at first while you are beginning to build a list and can't offer readers very much, but much higher later, after the exchange publication is well established and has many notices, which means many opportunities for readers to find suitable computer pen-pals. In fact, you should know, if you do not already, that all periodicals charge advertising rates based on their circulation, on the number of readers. (Radio and TV broadcasters charge rates for commercials on the basis of listeners and viewers.) It is, therefore, quite in your interest to build your circulation as high as you can.

## INCOME BASE

The presumed income base here is the revenue from the advertising you sell to readers. Every advertiser ought to get a free *checking copy*, a copy sent to confirm that the advertisement was run as ordered. There are some periodicals publishers who refuse to furnish a free checking copy to advertisers, but they are in the minority and it is probably a bad practice to be this miserly in your business practices. However, there is no reason for those who do not advertise to get a free ride, so you should charge a subscription fee, or at least a per-copy price to anyone who wants a copy but does not wish to advertise (even though he or she may have advertised in an earlier edition).

You now have two sources of income from the thing: advertising rates and subscription fees. There are other possibilities. For one, you need not confine yourself to being a matchmaker or lonely hearts publisher. You can do other useful things in your publication such as accepting advertisements from individuals wishing to buy, sell, or trade equipment and software, and perhaps even books and other items. In fact, listing such items and services in your advertising solicitations is likely to help bring in responses:

> Like to have a computer pen-pal? Meet, talk to interesting people? Buy,
> sell, trade hardware and software? Exchange ideas and experiences? Join
> a pen-pal club. Send name, address, telephone number to _____ .

Note that the focus has changed slightly: you are now offering a kind of computer club membership, with "meetings" through your periodical and computer-to-computer conversations. Your publication is no longer strictly an *ad sheet*. It's now a club newsletter which carries advertising, but also carries useful information, interesting "letters" (sent by computer-to-computer link), service articles, membership news, and other useful information every month. You are now justified in charging an enrollment or initiation fee to new members. The fee should cover a subscription to the publication. (Nonmembers must pay a relatively heavy subscription price to encourage them to enroll and be members.) You now have three sources of revenue.

That's not the end of the opportunities, either. There are other ways to diversify the activity as time goes on and you have built a customer base. Some of these are covered in a later chapter, but here, briefly, are some of the other areas, you will find, offer you profit opportunities as your venture becomes established:

1.   Selling special reports and software, either as the publisher or as the broker/agent for the originating source. (Selling your own published materials is, of course, more profitable.) The special advantage you have is that it is much easier to sell to established customers, especially subscribers you already have.

2.   Renting your mailing lists, either directly to noncompetitive renters or by brokering them through mailing-list brokers who take a commission for renting out your lists.

3.   Dealing in, selling, equipment to your customers and subscribers as a dealer/agent for manufacturers of hardware and accessories.

4.   Organizing special dial-up services that permit users to draw information on whatever you have to sell from a database or bulletin board you have established. The users would pay a fee to subscribe to and use your information service. The database ought to be built around that information you have collected in operating your pen-pal club or service, and should be unique. This item has great profit potential and merits its own separate discussion.

## SETTING UP YOUR OWN DATABASE

After you have operated your pen-pal service for a while, you will have built up a store of information that should contain not only names, addresses, and telephone numbers of your members or subscribers, but should also contain data on each that includes their systems, interests, and other such information. This is a database, or can easily be established as one, and should be on some accessible storage medium such as disk, accessible to dialing it up. Users would dial up the database and would be presented with a first menu, an index of top-level key words (or search terms). This is, in fact, a *library system*, in that the database is indexed at several levels as library indexes are. For example, if you want to look up a book by certain author but don't know the title of the book, or if you want to survey all the books by a certain author, you use the author's name as the first key word. The index then refers you to several other indexes, the equivalent of software menus. If the author writes different kinds of books, you will be referred to several other listings or indexes, and perhaps one or more of those will ask you to make still more narrowly defined choices for further reference.

The point is that an efficient system leads the searcher to a manageable number of selections. Too loose a system retrieves so many listings that the searcher cannot make use of them. Too tight a system tends to retrieve too few, sometimes zero, listings. The system must have at least two and preferably three or four levels or broad categories, depending on how large and detailed the database is.

One other important point: a good library system must be user-oriented as well as user-friendly. It should not only be easy to use and simple in general design, but should be designed with a view to what kind of beginning information—what key words—the user is likely to have. In the case of books, the key words might be these, for example:

Author.
Title.
Publisher.
Subject.
Year.

With these key words, a searcher can find any book listed or all the books listed under any key word recognized. The first key word will produce a list from which the searcher may choose an item, if the library is a small one. If the library is a large one, or has a large number of items to be listed under each of the categories, a second-level set of key words will be offered to narrow the number of items retrieved. Two factors, then, are the principal ones in designing the indexing system or menus: the information with which a searcher is most likely to begin and the overall size of the database or number of items each starting key word is likely to retrieve.

A user might wish to find others, one or more of the individuals you have listed, perhaps along one of the following lines:

A general pen-pal for regular correspondence.

Another hacker with similar interests to exchange information.

Software programs to buy, sell, or swap.

Hardware to buy, sell, or swap.

Books and magazines to buy, sell, or swap.

A source for answers to some specific problem.

Others to join in forming a local hackers' club or general computer club.

Usually, there will be more than one of these defining the user's objective. Perhaps the user wants to find people in a given area, with both hardware and software to buy, sell, or swap. It requires a series of menus, the first of which can be accessed or brought on-screen by using any of the preceding initial search terms. This means that you will have to have organized your database thoughtfully, coding many items for each entry such as the following:

| Name | Equipment | Software and OS |
| Address | General interests | Hours available |
| Telephone number | Software to buy | Hardware to buy |
| Age | Software to sell | Hardware to sell |
| Sex | Software to swap | Hardware to swap |

You will have to have each individual's permission to be listed, and some may object to being listed, although others may be so eager that they will be willing to pay to be listed. You will have to decide whether to make some charge for being listed.

As a variant, you may want to establish each of these as a separate database: a database of members, another database of software programs wanted or offered for buying, selling, or swapping, another for hardware equipment and accessories on the same basis. You may also want to discriminate between offerings and askings by members or subscribers and those by commercial vendors. That is, you may want to set up a database of commercial offerings and charge offerers to be listed, making the charges to users small or only nominal since the service is subsidized by the commercial acccounts to whom the listing is a form of advertising and, hence, a marketing expense.

All of this can grow out of a pen-pal service or club as described, and perhaps even more, if you are alert to opportunities. There are more opportunities for profitable commercial tie-ins than you may be aware. Suppose, for example, that you do not wish to rent your list of members' names and addresses to commercial users, but still want to make use of the list to produce income. One way to do this is to do the mailing for the commercial user. Here is one example of how that works, which also demonstrates that it is an established commercial practice which you have probably seen if you are the holder of an American Express card, a Diner's Club card, or any of several others. Note that when you get your monthly statement and invoice, you also get a number of multicolored brochures offering merchandise that can be charged on your card. Perhaps you have held the opinion that the credit-card company stocks all that merchandise and ships it out. Not so. The credit-card company simply has an arrangement with the vendors of the items, either on a commission basis or on a straight-fee basis, for enclosing the vendor's advertising brochures in the monthly mailings of statements.

Both methods are used. The first, the commission basis, is often referred to as P.O. advertising. That stands for per order, and it means that the credit card people get a percentage of the purchase price on each order, and that percentage can run as high as 40 to 50 percent of the purchase price.

This is a method also commonly used in advertising in the media, periodicals and radio and TV. Many of those late-night commercials of kitchen gadgets, for example, are P.O. arrangements. Many of the advertisements you see in magazines, where you send your order to the magazine rather than to the manufacturer or vendor of the item ordered, are P.O. advertisements. The publisher deducts the percentage (commission payment) up front, in fact, and sends the balance on to the vendor to fill the order.

If in your pen-pal venture you are making regular mailings such as bills and/or copies of a publication, for example, you may wish to seek such arrangements with vendors of hardware, software, and accessories. They need not necessarily be with OEMs (original equipment manufacturers) either; they can be with retail outlets or mail-order houses.

There are several advantages to doing things this way:

1.  You don't let out your mailing list to anyone; the only names they manage to pick up are those who order from them and to whom, naturally, they must ship.

2.  The profit potential is quite good if you insist on handling advertising only for items on which the seller can afford to give you a substantial commission, as much as 40 percent and perhaps even more, in some cases.

3.  You can advertise without doing so in your publication itself, which is an advantage inasmuch as some people believe that it cheapens newsletters or similar publications to use a lot of advertising in them.

There are some drawbacks, too, although they are less serious. One is that you can require advance payment on mailing-list rentals and advertising space in your periodical, but on P.O. advertising you must wait for the orders to come in from the customers before you get paid. Your income is tied to how successful the advertising is, so you may make less, not more, from P.O. advertising than you do from other advertising and list rentals.

In any case, be sure of one thing, if you do accept P.O. advertising. Be sure that the orders come to you—that only your name appears on the order form as the source of the item—so that you can deduct your commission directly, before sending the order and the balance of the payment on to the source of the item ordered.

However, if you prefer to charge the advertiser a flat fee for enclosing advertising brochures in your mailings, you can require that the client furnish the brochures ready to mail, and charge suitably. The charge should be more than would be the simple rental of your lists, since the client is getting the use of the list plus your own labor and postage. Therefore, if your list would rent for a somewhat typical $50 to $75 per 1000 names, you should at least double that price for enclosing the client's brochures in your own mailings, unless the brochures increase your own postage costs. In that case, you will have to consider that in setting the price. Be guided also by the fact that even a modest mailing will run advertisers $150 to $250 per 1000 pieces in addition to the cost of the mailing list itself. And, of course, as in the case of print advertising, get your fees up front, in advance.

One source of income a great many publishers of specialized publications tend to overlook is that of newsstand distribution. J. Norman Goode, publisher of the newsletter *Micro Moonlighter,* has succeeded in getting his newsletter on many newsstands, and Chet Lambert, Birmingham-based publisher of *Computer Trader Magazine,* has managed to get distribution of his periodical in many retail stores catering to computer enthusiasts.

By newsstand distribution we do not necessarily mean newsstands literally, but refer to distribution through any retail outlet by means of *counter sales.* By now you will have noticed that most specialty stores carry periodicals relevant to their specialties, and you will also find general-interest publications in supermarkets, convenience markets, drugstores, bookstores, and other retailers frequented by the general public. Wherever computer periodicals are sold to the public there is a potential distributor or dealer for your pen-pal publication, whatever it might be.

The usual arrangement is that the dealer pays you for only the copies he has sold. You take unsold copies as *returns*, for full credit, when you deliver each new issue and usually on something such as 35 to 40 percent of the cover price as the dealer's commission or profit percentage. All those unsold copies of last month's issue are not necessarily a loss to you, however. For one thing, you should have taken that into account in pricing your venture, and allowed for perhaps as much as 20 percent of the copies being unsold each month. Even then, you'll find individuals wanting *back* issues, copies of issues published earlier, and they are willing to pay for them. Therefore, you will want to keep a supply of back issues available for sale, and you may very well find that in some cases you could sell still more copies, if you had them. Do be sure, moreover, that you keep at least one permanent file copy for future reference and, possibly, for reprinting eventually, in whole or in part.

# Chapter Eight

## Training/Seminars

The thirst—and need—for new knowledge has never been greater, especially in the computer field. Wherever there's a need, there is a profit potential for anyone willing and able to fill that need effectively and efficiently.

## INFORMATION VERSUS TRAINING

Training, like education, is based on the imparting of knowledge, the delivery of information. Yet the mere delivery of the information, and even of the imparting of knowledge, is not of itself training. There is more—the need for the imparting of the ability to use the knowledge, to apply it properly in all situations requiring the application. That goes beyond knowledge. It becomes skill, and training has as its usual purpose the development of one or more skills in the trainee. Therefore, information is one basic essential of training, but the information must be delivered in such a way that the learner perceives how the information applies in actual situations, and is conditioned to make the transfer from theory to practice.

This is as true for computer technology, even on the level of users who do not wish to know more about the technology than is necessary to operate a personal computer successfully, as it is for anything else.

However, the amount of technical knowledge and the depth of technical detail that any given user requires depends on just what the user wishes to use the training for. Someone who buys a personal computer merely to get the latest information on stocks and play games in the evening has different information/knowledge/training needs than does someone who wants to write programs and experiment with a computer or build hardware devices.

To put this a bit differently, and in well-recognized training terms, the content of the training program must depend upon and be governed by the training objectives or, to use the educational technologist's own jargon, the behavioral objectives.

That latter technical term has a simple, commonsense meaning. A behavioral objective is a statement of what the learner shall be able to *do* as a result of the training. (There is a bit more to it, technically, but for our purposes here, that definition is quite enough.) Since by far the majority of prospective new computer users tend to be somewhat awed and frightened by this mysterious machine that appears to have a mind of its own, perhaps a first objective of training for the completely uninitiated ought to be that the learner will overcome any fear and awe of the computer by gaining enough understanding of it to realize that it is only a machine, and not really that "smart" a machine.

That is itself only information, knowledge, by the definitions given here. It is part of training, but is not training per se, because it is only part of the first part. It is, in fact, information delivered primarily to condition the trainee for what is yet to come. It is necessary for learners to grasp and *accept* that the computer is only a machine, and really a rather dull-witted machine by comparison with human intellectual abilities, so that they can relax and overcome any fears they may have had originally in preparation for learning how to be the masters of that machine.

## WHAT KINDS OF LEARNERS?

It is probably no coincidence that youngsters are so dominant in the population of new computer experts, or that the younger set "takes to" computers so readily, so much more readily than do more mature individuals. For one thing, it is characteristic of youth to be less afraid of the unknown and mysterious. For another, most youngsters are getting some education and even some hands-on experience with microcomputers in many schools today. Finally, youngsters have fewer prejudices, fewer things to unlearn, and so are more receptive to the "Buck Rogers age" we appear to have entered. Overall, computers appear to be much more a young person's game than an older person's game. Still, there are many mature adults who are interested and who want to learn more about the microcomputer.

A visit to any bookstore will lend evidence of this. There are literally hundreds of new titles (by far the majority of them stem from mid- to late 1982) about computers, almost all about microcomputers and so-called home or personal computers, and related subjects. A great many are of the how-to-buy-a-microcomputer genre. There are also many others, falling into identifiable classes:

All about BASIC.

All about PASCAL (or other languages).

How computers work.

How to write programs.

How to build your own computer.

Dictionary of computer terms.

Jobs in the computer industry.

Chips and other microelectronics.

Computer circuits and technology.

How to write programs for the _____ computer.

How to write programs in the _____ language.

By far the majority of these books are addressed to nonprofessionals in the computer field, knowledgeable hobbyists and aficionados and complete tyros. Many are about computers and computer subjects in general, but many are about specific computer models (the most popular ones) and specific programs or languages. The trend recently has been toward the latter, with publishers tending to more interest in books specifically about the most popular computers than in books about computers in general.

The same situation applies on the newsstands with regard to computer magazines. Probably about 15 to 25 such magazines are to be found on the majority of well-stocked newsstands, but there are several times that number of computer periodicals in existence. (One recent news item estimated that there are over 200 periodicals about computers.) Many of these are general in their coverage of computers, hardware, and software, but others are specialized, dealing with only a single computer (e.g., the IBM PC) or with only a single aspect such as languages and programs, software.

Does this answer the question "What kinds of learners?" or does it make the answer more difficult to find? Probably the latter, for some readers buy only one kind of book or magazine of the preceding types, whereas others buy several kinds. Let us sort out learners into at least the following generalized types or groups.

1.  The complete tyro who is fascinated by the micro as an interesting gadget (there are some who simply must have anything new and popular) and wants to learn enough to discuss computers intelligently and seek out one that would be most suitable to his or her own interests.

2.  The beginner who knows little or nothing, but has some specific use in mind such as investment analysis or word processing.

3.  The beginner who thinks a micro would be worth having as a tool for his or her business, but doesn't know how to begin to select one and wants to learn how.

4.  The beginner who has tried to plod through all the books and magazines, but is becoming more and more confused, rather than more and more enlightened.

5.  The beginner who has a micro, uses it successfully, but doesn't

really understand how or why it works and is now becoming more interested in learning how and why.

What all these people have in common is that they are all beginners, and all except the last one are tyros, who probably aren't even sure what a computer really is, much less anything of how it works. There are a few other things they all have in common, except perhaps the last one again.

All know or must be presumed to know absolutely nothing about the subject. In fact, it may well be that most (even that last one) "know" many things about computers that just aren't true at all. There are lots of myths being propagated and even originated by tyros who have read some popularized material in a Sunday supplement or one of those weekly tabloids.

All should get, at least in the beginning, purely functional information, as light as possible in technical detail, but definitely not talking down to them.

All should be made aware of one valid piece of conventional wisdom about computers: that it is important to select the proper software, at least by general characteristics and class if not by specific program, before choosing hardware because the requirements of the software dictate the hardware needs.

## THE LEVELS OF LEARNERS

The foregoing classes of learners are all similar in that they do not know the basics in most cases, are all beginners, and must all learn basics first, even if they plan to go on and learn more. However, there are those who already know the basics and are really interested in advanced study, perhaps how to write programs or how to service and maintain computers.

There may be still a more advanced class of learners: those who already know how to program, at least in BASIC or another higher-level language, and want to go on, to learn more of programming, and to learn how to work in other languages, perhaps to write in the more efficient assembly languages.

There also may be another kind of advanced class of learners: those who wish to learn more of computer design, logical or electronic (two different disciplines, although with interrelationship), and who are, therefore, interested in truly technical detail.

Some of this, especially some of the latter class of learners, is probably well beyond practical possibilities for home-based small businesses, at least as far as the possibility of full-blown study courses is concerned. It is not likely that even if you are a technical expert, you can organize full-scale study programs as a small or sideline business. Nevertheless, there are many practical opportunities at all these levels, the only limitations being your own capabilities and desires, and there is more than one way you can put your talent, capabilities, and desires to work as an instructor, and turn those characteristics into income.

## KINDS OF PROGRAMS

There are two basic types of learning programs that are most accessible and practical as small, home-based enterprises. One is the mini-course: perhaps two sessions a week, in the evening, of an hour or two per session, over a period of several weeks. If the size of the class is limited, you can do this in your own home. The other approach is the learning seminar, which can be an hour, two hours, a half-day, a full day, two days, or even longer. Again, you can do this in your own home with a small group, or you can rent space somewhere else such as at a local motel if you have a large group to address.

The seminar is probably most appropriate to the kinds of needs we are discussing here, although mini-courses are also conducted in individuals' private homes. The difference, philosophically, is that the seminar is normally more sharply focused on content and objectives. In fact, instead of a mini-course, you might wish to consider a series of short seminars (perhaps two hours each), each of which addresses another specific segment of the subject. You would write up announcements describing each seminar in the series, and customers could sign up for whichever interest them. Following are some typical titles as a starter list.

## Computer Fundamentals for the Layman

This would describe what a computer is and is not: separating fact from fiction; what you can and cannot do with a computer; how to decide whether a computer would be a useful addition to your home or office; basic principles in selecting the right computer.

## Computer Languages

Explanations would be given as to what computer language is, the three levels: machine language, high-level languages, higher-level languages; examples and explanations; pros and cons of each kind of language; how languages affect hardware and vice versa.

## Programming, the Basics

This would show principles of writing computer programs: what a program is; problem analysis; flowcharting; identifying routines.

## Finding the Right Software

Help would be given in identifying your basic objective or purpose; surveying software; where to find software listings and descriptions; what to look for; what the terms mean; how to determine how much memory you need; RAM memory versus virtual memory/data storage.

In practice, you would probably want to develop the descriptive listings of subjects covered under each title and ask for advance registration, explaining that attendance is limited.

If you feel qualified to do so, you can use this approach to teach the more advanced subjects in the field, even to computer professionals or

knowledgeable hobbyists. (Sometimes aficionados become more knowledgeable in a field than the full-time professionals are; it's not at all
unusual.) You might thus want to offer seminars on such subjects as
the following:

Chips and related technology.

Architecture.

Logical design.

Rewriting off-the-shelf programs.

Systems analysis and design.

Information theory.

Database management.

## OTHER APPROACHES

There are still other ways to put your knowledge to work as an instructor, at least these:

Individual tutoring/consulting.

Lecturing/instructing in local educational programs.

Individual tutoring is tantamount to consulting, a one-on-one advisory service as well as an instructional service. Even if you are called
upon as a consultant by individuals or business firms, you are almost
inevitably also cast in the role of instructor by the nature of the subject.
In most cases, the reason a consultant is called upon is because the
client does not know enough about the subject, and that will be true
whether the task is to help the client select a computer or to help solve
a computer-related problem. However, for practical purposes they have
to be separated to at least the extent that most clients who want tutoring
will find the service more palatable if described as *consulting*. This is
especially true when the client is a businessperson who wants the service in connection with business operations.

However, most communities have community colleges and other

local institutions of learning who conduct adult-education courses and summer courses in a variety of subjects, some for credit and some noncredit courses. The selection of courses offered is usually dependent on what or who is available to the institution in the way of instructors, who are most often individuals doing the lectures on a fee basis.

There are two basic approaches to winning such contracts. But, as a preliminary, first determine who offers such courses in your own area. Local colleges and universities are most likely to, but sometimes there are private-sector, for-profit organizations who do so as in the case of one in the Washington, DC, area that calls itself Open University. Lecturers usually teach in their own homes, although the sponsoring organization may also provide space for some of the sessions. In the case of educational institutions, they generally have the classroom spaces and facilities readily available.

Having determined who offers such sessions and what they offer, you can approach them: first, with a question as to what, if any, vacancies they foresee in their faculty and, second, to propose a session.

The latter approach usually works much better if you have made one or more suggestions they find valuable. (You need not confine yourself to only one suggestion, but may suggest several and let the institution decide which is of greatest interest to them.) Your chances are better if you propose a subject they do not already have coverage for but which appears likely to be of interest to many people.

The kinds of things people wish to learn in these special courses and seminars are usually self-improvement items such as dancing, singing, painting, computers, lecturing, writing, consulting, accounting, and other similar categories. Most institutions today have programs for computers, but they always welcome new ideas, and you will probably meet with success if you offer specialized ideas that others have not thought of, such as how to manage a stock portfolio with a micro.

## THE SEMINAR BUSINESS

The development and production of seminars is a distinct business today, and one that some operate on a grand scale. One company in

Washington, DC, began business a few years ago as a publisher of special information, newsletters and books on highly specialized legal/ business topics, and began to conduct occasional seminars on the subjects as other publishers often do. The seminars proved to be a more attractive business than publishing, and although this firm still publishes periodicals and books, its main business today is seminars and it books millions of dollars in registrations every year.

This firm does its seminars much like most others do, in basics, at least. It organizes a handout manual (most seminar producers have handouts for attendees) and a brochure that describes the program and the speaker(s). It engages one or more hotel/motel meeting rooms for the date(s) decided on, and mails out thousands of copies of the brochure to its mailing lists. (Lists can be rented from established list brokers, and information about this appears later.) It may also run print advertisements in newspapers or other periodicals. Some firms do most of their advertising by means of print advertising and mail only a relatively few brochures to their own mailing lists compiled from records of customers and inquirers over previous years. However, the mailing of brochures appears to be the more popular method, which suggests that most have found print advertising less effective than direct-mail using brochures.

By far the majority of seminar advertisers favor mailing the large (8½ × 11 inches) brochure, usually mailing it as a "self-mailer," sans envelope, under bulk mail rates. This is less effective than mailing a small brochure and sales letter in a regular business envelope as first-class mail (or even as bulk mail) as indicated by my own experience with seminars. However, most seminar producers appear to believe that they must mail many, many thousands of brochures, and the way they do it is less costly than would be mailing out the more typical direct-mail package in a business envelope. In fact, many make special arrangements with nonprofit institutions, getting an even more favorable postage rate as a result since bulk mail for nonprofits is heavily subsidized by the government.

Attendance fees vary widely for such seminars, but the ones presented with all the heavy mailings have a large expense to overcome, which probably accounts for the typical registration fees of $200 to $300 for one day, nearly double that for two days, and so forth. On the other hand, if you arrange to keep your costs small, you can do the whole thing for a great deal less money. In the chapter on marketing, we discuss some of the ways to promote—market—seminars effectively at relatively low cost. However, here are some rather typical costs you will encounter.

## Meeting Rooms

Rates will vary according to size of room, location of hotel or motel, day of the week, and other factors. However, they can run as little as $35 for the day, as much as $200. Shopping around will save you money.

## Coffee Service

Most seminars provide coffee service for attendees. Coffee prices vary, may run by the cup or by the urn. Oddly enough, hotels with high room rates often have low coffee prices and vice versa.

## Handouts

You can save yourself a lot of money by being smart here. Most companies will be glad to help you with free handouts that plug their products and services while also providing useful information. Write to many hardware and software companies, including major local computer retailers, explaining what you are doing and your need, and you'll be surprised at how much help you'll get. Also, don't overlook publishers of computer magazines and local government agencies with relevant interests; sometimes they can be helpful in providing materials (e.g., reprints and even whole copies of their publications) as samples.

Hotels are not the only place you can rent meeting rooms. Sometimes there are other facilities available at very low cost and even at no cost. You can often bring your own coffee and refreshments to these kinds of meeting rooms and save that cost too. Check around for availability of other people's meeting rooms such as veterans' associations, business associations or clubs, local-government facilities, public school buildings, or other such locations.

You can get some free advertising (again, refer to the chapter on marketing) by sending out news releases to newsletters and other periodicals, especially computer publications. Try your local newspaper publishers too; sometimes they'll give you a plug. Put up notices on the bulletin boards at local supermarkets, and leave some of your brochures around on the literature tables and bulletin boards of your local public libraries. Maybe you can drop a few judiciously at a few other places such as hotel lobbies.


## CONDUCTING A SEMINAR

A seminar presentation must be organized as any presentation is, focused on the general goal of the seminar. Bear in mind that, regardless of the classical or literal definition of the term, the general purpose of anyone attending a seminar is to learn something. And, to hark back to the thoughts with which this chapter opened, the information itself is of limited value if its use, application, is not also imparted to attendees. Therefore, the overall objective of a seminar ought to be HOW TO (*do something or other*).

To put this differently, the organization of an effective seminar is to present information in some logical order, with applications notes and explanations, and with ample opportunities for attendees to ask questions and get specific answers. Some seminars provide a great deal of applications practice, which makes them workshops, as well as seminars. We discuss this, too, in a moment.

Information can be organized in any of several ways, and usually one way is better than another for any given purpose. Sometimes it is even desirable to mix methods of organization, although this is risky: it can easily cause confusion and should be avoided whenever possible. If it cannot be avoided, use it with great care to avoid confusing attendees.

(Note, for example, how confusing a movie can be when it uses flashbacks excessively, a similar problem.) The basic methods of organizing information are these.

*Chronological.*   From earliest time to present or reverse, tracking back to origins.

*Order of Importance.*   From trivial to critical or reverse; reverse, usually, from most important to least important details.

*Order of Specificity.*   From general to specific (most popular and probably most often used) or reverse. (Latter useful if teaching is based in inductive reasoning, rather than the deductive reasoning more suitable to the first method.)

Teaching the evolution of computers has to be chronological and is probably most effective when taught from origins to present, rather than the reverse, but teaching the basics of how computers function is most effectively taught in order of general to specific and most important to least important details.

Lecturing all day without pause is difficult for both lecturer and listeners, even when the lecturer is talented and entertaining. However, a lecturer need not be especially talented or entertaining to hold an audience if he or she organizes the presentation so as to do two things: break the lectures up with frequent diversions to other activity and involve the listeners in the processes. Here are some ways to do this.

Use visuals, demonstrations, models, and/or other such supplements to lecturing. You can use slides, transparencies, posters, chalkboards, easels, or any other kind of adjunct presentation.

Use many examples and anecdotes. Hypothetical cases are acceptable if you have no live examples—case histories or anecdotes from direct experience—but hypothetical cases are less effective and less interesting than are cases where you can identify individuals or organizations and live examples.

Invite questions and comments. Far better to stop and interrupt a presentation to answer questions and clear up confusion or doubt than to allow the uncertainty to grow, as it will.

Encourage lively discussion, even difference of opinion. Controversy can be interesting and, even more than interesting, it can be exciting. Seminars always seem to work better and are more satisfactory to everyone when lively dialogue takes place.

If lively dialogue or discussion doesn't spring up spontaneously, you can encourage it by working some group exercises (a helpful practice in any case). Pose questions and ask for volunteer answers. This forces attendees to think a bit about the information and its uses, and is one of several ways to develop applications practice.

Set up the room in classroom style with attendees seated at tables or in chairs with writing arms so that they can do some work. (Classroom style is more comfortable than theater style for a long session anyway, even if the attendees are not going to do anything more than take notes.) Try to work up some exercises that will give each one an opportunity to do some applications individually. Then ask for volunteers to read their solutions and critique a few, also inviting comments from others.

## HANDLING STAGE FRIGHT

Unfortunately, many people find it difficult to speak publicly, even before a small group. It's a common enough problem. There are a few ways to ease the pain:

1.   Using the presentation aids, as already described, eases the situation by distracting the audience from concentrating on you, making you feel a bit less exposed.

2.   Speak from behind a kind of shield or barrier such as a lectern. Use one if you are nervous. It gives you a place to rest your hands, as well as a board on which to rest your notes.

3.   Better than standing behind a lectern is sitting at a table. If you can arrange to be seated behind a table on a raised platform, you will probably find it much easier to conduct your presentation.

4.   Have others at your table as a kind of panel. It's much easier to be part of a panel than to handle it all alone.

5.   Start out with very small groups. It's easier to speak publicly to a group of 5 or 10 people than to a group of 50 or 100.

All of these help when you are new to public speaking. In most cases you eventually overcome your fears as you gain confidence. It's true, perhaps, that some people never overcome their stage fright, but they are in the minority; most people do eventually learn to feel relaxed and comfortable on the platform, and most come to actually enjoy the experience after a while, for it is a gratifying experience to make successful presentations.

## THE TYPICAL SEMINAR GROUP

The typical seminar group for a public presentation in a meeting room is a variable, but small seminars tend to be on the order of 30 to 50 attendees, and even large seminars rarely run to more than 100 or, at most, 150 people. If you want to run seminars on a truly commercial scale, you should probably aim at the 20 to 40 bracket as a realistic goal, and price accordingly.

There is no doubt that high prices have tended to hurt the seminar industry in the past few years. Postage rates are high, printing costs are high, and meeting rooms are more expensive than ever. Still, there are many successful seminars, and it is not necessary for the small operator to charge high prices. It is usually viable to charge well under $100 per attendee for an all-day seminar and yet turn a profit, if you manage your costs and do not let them carry you away.

Probably you will do well to gain some experience by starting out with small groups, in your own home, if possible: 5 or 10 people in your recreation room, for example. (You will also probably feel more relaxed and less fearful of speaking to a group in your own home environment.) Charge a fee accordingly since your costs ought to be modest, and regard the whole thing as a learning experience for you as well as for your attendees.

## TYING IN TO OTHER ACTIVITIES

Many seminars are produced by people who are in other activities that give them some advantages as seminar producers. Publishers of newsletters and other periodicals, for example, have the advantage of having their own publicity/advertising medium, and can appeal directly to their own subscribers. If you run something along the lines of the pen-pal service or club discussed earlier, you have a similar advantage in your established customers. (It is always far easier to do business with your own customers than with total strangers, and a mailing to your own customers is almost always more productive than it would be if mailed to strangers. That's what makes a customer list a particularly good mailing list.)

## SEMINAR TIE-INS AND SPONSORS

Many businesses succeed because of cooperative tie-ins with related businesses, creating a mutual-support synergy. In this case, you probably have some commonality of interest with computer retailers in your area, perhaps even with manufacturers of computers and related hardware and producers of software programs. For example, if you teach initiates how to understand computer basics and use the information to buy the right computers for their needs, those who sell computers and associated products (peripherals, accessories, and software) can benefit from your work through sales to some of your attendees, through converting some of your attendees to their customers. A tie-in with a local retailer may thus produce several possible benefits for you:

Free guest speakers.

Demonstrations or demonstration equipment on loan.

Subsidies and/or sponsorship.

The last-named item perhaps needs some explanation. A local retailer of computer merchandise may be willing to sponsor you in presenting seminars, and the sponsorship might include any or all of the following:

Help in promoting the seminar through the retailer's facilities: perhaps mention in the retailer's own advertisements and brochures, posters in the several outlets, other such aid.

Subsidies to encourage maximum attendance by lowering the fees: the sponsor may supply a meeting place or pay for it or may provide other kinds of financial assistance.

The sponsor may offer a special inducement to anyone who attends, such as a discount or free gift of some kind, or may even offer to discount a purchase of a computer by the full attendance fee, making the attendance free for any attendee who subsequently does business with that retailer.

The sponsor may also pay the whole bill, with a fee to you, so that it is his seminar, which you do under contract, managing the entire thing (just as I do certain seminars for large corporations who contract with me to train their employees in certain matters).

All of this may be as true for the large manufacturing corporation as it is for the retailer. It's a relatively modest marketing expense for the sponsor, and it can be quite effective in winning customers. Certainly, it is not unlikely that many business firms would at least consider it, and some would try it for size. Moreover, the sponsor would get valuable feedback information on the kinds of questions attendees ask and what their concerns are. This information can be most valuable to a firm selling hardware and software in marketing their products. Large firms often offer the public free seminars which are held for obvious marketing/advertising purposes primarily, but that need not matter to you, since you would be under a fee arrangement.

There is still one more possibility (again, something I have myself done, so it is of demonstrated viability as a business option). There are those whose business is producing seminars and even other training presentations who are always interested in finding those who can do seminar presentations for them under contract. Such a sponsor (for this is another kind of sponsor, one whose business is seminars and training) will want you to write up a program, help with preparing a brochure, perhaps offer marketing suggestions, and will pay you an agreed-upon fee for each session you conduct plus your travel expenses if you must travel out of town for any of the sessions. In this mode, as in some of the others, you run no financial risk at all, although neither can you earn as much. However, there are some producers of seminars who will agree to pay you a guaranteed minimum fee and a percentage so that you can earn a good fee from a highy successful session and yet run no risk.

This is actually contracting your time and services directly to a sponsor. That sponsor need not be a manufacturer, retailer, or seminar producer, either: the field is still broader than that. You may wish to propose sponsored—contracted, that is—seminars with other business-people who might never have run seminars, but whose business is conducive and compatible such as publishers of newsletters and other periodicals dealing with computer subjects. You will find that the idea is not necessarily a new one or a novel one, but may have occurred to many of these people, with the only obstacle the fact that they had no one available or knew of no one who could do the seminars for them.

Approach, also, the program managers of associations. These are people who must plan meetings and annual events (trade shows, conferences, and conventions), and who are always looking for ideas and people to help them. Associations often sponsor seminars, and you are likely to find some of them welcoming your idea with great enthusiasm.

Situations change, of course, and conditions are different in different places and at different times. Seminars and training are highly fluid and dynamic activities, and you should be using what you have read here as stimuli to provoke your own imagination and motivation to probe your local situation. There is no doubt that you will find interest, especially in anything you offer that helps others market their computers and related products and services. Be sure to read Chapter 12, on marketing, for ideas for both marketing your own services as a seminar leader and trainer and to understand others' motivations and marketing needs.

# Chapter Nine

---

# Computer-Based
# Products/Services

The microcomputer has created entire new industries, but it also
creates new and better opportunities in older, established
industries if you take full advantage of what it can offer.

## SATELLITES: THE CHILDREN OF NEW INDUSTRIES

Every industry creates others, often called *satellite* industries or businesses. The major industry in this case is the microcomputer industry,
and it has created more than its share of satellite industries and related
enterprises. Perhaps "created" is not the proper term, for at least some
of the enterprises made possible by the *wunderkind* microcomputer
industry are industries of long standing which have adapted and expanded to accommodate the new markets created by this new industry.
Let us define that term *satellite* more clearly. It does not refer to those
industries and enterprises that are, in fact, part of the computer industry (hardware, software, and accessories), but to those that operate on
the periphery of computers in an indirect relationship. There are, for

example, many newsletters and magazines, including at least one tabloid, directed at serving information needs and advertising needs of everyone concerned with micros. There is a rapidly growing mountain of books on related subjects: listings alone could constitute their own databases. Special schools and special classes or courses in established schools have sprung up to train people in computers, and the public schools have created a heavy demand for instructional materials in the subject. Special computer furniture and fixtures have been designed and built for the burgeoning market. The advertising industry has grown to accommodate the demand for copy about the products. Airlines, hotels, restaurants, car-rental firms, and others offer reservation services never before possible, and banks offer more and more convenience in electronic transactions and 24-hour mechanical tellers. Databases make it possible to have virtual stock tickers and news teletypes in your own home, and information-services firms offer such service and convenience.

Where all of this will take us, we do not know. Some people see a virtual end to conventional publishing, even to books in libraries and on shelves—an end to conventional banking and bill paying—an end or near-end to conventional mail—a general metamorphosis in our traditional ways of doing things.

Whether the more extreme of these predictions will come to pass, certainly there will continue to be changes attributable to microcomputers. They have already begun and the trend will almost surely continue. We have discussed a number of business ventures possible for the microcomputer owner, most of which can be conducted from one's own home and on either a part- or full-time basis. For the most part, these ideas have tended to custom services and products, helping individuals and organizations on an individual, one-to-one basis, or on a group basis, but still primarily custom services and products. Now let us consider in this chapter some of the possibilities for proprietary, off-the-shelf products and services made possible by the microcomputer or linked to it closely in some manner.

## PRINTED/PUBLISHED INFORMATION PRODUCTS

For reasons that will soon be apparent, publishing your own newsletters, reports, and other special publications items is one of the easiest, lowest-risk home enterprises possible for the small entrepreneur. We touched on this type of enterprise earlier in connection with other venture possibilities, but we probe it more deeply in this chapter and offer a number of starter ideas. Publishing as a main enterprise is somewhat different than publishing an item as one function of another enterprise. It is also a somewhat different enterprise, a different set of problems and opportunities, to sell information in its printed and published form than in the forms we discussed in Chapter 6.

## HOME-BASED PUBLISHING

Earlier you read of the revolution in printing, platemaking, and typesetting, and some of what computers have contributed to that. Since that revolution took place (and it is still in progress) home-based publishing enterprises have become quite popular, and quite a large number of individuals are engaged in it.

Most of those engaged in this do their marketing largely through the mails. The product is almost ideal for mail order because it is light (goes easily and inexpensively through the mails) and the markup is high (sells for several times its basic cost), another mail-order requisite. Moreover, it is a product over which the publisher has complete control as the manufacturer and sole source. (Another principle of mail order is that the product should be one not easily available elsewhere, possibly not available at all elsewhere.)

The ease and convenience of the new offset methods led to the easy cut-and-paste methods described earlier in these pages, making it possible for almost anyone to enter into a small publishing venture in one's own home. And, as you have probably observed, you can get while-you-wait printing service easily today in any of the many "instant copy" shops. However, these shops also offer fast-copy services through use of modern office copiers as well as through their offset printing facilities. In fact, office copiers can be used to make offset printing plates if suitable plate material is used instead of paper. Many modern plate-makers do use that same process to make printing plates, simply copying the material onto a suitable plastic or foil plate.

Do not confuse the two processes, however: office copiers do not work on the same principles as do offset presses. In office copying, the image to be copied is converted to an electrostatic (electrical charge) pattern on a special master or selenium-coated drum. (The latter is the preferred method.) A powder is applied to that surface and clings wherever there is a charge. The powder is transferred to a sheet of paper by pressure, and the powder is then fused to the paper by heat. The most modern copiers do such a good job of duplication that copies are often sharper and crisper than the originals, and are also suitable as printed copies when only a small number of copies is required. For *short runs* (small number of copies), office copying is even cost-competitive with offset printing and offers other advantages which we explore here. Before going on, note that some people refer to copies made this way as *photocopies*, and the process as *photocopying*.

This is what makes small-scale, even home-based publishing a viable venture for small entrepreneurs. The costs of typesetting and printing have been brought under control. In the meanwhile, advancing technology has not neglected other industries and equipment, either: today's typewriters produce high-quality impressions which are quite acceptable as type for many publications, and most modern typewriters use changeable elements, so that a mix of typefaces (fonts) is possible also. Now word processing has carried the revolution still further: one can use a microcomputer to produce a variety of publications on a small scale at a higher quality than ever before and with a degree of sophistication formerly not available to any but fairly large publishers of newsletters, reports, and similar products.

## THE COMPUTER CONNECTION

Aside from the obvious application of word processing to composition (typesetting copy for publication), computers offer a number of advantages and special interests in connection with small-scale publishing. The relationships or connection between computers and publishing takes more than one form.

1.   The first connection has been mentioned already: it is that of word processing as a superior means of composing copy for printing.

2.   A second connection is that of several support services made possible by computers: services or functions that are made possible or at least far more effective by computer, such as data storage and retrieval capabilities, transfer of information by wire (modem and telephone line) to typesetters, printers, collaborators, reviewers, and others), and other such capabilities.

3.   A third connection is subject matter itself: the demand for printed information about computers and related matters continues to grow.

4.   A fourth connection is the swifter and readier access to information provided by computer connections to databases and to correspondents of one kind or another. In some respects, this is even superior to the traditional teletype and other wire services that once revolutionized the newspaper business for reasons you should soon perceive.

5.   Specialty publishing is a natural outgrowth or add-on to other ventures such as those covered earlier in these pages, and usually the two complement and support each other in a natural synergy. Each helps the other to succeed, and the aggregate of the two is often far greater than the simple sum of their combined worth.

Specialty publishing, then, is almost a natural for the microcomputer owner, and we now explore some kinds of specialty publications.

## NEWSLETTERS

Estimates of how many newsletters are published in the United States vary quite a lot because each source estimates on a different basis: all newsletters, newsletters published for profit, newsletters of major circulation, and other qualifiers. One estimate that appears reliable is that of some 30,000 newsletters, although other estimates quote both higher and lower figures, some of them much higher. In any case, it is obvious that there are a great many newsletters published in the United States. However, they vary widely in other respects: some are daily, some weekly, some even quarterly and semi-annual publications, with the majority published once a month. They vary widely in circulation figures, from a couple of hundred subscribers to many thousands of subscribers. They vary widely in subscription fees, from a few dollars to several hundred dollars a year. They vary in size, from 2 to 4 pages to 16, 32, even 64 pages. (The reason for these particular numbers will become apparent.) They vary in formats and physically: some typeset and printed on expensive papers, others composed by typewriter (even by old-fashioned manual typewriters, in some cases) and printed on inexpensive paper. They also vary in content, from an unvarying stream of terse, tight items to a potpourri of stories, articles, photos, cartoons, columns, and other features.

Some of these variations are of relatively small significance, being little more than cosmetic in nature (e.g., type and paper), but some are quite significant differences such as kinds of coverage. Let us discuss these differences first.

The basic philosophy of newsletter publishing is that of specialized coverage and brevity, covering only the essence (important kernel) of most matters and, in many cases, guiding the reader to the sources for greater detail. The idea is to save the busy reader's time by giving all the truly important information while also covering pertinent matters not usually covered in the general press. Medical journals, for example, might not cover an obscure item about some new treatment in a faraway country or a new electronic tool for medical practitioners, but a newsletter devoted to a specialized corner of the profession would. For this reason alone, some newsletters can never have large circulations: their population of interested readers is limited to perhaps a few hundred individuals, although those individuals might be willing to pay enough for their subscriptions to make the enterprise of publishing the newsletter a viable one. For example, here are a few newsletter titles that reveal how narrowly they are oriented in their content coverage and readership appeal:

| | |
|---|---|
| Off-Street Parking | Cable TV Advertising |
| Alfa Owner | Cable TV Regulation |
| Crow's Plywood Letter | Speechwriter's Newsletter |
| Telecom Insider | Chocolate News |
| Trademark Trends | Schoolboard Notes |

To put this another way, let us consider why subscribers will pay more (usually) to subscribe to a small newsletter that comes out once a month or thereabouts than they do to subscribe to a fat weekly newsmagazine or a daily newspaper. All are motivated by one or more of the following objectives and reasons:

1. Get information not published elsewhere.
2. Save time by having an expert search a wide variety of information and abstract important items.
3. Get interpretive analysis of developments from an expert.
4. Get advice from an expert.
5. Get valuable, little-known insider tips and leads.
6. Get lots of good ideas.

## TYPES OF NEWSLETTERS

The list of reasons for or objectives in subscribing to the reading newsletters furnishes the clues needed to analyze the several basic types of newsletters—types, with respect to content and coverage.

1.   Obscure data, of interest to only a relative handful of specialists in something or other, but not readily available to them or anyone else except by intensive and extensive research conducted continuously (e.g., technical data).

2.   Roundup of key items from a large number of periodicals, summarizing for the busy executive or professional who hasn't the time to read all these publications, but wants the essence of them anyway (e.g., marketing news).

3.   Advisory newsletter such as securities analysis and investment counsel, forecasts, special reports, and other such coverage by an acknowledged and qualified expert.

4.   Tips and ideas for people in some specialized profession or business such as sales promotional ideas and advertising guidance.

Getting this down to the immediate case of your own interests, you may consider a newsletter connected with computers, although that is not necessarily a condition. You can consider doing a newsletter in any field that interests you. Suppose, for example, that your chief interest—and perhaps your main profession—is that of sales and marketing. You might very well do a newsletter on that subject, or perhaps combine interests and publish a newsletter on marketing and sales in the computer industry. Whatever the subject, you must reach decisions on what the general objective of the newsletter is to be. But remember these factors and principles, in reaching a decision here.

It is difficult to deliver true news in a monthly publication or any publication published less often than every day. Don't attempt to do what newspapers and news magazines can do far more effectively than you can. If you intend to present news, it has to be news of a nature not generally covered in the regular press, such as some of these items:

Personnel changes within an industry and within companies, generally those involving personnel at less than top levels.

Technical developments, again those of less than headline-grabbing prominence.

Other obscure items that would be of significance to certain specialists or others who are readers of your publications.

It is difficult to sell subscriptions to an advisory newsletter if you cannot show persuasive credentials as an expert. This does not mean that you must be a celebrated or recognized authority, but it does mean that you have to show that you are qualified to advise others.

You must give your readers something they can't get elsewhere as easily, as conveniently, as inexpensively, or at all, if you are to show prospects why a subscription to your newsletter is a good idea. Therefore, don't imitate competitors (why should anyone buy an imitation when they get the original?); improve on them, be innovative, be different, but be BETTER. And demonstrate that you are better, not merely different.

## MARKETING A NEWSLETTER: GENERAL OBSERVATIONS

Newsletters are notoriously difficult to market according to conventional wisdom. Yet some take off vigorously and earn a great deal of money for their publishers. This leads me to believe that what is difficult to market is the newsletter that is not really that good to begin with. Like most things, only a small percentage of the newsletters published in the United States are really good; most are on a scale from pretty good to pretty bad.

This is not to suggest that if you create a good newsletter success will follow instantly or automatically. It is possible to be good and yet not be popular or succeed easily. Be prepared to work at it; most worthwhile results do not come easily, and newsletter publishing is not an exception although it is less risky than many other ventures, if you pay heed to what you learn here.

The traditional way to sell newsletter subscriptions is through direct mail. Many have tried other methods such as print advertising and have usually found that nothing works quite as well. Therefore, it has become conventional wisdom to rely on the Postal Service to deliver your sales messages.

Some publishers offer free sample copies. This rarely works well and is, in fact, usually a grave mistake. Tests and experience have demonstrated rather clearly that the closure rate (orders received) on leads to whom sample copies were sent is abysmally poor. Evidently, a great many respondents either are merely looking for something for nothing or are severely disappointed with what they see. Probably both factors are contributors to the poor showing this marketing method makes for those who have tried it.

Some of those who offer free samples do not send a true sample issue (one of the regular run), but send a special issue which is not really a sample, but a thinly disguised advertisement made to appear as though it were a regular issue. This seems to work somewhat better.

Another variant that appears to work well is one in which the prospect is offered the first copy free if he or she subscribes. Or, as a twist on this, the prospect is advised that if, after reading the first copy, he or she doesn't like the thing, he or she can simply write "cancel" across the invoice and return it, keeping the first issue and owing nothing. This works better because it compels the subscriber to make an effort to cancel, and most people don't bother. Instead, they pay the bill, whether they later renew or not. (Book clubs work on the same principle, relying on the nature of many to procrastinate and let things take their course, rather than exerting effort to change things.)

Many prospects who won't sign up for a full year's subscription will sign up for a "special" or "trial" subscription of a lesser period, six or even three months. And "penny" sales seem to work, too: for example, one year for $18, two years for $18.01, or some such thing.

## SPECIAL SALES

In many cases, it is possible to make a deal with organizations to sell their members subscriptions at special rates, or to have the association buy subscriptions for all members at some special rate. Since the largest expense by far in newsletter publishing is marketing, it is economically possible to make special deals that are profitable for all concerned.

It is also possible to make deals such as those suggested for seminars if you publish a newsletter that lends itself to supporting the interests of other, larger business firms who might wish to consider subsidizing your newsletter as a sales/marketing effort of their own. In this respect, a newsletter offers one great advantage: it can be imprinted, as was suggested earlier, with different sponsor's names and distributed directly by them. (In fact, you may wish to consider this possibility in developing your newsletter ideas.) You can do this for associations, too, and allow them to distribute your newsletter as their own.

## COST AND PROFIT FACTORS

Subscription renewals are critical to success—allegedly. Some experienced newsletter publishers say that the first year of a new subscription is only a breakeven year due to the high cost of winning subscriptions, and that if the enterprise doesn't win a renewal rate of at least 50 to 60 percent, it will not earn a profit at all.

The problem with that thesis is that it overlooks other avenues for profits open to newsletter publishers. The fact is that many newsletter publishers do not expect to turn a profit on subscription fees at all, but hope only that the fees cover basic costs. Profits will come out of ancillary sales, or what some in the business call *bounce-back sales*. These are sales of items the publisher offers readers in the newsletter such as manuals, books, special reports, software, or other items, preferably other items the newsletter publisher also publishes. In short, some newsletter publishers operate their newsletters primarily to establish and maintain a customer network that serves them as a good market for their other publications, which are the real heart of their ventures.

In that sense, at least, the newsletters published by these individuals are marketing tools rather than profit centers, and in some cases they are self-liquidating. They return their own costs, sometimes even with a profit, but at least they always return part of their costs. It is for this reason, too, that some newsletter publishers will offer their newsletters at modest, even nominal subscription fees, thus encouraging a large circulation and a high renewal rate.

The economics of specialty publishing are highly favorable in terms of costs, markup, and profit ratios. A four-page newsletter will cost on the order of $2 to $3 per year per subscriber to print and mail. This will, of course, be somewhat higher for an eight-page or larger newsletter, will also go up for newsletters printed on more expensive paper, with photos (which require more expensive processing and plates than does straight text or other line copy), and may go down for longer press runs. However, this serves to illustrate the general markup, since even a modest four-page monthly newsletter will usually bring a $24-per-year subscription fee.

Probably the most profitable of the ancillary publications is the special report, which does not have to have expensive paper or costly bindings. Most buyers will accept these as typed copy, bound with a corner staple if they are brief, or in a simple binder or between simple covers if they are more extensive in size. Such reports can sell for a few dollars or many dollars, and the size of the report (whether 8 pages or 228 pages) has little to do with the price. The price is set by other factors, such as these.

Nature of the information such as how exclusive, how difficult to gather, how valuable.

Estimated number of copies that can be sold: a limited edition must necessarily bring in more per copy to bring back all costs and a profit.

Cost of gathering the information, which is far more an item of original cost than is the cost of typesetting, printing, and binding.

Bear in mind at all times in specialty publishing that it is an information business: buyers are buying information and they are paying for useful, even valuable, information, not for ink and paper. This is true for the newsletter itself, it is true for the reports, and it is true for the enterprise in general. You must set prices that reflect the value of the information as well as the cost of gathering and presenting it.

## KINDS OF INFORMATION NEEDED/WANTED

In discussing newsletters we have already considered several types of information such as inside tips, advisory services, technical details, and others. There is another way to characterize the types of data readers want and will pay for. The kinds of information people want can be listed as one or more of the following classes:

1. How it works.
2. How to do it.
3. Where to find it.

Let us consider each of these individually to gain more insight into what each constitutes as information.

## HOW IT WORKS

How-it-works information includes exposés, news behind the news, technical narratives, and a variety of other such information. For example, some of my own reports in the past have explained how the government procurement system works, how advertising agencies operate, and how list brokers operate. Many other kinds of books and reports fit into this category, even such books as *The Price of Power*, an exposé on government at high levels in international and military operations.

How-it-works information is often part of and closely related to the other two kinds of information, however, and in at least some cases the reader is interested in how something works only in connection with learning how to do something or where to find something, so that how-it-works information is not always separable nor even of great value of itself.

## HOW TO DO IT

How-to-do-it is probably by far the most popular and widest selling category of special reports, magazine articles, and books overall, despite the appearance of exposés and other how-it-works information on best-seller lists. The more complex our society becomes, the more important how-to-do-it information becomes, and the greater the demand for it becomes as well. Today, there is a great demand for such information about many things: computers and related items, tax shelters and tax returns, how to see Europe on $25 a day (or some other ridiculously inadequate budget), and a host of other things.

What your readers will want to know about will depend primarily on the kind of readers you have, to whom you have addressed your sales appeals. If they are computer hobbyists, for example, they will want how-to information on writing programs, how to find free programs, how to join a computer club, how to build or modify a computer, and perhaps a thousand other items limited only by your imagination.

If how-to is the most popular and most demanded information, it is also the area of greatest opportunity in newsletters and reports: our modern technological society has created a great need (and, therefore, a great hunger) for such information. One can hardly survive today without study, formal or informal, of how to cope with our society. To carry out simple banking operations, for example (i.e., use automatic teller machines), one must cope with a computer, albeit one that has an extremely friendly set of help menus. Even to find something in a modern shopping mall one must read complex directory boards or cope with another computer terminal that offers a set of help menus.

It is likely that it is nearly impossible to go wrong with how-to information if the information is sound enough; there are candidates for virtually all kinds of how-to information. Place this category high on your calendar when planning newsletters and/or special reports.

# WHERE TO FIND IT

The complexity of today's society makes where-to-find-it information (directories) almost equal in importance and popularity to how-to-do-it information. Where-to information is also a great necessity in today's society. One needs to know where to find things. As the author of a number of books (both how-to and where-to) I receive letters and telephone calls frequently from people who cannot find my books in their local bookstores and call me to find out where and how to order them. They see the book or an advertisement listing the publisher, and perhaps their local bookstore does not have the book. They fail to ask the bookstore people to order for them, or to tell them how to order it, and yet they think to track the author down. Why? How? Who knows; somehow they manage to do so. It illustrates how little they know the logical thing to do or the logical place to turn.

For example, among the directories I have produced was one on government purchasing offices. Unbelievably, even the government itself does not have such a directory! Perhaps more surprising are the following stories.

In Washington, DC, there is the central office of what is now the Office of Personnel Management, formerly (and for many years) the Civil Service Commission. Incredibly enough, this office has one of the poorest lists of vacancies in the federal government; several other government offices have better lists of openings. (Examples: The Department of Transportation personnel office and the General Services Administration personnel office.) An enterprising individual developed a good biweekly listing of openings in the federal establishment and has built a good business, of which one of his best subscribers are government offices. Now there is more than one such service.

Most major government agencies publish a telephone directory of their offices and executives every year. Unfortunately, like most bureaucratic efforts, this produces something considerably less than perfect. However, an individual produces the *Federal Telephone Directory*, an annual publication listing some 18,000 federal executives, sells it at a highly satisfactory figure every year to many government marketers and lobbyists, but counts federal offices among his best customers. Federal executives find his directory far better than those produced by the federal agencies (far more accurate and up to date) and are more than willing to pay his price.

Where-to books are almost as popular as are how-to books, and are becoming more popular as society grows more complex. Most people do not know where or how to begin researching, and Matthew Lesko, who founded his Washington Researchers firm in Washington, DC, a few years ago, makes a business of teaching others how to carry out their own where-to research. His firm publishes material on the subject and conducts training seminars. Originally, his firm also undertook researches on a fee basis, but he now turns that work over to another organization. Lesko is also the author of two commercially published where-to books, *Getting Yours* and the more recent *Information USA*.

Many other directories have been highly successful. There are several that list toll-free numbers, usually organized by the types of goods or services offered, for example. The *National Directory of Addresses and Telephone Numbers* lists banks, corporations, state and local government agencies, and many other such addresses and telephone numbers, and there is at least one other directory covering essentially the same ground. A newspaper reporter compiled a listing of sources a newspaper reporter would want to have available, and succeeded in having it published commercially.

The idea will work in any field of great interest. Directories of computers and related equipment and accessories appear regularly in popular magazines devoted to the field. Unfortunately, because the market is so dynamic, these listings have only fleeting usefulness; they are obsolete almost as quickly as they are published, which makes the idea useful for a real-time publication such as a magazine or newsletter but not for a batch-type publication such as a book. However, a newsletter devoted at least in part to listing new offerings in hardware and software is viable, and most computer magazines do have some sort of new hardware and new software coverage.

A local firm (Phillips Publishing, Inc., of Bethesda, MD) publishes what they call *The Local Area Networking Directory* in which they list systems, manufacturers and distributors, support services (e.g., consultants, engineering firms, associations, and others), standards, and many other items of useful information. Evidently, it is a successful publication for they revise and republish it periodically. It is currently in its third edition.


## REFERENCE GUIDES

Somewhere along the spectrum of how-it-works/how-to-do-it/where-to-find-it materials is the reference guide, that directory of facts that is something of a hybrid of all the other categories. The computer dictionary is such a reference, as is the index to dot matrix printers and the list of microprocessors with their specifications, characteristics, manufacturers, and other details listed.

The reference guide is almost any publication you would keep on your desk or library shelf for ready access when you need some specific piece of information. In some cases, even how-to guides are used for reference intermittently, as are where-to directories. In short, a reference guide is one of any kind of information that the user is likely to want to refer to again and again as one does a dictionary or encyclopedia; therefore, it may be a collection of any or all of the several kinds of information we have been discussing here.


## GETTING THE INITIAL IDEA

Whether you plan to launch a newsletter, a series of reports or manuals, or some combination of the two, you need to start with a basic idea of what kinds of information you will provide and to whom. The accuracy with which you judge the needs of those you reach—or, conversely, the efficiency with which you reach the right prospects for the information you wish to offer—is the single most important factor in your success.

Obviously, you can start from either end: with a view of the people you can reach and your judgment as to what they will be most interested in and attracted by, or with some certain kind and class of information you can produce and your best estimate as to whom this should be directed and how the offer should be presented. Most people, however, begin with an idea for the product, although with some user in mind, usually an obvious deduction. If, for example, you decide that you are in a good position to begin a newsletter for amateur or hobbyist programmers, you obviously must address those who already own a computer of some sort, and who already know the rudiments of programming and are practicing programming. On second thought, you may decide that your readers need not be those with some prior experience or skill in programming; perhaps you want to help complete tyros learn to program. In fact, that not only broadens your list of prospects, but perhaps increases your probabilities of success. But does it? Perhaps a little research is in order.

## RESEARCHING THE IDEA

One way to research a newsletter idea is to see if there are already some newsletters on the subject. You can check this out at your local library. The librarian will be glad to help you look up some directories of newsletters (or see the data listed in Chapter 14). It won't take you long to find out whether your idea has occurred to anyone else.

Conventional wisdom says that if you find no newsletters on the subject, go carefully: this may be a sign that there is not enough interest in the subject to support a newsletter. However, if there are a dozen or so newsletters on the subject, be aware of how much competition you are going to have to combat in your efforts to make a place for your own newsletter. If there is a corporal's guard of newsletters on the subject (perhaps three to six), that is probably an encouraging sign.

Still, be careful. Do not assume that newsletters about computer programming are of the same genre as the one you plan. They may be entirely different and addressed to an entirely different audience than the one you envision. It is necessary to study these newsletters and be sure that you know to whom they are addressed, what they cover, and any gaps—*what or who they neglect to cover*—to evaluate how they relate to your idea.

That is not all. Survey the magazines on the general subject, and see whether any address the same audience on the same subject, how to write programs, that is. This, too, will help you gauge both how much coverage is now provided and how much interest there is, that is, how interested readers are in the subject.

Read letters to the editor in these magazines, and see what impressions you get from those as to interest in learning how to program or getting free programs and other related information.

Contact computer clubs, local ones and others (as many as you can reach), and inquire as to their activities and the interests of their members. Try to determine what members want to know about or learn to do.

You may get reinforcement of your original idea. You may decide that it was not a good idea. You may decide that with a little modification it will be a sure winner. Or you may get a far better idea as a result of your research. But do the research. Not only will it make your venture more likely to succeed in general, but it will be an excellent experience for you in several other ways and will help you to market your newsletter and/or other publications more successfully.

You can even research the idea by a very special method that includes its own bonus pay off. You can run an advertisement and/or make a mailing that announces that your new publication will soon be available and ask for advance orders, offering some bonus as a reward for ordering in advance and waiting perhaps 30 to 60 days to get the product. (Once, using this approach produced about $2500 in advance orders for a report I planned to prepare, a sound indicator that it was a viable idea.) If you get only a few orders and become convinced that the idea is not a good one, you can return the money with your apologies and regrets. If you get a good response, you can be fairly sure you have a viable idea.

Caution: Don't accept promises of purchase as evidence. If you ask respondents to express only their reaction or interest, the response is meaningless. Many will say "Yea" just to be kind, but only actual prepaid orders are *proof* of interest and acceptance. Do, however, offer an inducement such as a free report, a discounted price, or some such thing. (In the case I cited here, I included a free three-month subscription to a newsletter as a bonus for the advance, prepaid order.)

You can also check out bookstores and libraries for books on the subject you plan for your newsletter and/or other publication to see how much interest in the subject is indicated by the books available. Ask bookstore dealers whether books on programming written for the non-professional are moving well. Ask your librarian, too.

## HOW/WHERE TO GET A SUPPLY OF INFORMATION

Earlier we discussed some of the ways to get a stream of information such as by asking those who send out news releases to put your name on their mailing lists so that you begin to get such information regularly. Let it be known generally to as many others as possible that you are in the publishing business, especially if you are publishing a newsletter. Send sample copies to potential news and information sources such as manufacturers, software developers, research laboratories, universities, retail chains, and whoever might be a source of information useful to you. Also trade *comp* (complimentary or free) subscriptions with other newsletter publishers, with permission granted to each other to use material from the other's publication. Many newsletter publishers also invite freelance writers to contribute material for which they pay small sums.

Although you may not want to reprint other's information word for word, it is still a good idea to get formal, written permission (releases) to do so. This gives you protection against lawsuit for copyright infringement. A sample of such a form appears as Figure 9.1. However, although some people will give you such a blanket release, others will only agree to specific material: you must tell them precisely what it is that you propose to reprint, cite, quote, or reproduce in some manner, and the copyright owner will then make the release specific for that item alone. The form shown works well for me when I am gathering

# Herman Holtz
Proposals - Seminars - Support Services

P.O. Box 6067
Silver Spring, MD 20906
(301) 460-1506

I am the publisher of <u>Microcomputer Programming</u>, a monthly newsletter for amateur and hobbyist computer programmers. In this newsletter I include information about standard, off-the-shelf programs they can buy, tips on writing their own programs, sources of free programs, information about computer clubs, and a variety of related information. I also publish information about firmware, new equipment, and industry news.

I am always seeking good material, and trying to make my readers aware of new products and services of interest. I review products now on the market, and often include manufacturers' own literature, including drawings, specifications, and general descriptions. I will, of course, credit the source.

I am therefore interested in any materials and information you can supply about your own products and services, and in getting your permission to reproduce these. If you can supply such materials and wish to gain the free publicity of such coverage as that described above, please send all materials to the above address, along with the signed form below.

Thank you for your help and your cooperation.

Cordially,

Herman Holtz

## RELEASE

Permission is hereby granted to reproduce the materials supplied herewith, as stipulated and requested above, to publisher Herman Holtz. It is understood that this permission is conditional on the publisher making suitable attribution, fully identifying the product and source.

Name and title, typed or printed          Signature

Name of company

NOTES: _____

**Figure 9.1.**   A simple letter and release.

materials for my books, but you must adapt it to your own purposes. When you want to quote something specific, cite the specific example in your request and release. You definitely need a release to make verbatim quotes or use other people's materials in some way. The following paragraphs on copyright will clarify this for you.

## COPYRIGHT

The very word *copyright* is self-explanatory: it refers to the author's rights to his or her own copy: text, music, art, or other creative product. (And, also, to the publisher's right to such material when the author has assigned or sold that right, for it is a negotiable commodity.)

The old copyright law was changed several years ago to meet modern conditions and to satisfy what many agreed were flaws in the older copyright law. Briefly, the major difference in practical terms is this: under the old law, copyright began when the author or publisher issued a number of copies (perhaps as few as 10) with the announcement of claim of copyright. That claim is the word *copyright, copr.,* or ©, with date (year, for books) and name of owner. Too, the copyright could be registered with the Copyright Office, an agency of the Library of Congress, by filling out a form, supplying two copies of the published item, and paying the small fee required. However, registering the copyright with the Copyright Office was not a requirement since publishing the material with the copyright notice, the date, and the name of the copyright claimant was itself quite sufficient to establish copyright in common law. Should the publisher neglect to make this claim of copyright and publish the work without that notice or with the notice in some defective form, the publisher surrendered all rights to the copy and allowed it to automatically enter the public domain, under which condition anyone could use the material as he or she saw fit, and did not even have to acknowledge the source. The copyright was thus lost forever and could not be reclaimed. However, under the current law, acutal distribution is not necessary as a prerequisite to copyright, nor does the publisher lose all rights as a result of neglect, but is permitted to correct the error of publication without the copyright notice and still retain copyright. Copyright is thus presumed to have begun with creation of the work, rather than with distribution.

There are other provisions, not all of immediate concern here. One is the doctrine of fair usage, which permits quotation of excerpts from a copyrighted work without violation of one's rights such as the quotations a book reviewer or critic might use in a review. However, it is most difficult to determine what fair usage is, and it remains a problem to know what you may quote without having infringed on someone's copyright and exposed yourself to the possibility of being sued for infringement.

In that connection, let it be clear that although you are legally protected under common law by the simple act of printing your copyright notice on your publication, should you wish to sue someone for infringement, you will have to have had that copyright registered with the Copyright Office. However, you can register the copyright at any time, so you can do so when and if you expect to get into a legal battle.

One other matter about copyright. You cannot copyright titles. You can appropriate anyone else's title, and they yours, perhaps. *Perhaps* because a title can be protected as a trade mark, but if it is not identified as such, it is not so protected. (Trade marks are protected under patent law, within the Department of Commerce, rather than within the Library of Congress.)

Still one more final comment. It is wise to spell out the full word *copyright* in your publication because some other countries' governments do not recognize or accept the copyright symbol, and will not give you legal protection if you rely on that symbol alone to claim your copyright.

You should know also that some publications will grant permission to others to use their copyrighted material only upon payment of a fee of some sort. Usually, this is the case only if you want to make use of an extensive piece of someone's work; most others rarely insist on payment for fragmentary quotes or citations. Anyway, there is another "out" if you are interested only in the information itself, and not the words. It is this: copyright protection is extended to some given combination of words and/or other original material. You cannot copyright basic ideas or information. You cannot, therefore, quote a passage from an encyclopedia verbatim without infringing on that encyclopedia publisher's copyright, but you can use the information or idea in the passage as long as you write up the material in your own words. Do not make the mistake here, however, of believing that a few minor cosmetic changes in the language or in the wording will do; it will not. You do have to make an original work of your own, even if it is based on ideas or information you have borrowed. How much does it have to be changed? It is impossible to say; too often, the courts have had to decide whether a given piece of work was plagiarism and infringed on someone's copyright or not. There is an ancient witticism that illustrates the point, and is largely a truth, even if a sardonic one. It is this: stealing material from one or two sources is plagiarism; stealing from 50 sources, however, is research.

To illustrate the point more clearly, however, there is a case current at this writing of a novelist who appropriated the entire plot of another, published novel. Although he created his entire novel in his own language, the resemblance in plot details was so startling that it was soon discovered. The writer admitted that he adopted the other's plot, but did so innocently, he said, thinking that he had a perfect legal right to do so, if not a moral one. Morally, it seems to be a clear case of plagiarism. What the legal decision will be is impossible to say, nor is it certain that the matter will go to a lawsuit and trial to be decided in the courts. It illustrates the inherent difficulty in making determinations of what is the exact protection given by the law; that is, what is plagiarism (i.e., in the legal sense, not the moral one) and what is infringement (for plagiarism is one form of infringement, but there are others).

## NEWSLETTER FEATURES

Aside from the overall objective of your newsletter, whatever it may be, there is the matter of what kinds of features you will offer. Magazines and newspapers generally have many features such as columns of various kinds (opinion, advice, sounding off, commentary, and others), new-product descriptions, crossword puzzles, and others. The newsletter is generally tightly restricted for space and cannot offer all these features, although they do offer some. In fact, here are the features listed by newsletters appearing in Howard Penn Hudson's *The Newsletter Yearbook Directory*:

Industry news.

Personnel changes.

Financial news.

Product news.

Photos.

Cartoons.

Publishers listed here also indicate which features they will buy from freelance contributors, if they are willing to buy material at all.

The use of photos and cartoons in newsletters is more the exception than the rule, due to space limitations. However, the other features listed suggest areas of coverage suitable to newsletters as they relate to the general objective of the newsletter. They are not the only areas you may wish to address, however. In fact, the kind of coverage you offer will probably conform, in kind, to one of the areas already discussed. In periodicals coverage that helps the reader understand, do, or find things are often referred to as *service articles*, denoting the fact that they service reader needs directly. Among the kinds of material that this covers, in addition to the how-to, where-to, and such coverage already discussed, are these:

Columns answering reader queries.

Columns in which readers can exchange opinions, information, answers.

Buy/sell/trade offers.

Some periodicals are slanted to such objectives. The *Computer Trader*, a monthly periodical published by Chet Lambert of Birmingham, AL, for example, suggests in its very title that its *raison d'être* is to provide a medium of exchange between individuals buying, selling, and/or trading computer equipment. (*Computer Trader* is something more than a newsletter, however, more closely resembling a magazine in format although newsletter-like in coverage.) *Computer Trader* invites contributions and pays for them in advertising space since the publication accepts advertising. (Most true newsletters do not, although there are exceptions.)

If your appeal is to hobbyists and aficionados, the buy-sell-swap exchange will be an appealing one, almost certainly, for invariably those whose hobbies entail physical equipment are always trading, buying, and selling items. It would make good marketing sense in such case to make this as prominent a feature as possible since it will be a feature of great appeal. But how-to, where-to, and how-it-works features are also appreciated by hobbyists, especially those who are still relatively green.

Another appreciated service is job-finding help, and this is a service that is useful to both parties, job seekers and employers. As a publisher, you can invite subscribers to use your columns to invite resumés from prospective employees and describe job openings to readers. And, since employers often want to run such advertising "blind," so as to avoid having a horde of job seekers descend on them, you might wish to offer a box-number service also.

You might also do the reverse of that, and run positions-wanted notices for readers, perhaps again with box numbers to screen the individual's identity from general view.

## COMPUTER-BASED DIRECTORIES

The main weakness of directory publishing in the microcomputer industry can be turned into a main strength. (Astonishingly enough, most liabilities can be turned into assets with enough imagination.) The weakness is the extraordinarily dynamic nature of the industry at present. It is all but impossible to devise a directory or compendium of any sort that will not start becoming obsolete almost immediately. However, your own computer offers a way to turn that problem to advantage and make a commercial asset of it. The principle of finessing such problems is to accept the problem—do not even attempt to overcome it—and devise a *system* that will work despite the problem.

In this case accept the fact that any directory of computers, printers, modems, programs, disk drives, or other computer components and accessories is of fleeting value, useful for only a short time. Concentrate on the fact that there is need, nevertheless, for such information despite the fact that it cannot be kept on the shelf. Therefore, it must be stored in some more dynamic and more flexible medium than the printed page, and it is obvious to all of us that that medium must be magnetic disk, a medium that enables us to update (maintain) the directory continuously.

The trick, then, to make this commercially viable is to devise some scheme for marketing the contents of the directory file, but being able to offer reports at an acceptable price.

Doing this is not difficult if we accept that most people who buy directories do so to gain access to only some relatively small part of the directory. Someone buying a directory of computer hardware, for example, might be interested in only printers, and perhaps not even all printers but only formed-character impact printers. The publisher does not find it viable to publish many thin directories (i.e., highly specialized directories) and so combines many categories to create a large enough directory to command a viable price, in effect forcing buyers to pay for more information than they want. But they've no choice.

It is possible now to change that to the benefit of both buyers and sellers. You can set up a large number of specialized computer files of all these fast-changing items, maintain them, and allow users to have access to the contents of any files of interest on some fee basis, either by means of computer-to-computer link accessing the files of interest, or by printout of the file(s) of interest. Your database is the entire set of computer-file directories, but users need not buy everything to get what they want. Buyers of such information might be individuals, but they might also be companies and retail stores, and some might even be interested in a regular weekly or monthly service offering them the newest compilation.

This need not be confined to computers and related products. There are other industries to which this philosophy might be applied, industries where change is almost constant and people need up-to-date information. For example, restaurant and hotel owners might want daily or weekly quotations on different foodstuffs to guide their menu planning and purchasing, or perhaps the latest long-range forecasts on foodstuffs. Some users might want weekly or monthly guides to special tours, special airline rates and travel packages, cruises, and other such items that change frequently or in which special offers arise frequently. Some people want the most up-to-date information on business meetings, conventions, conferences, and trade shows or exhibits and fairs. Or, on a local basis, many merchants (restaurants, hotels, tourist attractions, bus lines, taxicab companies, and others) want to be alerted to or reminded of such events coming to town.

Your micro is also a convenient place to store and maintain a roster of local services such as that of baby sitters, which is also data that tends to change. Aside from individuals utilizing your service (you can charge either the client or the baby sitter for your service), hotels have use for this service as a convenience for their guests. You can either provide a list of most appropriate names or you can actually make the specific arrangements yourself, acting as a booking agency. (In that function, you generally charge the baby sitter a fee or commission for your service.)

You might wish to establish a day-care guide for your own town or area, as did Nichol Publications, cited earlier, but keeping the directory on disk, rather than in hard copy. Again, you might offer a service, charging the centers for listings or placements, or charging the user for the listing which you print out. Here, too, the buyer does not need to buy the entire directory, but can ask for only those centers in some specific area, getting a list of perhaps 10 or 20, rather than 200, and paying accordingly. To do this, you would simply arrange the database (the entire list of centers) into a set of files organized by geographic location. You might set each center up as a file with several labels by which you can access them and retrieve them in a kind of library system by any of several characteristics (key words), according to how you have labeled them.

The possibilities are almost endless. Suppose you study the Thursday newspaper advertisements and circulars distributed door to door by the local supermarkets, who usually advertise their weekend specials on Thursday. You might then collect lists of the various leader items, including those for which coupons have been made available, and print up a report that you would mail out to subscribers for their weekend shopping. However, there is a better way to do this. Approach the supermarkets with the proposition.

In this mode, the supermarkets would provide data for their specials, and could thus make the information available earlier in the week. They might even consider paying you to support their advertising in this way, either as advertising fees per se or as a subsidy to enable you to increase distribution since you can afford to make the publication available to customers at modest prices, and thus boost circulation. Note: Charging a small, even nominal price for the publication is better than giving it away free, even if you could afford to give it away free, for then people regard it as a circular and attach no value to it. Always make some charge, no matter how small.

This idea need not be confined to supermarkets, but can be applied to any large stores: department stores, large drugstore chains, and others. It can even be applied to small stores by soliciting information and fees from them, one by one, and urging them to feature only specials, thus giving your publication a certain exclusive value: it carries only special offers and is thus well worth reading.

## IT'S ALL INFORMATION HANDLING

You may note parallels between some of these ideas and those of Chapters 6 and 7. In a sense all are closely related because all deal with gathering, compiling, organizing, and disseminating information. But isn't that the essence of the computer in the first place, the special advantages it offers us in those functions of processing and managing information? The true difference among these several explorations of ideas is only the main theme of use or purpose, and this has more to do with the markets and marketing of the products and services than it has to do with the kind of products and services or the methods of creating them. If you go back and review some of the earlier chapters you will see that this is true, and that ought to be helpful in stimulating new ideas, ideas that might fit any of these categories—or fit them all.

# Chapter Ten

---

# Overload Support Services

Service industries continue to grow even as smokestack industries
decline because the demand for service is increasing steadily
despite other economic trends. A useful and dependable service is
a sound basis for a business venture today.

## INFORMATION *IS* A SERVICE BUSINESS

Earlier in these pages we touched briefly on the business of helping
organizations whose own systems were overloaded, had more work to
do than they could handle. If you have doubts about the viability of this
notion, consider the case of a firm that is today known as Volt Information Sciences, Inc. Launched over 30 years ago at the kitchen table
of its founder, it was based almost exclusively on supporting larger
companies (some of them major corporations) with work that involved
information products: parts lists, technical manuals, proposals, and
other such developments. For a number of years, growing to an annual
volume counted in many millions of dollars, the firm was still devoted

almost exclusively to supporting larger companies. Even today, itself a rather large corporation, the company deals primarily in information products and services and supports other companies.

What makes this support service such an important industry is the vast growth in demand for information. The technological revolutions have spawned that demand both directly and indirectly: directly because we need to "document" jet airplanes, radar, TV, satellites, video-cassette recorders, stereo players, robots, moon landings and other space flights, office copiers, and that whole, vast family of new technological achievements; indirectly because these things have brought about other developments that require further information gathering and dissemination: global communications and global travel by millions of people, new industries created by many of these inventions, and their overall effects on society in general.

There is another factor at work: the computer itself, which exists in a symbiotic relationship with that burgeoning technology, each dependent on the other. The computer is itself a product of modern technology, but at the same time the computer has made much of the technology possible. The space program, for example, could not have come as far as it has without computers. (The Goddard Space Flight Center alone, only one of a number of NASA centers, has well over 200 big computers and micros on the same scale as typewriters.) Even that does not explain everything, for the mere existence of a new capability creates its own demand or need. The mere fact of computers and printers exploded the demand for printed reports, even beyond real need. (Is there a manager in business and industry today who does not wonder what he or she will do with all the stacks of 11 × 14-inch printout that arrives almost daily from the computer room?) Whether the need is real or not, in practical terms the demand exists and will grow, inevitably. And therein lies opportunity for the entrepreneur. As you read earlier, no organization can do everything, and all organizations become overloaded from time to time. When they do, they have only a limited number of alternatives. If the work is not obligatory, they may decline it (something most firms are reluctant to do), they may work overtime, they may choose to suffer whatever penalties they have to suffer by being behind schedule, or they may turn to outside services for help.

Quite often, the decision lies primarily in the question of whether they can do the latter satisfactorily, in whether there is a reliable support service available. In managing an organization that derived most of its business from contracts with federal agencies, I relied heavily on a network of home-workers to get many tasks done on time such as typing, proofreading, and editing. Most of my network consisted of women who could not devote eight hours during the business day to the tasks because they had families to look after. They could, however, devote many more than eight hours, if the hours were of their own choosing. Therefore, working at home was a viable idea for them and for the company. They chose their own hours, set their fees (or negotiated them), and took care of their own taxes and fringe benefits. The company worked at a lower overhead, was not forced to pay for idle labor during slow periods, yet could respond to sudden demands and peak loads through what was really subcontracting in most cases.

## EVERYONE NEEDS SUPPORT

You may have gotten the impression that only large organizations have situations where they require support to help them handle overloads. If so, the impression is a false one. The work overload is a condition that falls, like the rain, on everyone alike. The one-person enterprise gets into the same predicaments that large companies and even supercorporations do, and needs the same help.

In our earlier discussion of this we talked principally with reference to word-processing services. However, overload burdens do not confine themselves to any single area but can affect any kind of work. A client may need help simply in organizing a list of parts or an index to something or other. A lawyer may need help in researching precedents or obscure provisions of the statutes. A writer may need help in searching out some arcane fact tucked away somewhere in someone's database. An accountant may need help at tax time.

## SOME SOUND BUSINESS PRACTICES

In some cases, especially where the overload the client faces is not unanticipated (as that of the accountant at tax time when the overload is a typical one), the client may supply the applications program as well as the raw data. (If, of course, the program will run on your system.) In others you will be required to supply the program. If you do not have the proper software but must purchase it especially for the use, you must proceed with caution or run a serious risk of loss on the job.

Suppose the job is worth $300, but the program will cost you that much, perhaps even more. Will it pay you to buy the program? No, not if you have no guarantee that the program will be of further use to you. It is exceedingly risky to accept mere assurances by a client that you will be able to use the program in future assignments. You've no guarantee of future assignments and, perversely enough, those verbal assurances rarely prove out. It is worth your investment only if it can meet one of the following conditions:

1.  The job is large enough to absorb the cost of the program in overhead and leave you a profit, even if you never use that program again (i.e., if you write it off on this one assignment).
2.  The program is one you want, anyway, because you *know* you will have other uses for it and are sure that you can write it off (amortize it) over a number of future uses.
3.  The client will give you some kind of acceptable guarantee (perhaps a term contract) that eliminates or at least reduces the risk to an acceptable level.

Otherwise, you will be wise to ask the client to supply the program necessary to produce the result asked for. However, if the client insists that you will be using the program in his or her own behalf regularly, suggest that the client should then buy the program and deposit in your care, although it will remain the client's property. This is not an unusual arrangement, nor is it without precedent in other businesses such as printing and publishing, where the printer often retains possession of negatives and plates, although they are the property of the customer and held in care.

The same consideration obtains with regard to files, which will usually be on disk. They are the client's property if generated for the client and paid for by the client, but you hold them as a matter of convenience for both of you. The client need not be bothered with filing them away and keeping track of them, to search them out each time you are to do some new work. However, it is very much in your interest to store these free of charge for clients since having them in your possession makes it far less likely that the client will go in quest of other suppliers. It is far more convenient to have you do the work and convenience is a powerful motivator. Never forget that what you offer here is a service, and an important part of any service is convenience for the customer. Always consider how you can arrange your service for the greatest convenience of the customer. It will always pay off in the end, especially since it may be the only or at least the chief difference between your service and someone else's, hence the only argument you have for choosing your service over your competitor's service. A cardinal rule of selling is to make it as easy as possible for the prospect to become a customer and to do business with you. Later, when we discuss marketing in more depth, we examine this again.

## PROSPECTING FOR LEADS

Before you can develop accounts—sign up customers or clients (*clients*, if you consider yours to be a professional service)—you have to develop *leads*: those who appear to be good prospects for the services you offer and whom you should approach. In studying this it might appear to you that your best prospects will be those who have no computers of their own and who should, therefore, be in need of support by those who do own computers. The facts are different. Those who own computers do so because they have need of computer assistance in whatever they do, and since overloads are inevitable, at least occasionally, they are always good prospects for overload support contracts. Therefore, a list of all those who use microcomputers in their business or work is a useful list for marketing purposes.

That list may include all kinds of business firms, small and large, plus all self-employed professionals, all associations, and all government and quasi-government agencies. (Overloads may also be the consequence of computer breakdown. Computers, following Murphy's Law faithfully, will do as other machines do and pick the worst possible times for their breakdowns, forcing their owners to an almost desperate quest for alternatives.)

If, therefore, you can acquire a list of all those in your service area who own and use computers for business purposes of any kind, do treasure that list as a valuable resource, and do be sure to do at least occasional mailings to those on the list, advising them of your service and availability. If there is no such list in existence or none that you can acquire, begin to develop and compile such a list by whatever means possible, such as the following:

Local computer-club membership lists.

Information from retail computer stores.

Local advertising.

Local newspaper features.

Miscellaneous.

Let us expand on these briefly since simple listing of a possible source does not explain how to use that source.

## Local Computer Clubs

If you have one or more local computer clubs, you may be able to get membership lists from them. These may or may not be helpful since those who buy computers for business or professional use do not necessarily join computer clubs, but it's a possible source.

## Retail Computer Stores

Retail merchants may be willing to help you acquire some of this information, especially if you make use of some subterfuges such as asking for the names of some people who own computers bought from that merchant so that you can use them as sources of information on how satisfactory it is to deal with that merchant. Or perhaps you can exchange services of some sort.

## Local Advertising

Sometimes the advertisements people run in local newspapers, Yellow Pages directories, and other media reveal that they own computers.

## Local Newspaper Features

Stories about local businesses and associations appearing in the local press may give you clues.

## Miscellaneous

You may be able to rent mailing lists of local computer owners from one of the established list brokers, listed in the reference data provided in Chapter 14. Or you may draw inquiries, either casually or by design (e.g., your own inquiry advertising), which gives you some of this information. In any case, be alert for such information at all times and you will surely compile such a mailing list, even if slowly and name by name. (In addition, other activities you are involved with may provide some of this information.)

## SERVICES OFFERED SUGGEST PROSPECTS

Reviewing the array of services offered by others itself suggests many of the prospects: those who have use for overload support. Here are some of the lines appearing in advertisements which suggest uses, services, areas of application, and various kinds of prospects for support services:

| | |
|---|---|
| Transcriptions from tapes | Reports and proposals |
| Mailing list maintenance | Invoicing/accounts receivable |
| Sales analysis | Inventory control |
| Accounts payable | Communications |
| Magnetic storage of data | Data preparation for laser printing |
| Tape-to-disk conversion | OCR conversion |
| Weekend service | Airport hotel service |

The notation of airport hotel service is a particularly interesting one, and suggests an entire service area: that of traveling executives who need help while in the field. An executive traveling on business often discovers after arrival a sudden need for help in preparing a report, perhaps taking input information over the telephone from a home office. The executive tends to turn to the hotel management for help, and most hotels have reference lists of people who can help such as baby-sitters for families traveling for private purposes and public stenographers for people traveling on business missions. If you are within reasonable range of hotels in business districts or near airports (those hotels which are generally occupied on weekdays by people traveling for business and professional purposes), you would do well to register your name and services with the hotel's management. If you are in a position to give *sudden service* (quick-response), so much the better, but make sure to make the hotel management understand that this is a specialty and is always available to those with need for extraordinary effort. It is also helpful to leave a supply of brochures and/or business cards with the hotel, but be sure that these explain what you offer. (Advertising is no place to be subtle or cute; it's important to be clear.)

If you are in a key city, one that receives a steady stream of business visitors, you might do well to make your services known to companies away from your city, explaining that your services are available to those traveling to your city. For example, if you are within service range of downtown Chicago or, especially, O'Hare Airport, almost any company of size is a good prospect for you. This will be true also for most major cities and their airports such as Los Angeles, Washington, San Francisco, Denver, and others. It may be especially true for some cities, more than for others, where there are major government facilities (because of the stream of proposals and reports arriving at many of these). Washington, DC, is, of course, one example of this, but not the only one; there are San Diego, Los Angeles, Atlanta, Denver, and New York, also, among others.

As an example of this kind of need, on one occasion a team of people arriving in Washington to make a presentation to a government agency the next morning discovered that they had neglected to prepare certain presentation pieces. Fortunately for these gentlemen, who had come from the home offices of their major aircraft-manufacturing corporation in California, their Washington-area office knew a small firm who specialized in solving this kind of problem, and this small firm worked until the small hours to equip this team for their early-morning task.

## OFTEN IT'S A RESCUE SERVICE

There is a vast amount of such rescue work in most cities and especially in busy airport areas, which tend to take on a special life of their own and become satellite communities of the cities they serve. However, wherever there is a government facility of any size or a group of government facilities, there is often similar opportunity. Government agencies are staffed by people with the same traits as the people staffing private-sector organizations and they find themselves in the same straits quite often. Both tend to be overly optimistic about what they are going to accomplish and about what their own staffs can accomplish, so that it is not the slightest bit unusual for them to find the deadline almost on them before they realize that they cannot meet that deadline without special outside help.

For example, a group at Goddard Space Flight Center a few years ago was scheduled to take a 6:00 AM flight to Paris on a Monday for a special symposium. The American group from NASA was to bring along 30 packages of their presentation materials, each package comprising hundreds of pages of material, some of it already in printed form, but much of it yet to be printed and bound.

On the previous Monday, the group's manager confidently assured the Goddard center's technical-documentation support manager that there was no need for help; the group's own staff would handle it all. The manager was skeptical and he had a support contractor ready to provide help, but the engineering manager was calm in his assurance that he did not need help.

By Wednesday he began to have some doubts. On Thursday he was whistling in the dark, and by Friday he began to beg for help. The support contractor worked around the clock all through the weekend, almost to the 6:00 A.M. departure time, to prepare the 30 packages and get them to the airport.

It's not an unusual story, but a typical one. Be sure that everyone in your service area is aware of your service, especially if you are willing to handle these desperate emergencies that arise constantly in both public- and private-sector organizations. Overloads come about for at least five separate reasons or as a result of at least five different situations:

1.  A sudden surge of work for any of many unpredictable reasons, but as the result of a special set of circumstances which may or may not ever occur again.

2.  A seasonal peak, but one for which the organization cannot or prefers not to gear up the permanent staff and facilities, preferring to contract out overloads.

3.  An internal condition such as a breakdown of the organization's own computer, illness of key employees, a labor dispute, or other such unexpected circumstance.

4.  Failure to plan adequately, internally, or failure to appreciate, realistically, what will be required to meet an objective.

5.  The organization's workload or business grows faster than their ability to recruit qualified people or train new hires for the jobs so there is a continuous overload at least until the organization's capability catches up with sales.

# PROSPECTING THE WANT ADS

You can see that handling overloads can be a major business in itself, particularly in these times of increasing need for special skills in the business world. If you scan the want ads in any large newspaper, under *WORD PROCESSING*, you'll see that in this one area there is enormous demand, far more than the supply can satisfy. If you need further evidence, have a look at the advertising of the office-temporaries agencies, and you'll see further confirmation of this demand.

This is another way to search out prospects for your services—the help-wanted advertising. Such advertising reveals which companies are most in need of personnel who can handle their various computer facilities. Many of these firms who are advertising heavily for help to operate their word processors and other computer facilities are in the position of those described a few paragraphs ago as suffering a work overload through a shortage of skilled employees, whether the shortage is due to rapid growth of the organization or to other causes. Still, careful study of help-wanted advertising is highly revealing, and furnishes many clues—even actual sales clues—to people who need help.

The approach to such people is, of course, one of offering help as a vendor or contractor until the organization can recruit skilled help and handle their workload in-house. In the meanwhile, you can help them keep up with their workload, relieving some of the pressure. (Despite the many agencies offering the services of office temporaries, the supply of those who can operate even word processors, let alone other computer programs, is severely limited and temporaries are, therefore, not a practical answer for many organizations who need help if they need it immediately.)

# ANCILLARY SERVICES

It is noteworthy that many who advertise such services as we are discussing here stress in their advertising that they provide pickup and delivery as part of their overall service. This is no minor matter, but is an integral part of making the service convenient for the client. However, this does not necessarily mean that you must chase around in your own car or station wagon or even hire an assistant to do so. Quite the contrary, it is much more in your own interests normally (we discuss an exception to this in a moment) to stick to doing the best possible job of the main service. Fortunately, it is not necessary to worry overmuch about it; most cities today have a variety of courier services to offer. It is usually possible to have a courier make local deliveries within the area for $5 to $10, which is far less than the cost of taking your own time or sending an assistant of your own to make a pickup or delivery. The fees for such can be charged to the client as a cost item, or absorbed into your own overhead (or priced into the fee for the job) if you wish to offer "free" pickup and delivery service. It's rarely a problem, and as a rule the client does not object to being billed directly for the service, although there is some advantage to making the service free in that you absorb it into your own costs or fees.

The exception to the rule is that occasion when it is good marketing practice to meet the client personally such as in the first contact or when the job is of special importance and you wish to stress personal service.

## WINNING OUT-OF-TOWN CLIENTS

There are occasions when you can do business with clients located some distance from your normal service area, especially if you are in the sudden service or quick-reaction business. Providing such services to visitors from out of town, for example, is a natural lead to providing your services to them at their home offices, especially if those home offices are not too far from your own. Telephone lines, modems, and overnight-express services make it possible to do business between cities conveniently and easily. And providing services to visitors from out of town is an even stronger lead to continued business with the organization.

It is easy to compile mailing lists of such organizations from a variety of sources, one of them the help-wanted advertisements, but especially those seeking professionals and executives. These are display advertisements, rather than classified advertisements (although many firms use both in seeking people), and are generally run in the financial or business sections of newspapers such as the *New York Times*, the *Washington Post*, and others. The *Wall Street Journal* also carries many such advertisements. The latter has the majority of such advertisements in Tuesday and Wednesday editions; the others usually in their Sunday editions.

You can also compile lists from such publications as the *Thomas Register* and Dun & Bradstreet's *Million Dollar Directory*, although you can also rent suitable mailing lists from commercial list brokers quite easily.

## SOLICITING NEW ACCOUNTS

The typical method you are likely to use in soliciting accounts from business organizations who need help is the direct-mail package. Although we describe the typical direct-mail package more thoroughly in Chapter 12, one observation that is appropriate here is this: most organizations are divided into a number of departments (see Figure 3.1 to refresh yourself on this), each with its own mission and its own needs and problems. Sending your mail package—sales letters, brochures, cards, and other such items—to the company without addressing at least a department or specific function is wasteful. All too often the mail room will open mail not addressed to anyone in particular, trying to decide where or to whom to send it in the company, with the result that it may be discarded as advertising of no particular appeal to anyone. (That may mean that the mail clerk did not know where to send it.) It is important, therefore, to address someone by name, by department, or by some more or less standard and typical function. There is a way to do that which works pretty well because a mail clerk will recognize it as a familiar device. That is a *routing* or *distribution* box at the head of the main item, usually the upper right-hand corner (see Figure 10.1) . One or more lines include suggested destinations within

## Herman Holtz
Proposals - Seminars - Support Services

POST OFFICE BOX 6067
SILVER SPRING, MD 20906
(301) 460-1506

| ROUTE TO | |
|---|---|
| 1. MARKETING MANAGER | ☐ |
| 2. ADVERTISING DEPT | ☐ |
| 3. _____ | ☐ |
| 4. _____ | ☐ |

**Figure 10.1.** Typical routing box and its use.

the company, particularly the first line or two, but there are several blank lines also. This results in the piece being routed around to several people usually, especially if the first one or two find that they have no use for whatever is being offered but suspect others in the company will. It's a method that has worked well for many people and is well worth adopting.

To use this effectively you must prepare your copy in such a way as to have wide appeal, suggesting several uses of applications of your service. Consider all the departments or functions within an organization which would be able to make good use of whatever you have to offer, and prepare your copy accordingly. Remember that every organization must carry out at least the following functions, even if they are nonprofit or government organizations:

| | |
|---|---|
| Income Producing | Sales, marketing, membership drives, grants, contracts |
| Accounting | Bookkeeping, financial management, financial reporting |
| General Management | Directing operations, making decisions |
| Services | Providing whatever the organization provides as the reason for existence |
| Information | Brochures, advertising, news releases |
| Correspondence | Letters, notes, telephone, filing |

Think about any and all the functions in the organization that relate somehow to what you do and can offer, and especially of the kinds of problems the relevant departments are likely to encounter that will require outside help. Gear your sales appeals accordingly, and use a title or headline that suggests what you do to help while reminding the recipient of the problem (fear motivation). For example, something along the lines of BUSINESS RESCUE SERVICE or EMERGENCY OVERLOAD RELIEF might serve well as a one-line descriptor that conveys your main message and sales appeal in a single glance with a great economy of words. Or, if you want to be more colloquial, you

might try something such as BAIL-OUT SERVICE or DESPERA-
TION-TIME SERVICES. Such headlines as these are almost sure to
command attention, the first requisite for advertising effectiveness.

Obviously, you want to try to select the types of organizations most
likely to need the type of service you offer: the types of organizations
that are most prone to encountering the problem of work overloads and
are also most likely to be forced to do whatever is necessary to meet
their deadlines rather than to simply shrug and let them slip (as some
government organizations and other nonprofit groups seem able to do).
The companies' advertising is a good indicator of the kinds of business
environments in which each operates. Those most likely to have overload situations are organizations that do contract work (in contract work,
peaks and valleys of activity vary widely and, often, unpredictably) and
those generally in high-technology industries. Obviously those whose
advertising appears to be almost desperate in the quest for word-processing operators and other computer-related help such as programmers
and analysts are also likely to welcome offers that promise at least
temporary relief from the pressures of overloads or, to regard it from
another angle, undermanned operations.

## WHOM NOT TO ADDRESS

In pursuing the leads represented by such advertisements, do not address your material to the individuals named there as the people to
whom responses should be addressed. The reason for this admonition
is simple: the individual named in help-wanted advertisements is normally a personnel manager, and personnel managers are the last people
to whom you want your advertising solicitations to go. If the personnel
person understands your offer, it will promptly find its way into the
nearest wastebasket. Personnel people do not want anything to obscure
their own functions of recruiting new help. Surprisingly often what will
happen will be that you will receive a typical "Dear John" letter in
response to your brochures and sales letter, advising you that no suitable
opening exists at the moment but your resumé will be kept on file.

Whether this happens because personnel specialists can't read or because they just don't know what else to do about your solicitation is unclear. But it does happen, distressingly often.

Do not address your appeals to "President," "Chairman of the Board," or "Chief Executive Officer," either. Rarely will that help your case. Rather, if you want to address the envelope to a functional title of some sort, it is best to address a manager, probably the one that heads up your routing box. The routing box will then send its own message.

If you want your letter circulated, as you have suggested by your routing box, it is best not to address anyone by name, even if you happen to know the name of a manager. That makes the sales letter a personal one and militates against circulating it. People rarely send around a letter that has been addressed directly to them.

# Chapter Eleven

## Doing Piecework or Other At-Home Work as an Employee

*Owning a micro, especially with a modem so that you can be an extension of an organization, opens up a number of new career possibilities.*

### OUR LAWS NEVER ANTICIPATED MICROCOMPUTERS

The microcomputer has ushered in what may well become another revolutionary trend in employment. It has made it practicable for many people to work at home while carried as regular employees. The trend has already been set in motion with individuals operating their own microcomputers at home while connected to the company's computer by means of modem and telephone link and to people in the company

221

office by means of voice telephone link. Long predicted, it is now a reality, although still an infant movement, admittedly.

There are many problems to be solved before this becomes a widespread practice. There is the problem of prejudice. It is against tradition for one to have an employee on salary working at home. How does an employer verify time records of employees who are not under direct company supervision? There is the problem of insurance. How will insurance companies regard coverage of people whose premises have not been inspected and approved for coverage? There is the problem of federal regulations. How can EPA (Environmental Protection Agency) and OSHA (Occupational Safety and Health Administration) verify that government regulations are complied with in the workplaces? For those companies working on government contracts, how can they certify to the government auditors the labor hours charged to contracts by employees not observed directly by the officials of the contractor company?

There are also labor union problems. What kinds of labor rules apply to these special employees (for there is no denying that they are special)? Are they really employees or are they actually contractors and subcontractors? Those questions, in turn, bring up sundry other questions of overhead burdens and regulations regarding the letting of subcontracts.

Until these and other problems are ironed out and resolved, hiring salaried or hourly employees to work on their own premises is going to be the exception, rather than the rule. Yet some of this special employment has taken place, usually with the employee working at his or her own micro or word processor, tied to the employer's system by means of modem and telephone line.

## WORK STATIONS AND LOCAL AREA NETWORKS

Hooked up in this manner, the remote employee's micro actually represents a work station and part of what has come to be called a *local area network*, or LAN. This is gaining prominence rapidly as the key to office automation, and a LAN is, by definition, confined to a relatively limited geographic area, even, in many cases, to a single building or group of buildings.

A growing number of manufacturers are building equipment systems designed especially to function as elements (terminals and work stations) within such networks, and many other companies are supporting such systems with related components, accessories, and technical services of various kinds. Some of these systems are designed to accommodate hundreds of stations and operate over distances of several miles, whereas others will support as few as two or three stations and operate over only a few hundred feet.

Obviously, if you are to work as the employee of a company with your micro tied to the company's computer as a remote terminal or work station, your hardware and software must be compatible with the employer's hardware and software.

If your system is self-sufficient (contains all the elements and capabilities to support others), working as a piecerate employee or as a subcontractor may prove more practicable. In fact, there are actually three different situations possible, although the work you would be doing would be the same.

## NEITHER FISH NOR FOWL

The first situation is, obviously, that which we have just discussed: being a regular employee, full- or part-time, but an employee nevertheless.

The second situation is being a contractor or subcontractor, operating as an independent, self-employed person and negotiating your prices as you see fit, doing work for anyone you see fit.

There is a hybrid situation in which you are not an employee but are, technically, an independent contractor. At the same time, you function as though you were an employee, despite the fact that your legal status is not that of employee. That is because in this situation you do all your business entirely with one customer. That is what makes the relationship virtually that of employee and employer.

Microcomputers are rather new, and there is not yet much history of such arrangements as this in connection with privately owned micros and working relationships with companies. However, this arrangement of doing piecework or contract work exclusively for one customer and thus being a virtual employee, although not an employee legally, has been common in a number of fields. For example, there are many in the construction industries who specialize in hanging doors or installing windows, and do so under such an arrangement as that just described. It was once quite a common practice in the garment industry, even in modern times.

## PROS AND CONS OF EACH ARRANGEMENT

Not surprisingly, there are pluses and minuses in each arrangement. Being an employee offers certain benefits which have a cash value (e.g., paid time off, insurance, hospitalization) and some which do not have a quantifiable value such as relative security. Being an independent contractor—a totally independent contractor—confers the freedom to seek business everywhere, to ask for whatever prices you think you should command, to work when you wish and stop work when you wish, and sundry other, related benefits such as setting whatever hours you wish and even working in your own home. On the other hand you have little security, must work hard, spend money to market (seek business), and undertake some degree of risk.

In that third, hybrid arrangement, you get the best and the worst of both situations. Frequently, in such arrangements the customer will keep you busy as many hours a week as you wish, and the work may go on for many years (may thus offer security). But you will be dominated by this one customer, will not be able to seek other clients (for lack of time or because this one customer demands your services be dedicated solely to him), and will therefore be totally at the mercy of this one customer who may then dictate all terms and conditions to you.

You will have no marketing expense and no idle time, unless you want to be idle, so you may be better off financially, after all. However, if for whatever reason the arrangement is suddenly terminated, you will have to begin from scratch to find new customers, so there is also that risk factor.

Helen H. has such an arrangement with a New York company that is a manufacturer of technological products used by the military organizations of the government. Helen lives in the Washington, DC, area, operates from her home, and maintains an office there complete with her own microcomputer system and other office facilities. She represents the company, in a limited sort of way, by handling many administrative chores. Using her own computer, tied to the company's computer, Helen can print out quotations, letters, specifications, reports, letter proposals, and whatever other "paper" the company decides must be hand-carried and/or delivered the same day. The reverse is true also: Helen often picks up bid solicitations and transmits the important essence of them through her computer, printing it out on the company printer in New York.

This saves the company a great deal of time and expense and even enables them to accomplish some things not otherwise possible. It is especially economical of the time of managers and other executives who would otherwise be compelled to travel more frequently to Washington than they do.

In this case, Helen performs similar services for several companies as an independent contractor who is treated as a virtual employee. The services she renders are unique in many ways and are not totally dependent on her computer, but without the computer her services would not be nearly as valuable.

Of course, Helen happens to live in the Washington, DC, area, and is thus in a position to be an asset to companies who do business regularly with the federal government but are not located near Washington. However, if you live in or near any major metropolis, there are probably parallel situations you can exploit and benefit from; the cost of travel is high, and the cost in time of high-level executives is even greater. If you can help client companies reduce those two expense items, not to mention providing the convenience to executives of reducing some of their traveling, you are bound to find sympathetic ears.

## HOW TO BECOME A LOCAL REP

There are several ways to pursue such arrangements, some of which you will find discussed in detail in the next chapter, which is devoted to marketing: finding clients, that is. Let us talk a bit about the services and preparing to go to market and seek clients for such a service.

The service is that of being the client's local representative, or *rep*, as many put it. Companies often work through reps. Some companies do all their selling through independent salespeople, who call themselves *manufacturer's reps*, and who usually represent (sell for) more than one manufacturer. Then there are individuals known as *marketing reps*, who may or may not do actual selling; many simply do continual scouting of the market and pass on ideas, tips, and leads to the company for their action. Newspapers and magazines sometimes have reps in other cities where they think it necessary to have a more or less permanent and full-time coverage or, at least, someone on whom they can call when they need something done there immediately. Some firms retain a consultant or lawyer as their local rep in other cities where they believe they need someone highly specialized in some way to represent them there.

## SPECIAL CASES

If you happen to have some area in which you have special skills or knowledge, particularly if it happens to be a rare or highly technical specialty such as super-computer technology or foreign markets, there are some special situations into which you might very well fit: that of subject-matter consultant. A brief explanation is necessary.

Publishers of books and magazines, as well as some others who will be mentioned shortly, are not experts in everything under the sun nor do they have staff members for all the myriad of specialized sciences and activities of this modern and complex world. Yet the nature of their businesses requires that they publish books and articles about an almost infinite variety of subjects and in an almost infinite variety of specialized fields of endeavor. Accuracy is important, too, if they are to establish and maintain a reputation as reliable sources of information. Therefore, publishers and others turn to specialists in each field to review proposals, queries, and manuscripts for technical accuracy and often even for estimates of marketability of the projected product.

The ready availability of such specialists by microcomputer and telephone lines is a decided asset in this, and more and more we are turning to this method for speeding up the process and overcoming the increasing delays of depending on the mails.

It is not only the many publishers who are in need of such services and use them. Others also rely on subject-matter experts and for-hire researchers for help. The National Home Study Council, for example, which gives or withholds its accreditation for home-study courses, utilizes consultant experts to review text manuscripts and pass judgment on both their technical accuracy and on their validity and effectiveness as teaching presentations.

If you are expert in some field or for some reason are in a position to do helpful research to gather raw data or to verify projected material, you are likely to find many opportunities to sell your services in some relevant function.

The idea of a local rep, then, is of itself not a new idea, although the microcomputer and the ability to transmit data and have it printed out spontaneously as hard copy at reasonable cost is almost revolutionary. That makes a different kind of representation a practical possibility: a general representation that does not require ultraspecialized skills and abilities such as marketing, consulting, and legal practices do.

The first step, then, is to analyze the local situation and decide what kinds of needs you can satisfy as a local rep (whether as employee or contractor):

1. What kinds of companies located some distance from your locality have frequent occasion to do business in your area?

2. What kinds of things must they do in carrying out these transactions (e.g., are they architects and engineers or construction companies that pick up bid solicitations and submit bids, proposals, and quotations frequently?)

3. What are some of the services, specifically, you can provide?

4.  How do you reach these companies and sell your services to them?

We defer the fourth question to the next chapter as noted already, and discuss the first three items.

## LOCAL REP SERVICES

Consider first of all that your micro and printer, together with a modem, constitute a teleprinter: a device that prints hard copy out at distances remote from the point of origin of the data. The immediate capability this represents is obviously that of rapid transmission of material to be delivered at a distance. These can be bid and proposal announcements, proposals, reports, parts lists, specifications, and sundry other material, as in the case of Helen H. and the companies she represents.

Governments and contractors to governments are one major area of such communication needs and opportunities. Among federal, state, and local governments procurement runs approximately $512 billion annually and is growing every year. $512 billion in sales and contracts generates an astonishing volume of paper and various kinds of communication and correspondence. To get just a small idea of the approximately $350 billion spent by state and local governments each year for procurement, open the newspapers of any major city to the section headlined *BIDS & PROPOSALS* and see the variety and volume of contracts solicited and let almost daily.

A great deal of state and local government procurement goes into construction work of various kinds: highways, streets, buildings, bridges, tunnels, industrial parks, overpasses, underpasses, bypasses, dams, and renovation of all these. These contracts alone account for a great deal of money, paper, and communication because almost all are let through competitive bidding. If you live near a state capital or county seat, you are in somewhat the same position as Helen H., who lives near the federal capital. If you are in or near any city, you are not far from the city hall, which is the purchasing headquarters of the city government, ordinarily.

The services you can offer those who bid to these governments for contracts are similar to those Helen provides. You save the company executives' time and you save the company money while you make some things possible not otherwise possible.

For example, in some cases a contractor may call a government purchasing office and request a copy of the bid announcement and solicitation, but there are many cases where a verbal request is not acceptable, and a written request is required. There are at least these reasons why this is often a problem for the bidder:

1.  Relying on the mail to deliver a written request means a delay when delay is a hardship because there is hardly ever enough time to prepare bids properly.
2.  Delay may mean not getting the bid announcement at all because sometimes the demand is so great that the purchasing office runs out of copies and generally will not print more copies (even if there were time to do so).

This means that the bidder must usually manage to get someone there in person with a written request, and aside from the expense of doing this, it is not always possible to do so. The local rep can solve that problem quickly.

Delivering bids and proposals is always a chancy business because there is always a limited time allowed to prepare them, and late bids are not accepted. Local reps are sometimes the only satisfactory answer to this problem. (Some government procurement offices will not accept bids wired, telegraphed, but they can't refuse one delivered by a rep authorized to sign the bid for the company.

Local reps may be pressed into service in some cases to attend pre-bid conferences. In some cases, attendance (representation by the bidder) is mandatory in fact, but even when it is not, most bidders want to "cover" the conference and get a report on it.

Local reps often provide their employers or clients (whichever is the case) an information-gathering or research service. For example, one California firm that manufactures mannequins for automotive testing (e.g., crash survival tests) has frequent need for information searches at the Department of Transportation and other government offices, and relies on a local rep to handle this for them. A large Chicago meat packer has a rep covering the Department of Agriculture for similar purposes, whereas a publisher of various newsletters has a local rep searching out information released daily on two-way radio licenses granted and certain banking information available every day. That rep is busy at his micro every night, inputting copy to be printed out many miles away for a newsletter to be printed that night.

With a little imagination, some research and discussion with friends, and a questing mind, you will find a great many more services than these which people need.


## WHAT KINDS OF COMPANIES NEED THESE SERVICES?

The quick answer to what kinds of companies need such services as we have been talking about is that almost any and all companies can use such services. That kind of answer is not very helpful, so let us name some kinds of companies specifically.

We have already identified a manufacturer of high-technology equipment, a meat packer, a newsletter publisher, the manufacturer of mannequins for automotive testing, architects and engineers, and construction companies as some of the kinds of companies likely to have continuous or ongoing needs for local representation. One way to get some information about this is to monitor the BIDS & PROPOSALS announcements to see what kinds of things, products and services, are being purchased regularly. If, for example, there are many street and highway construction contracts let in your locality, look to construction and paving companies, the kind that do such work.

One way to monitor this is to read the classified advertisements in the daily newspapers, but also read business and financial sections of your local newspaper, and as many business periodicals as possible: the *Wall Street Journal*, the *New York Times* business section in its Sunday edition, and some of the business magazines, such as *Forbes* and *Business Week*.

Call on your local Chamber of Commerce and inquire there. Ask also at local government purchasing offices for lists of suppliers and contractors, explaining why you are seeking such lists. Go to your public library and ask the librarian for back copies of Dodge Reports, which is dedicated to information about the construction field, and to other such reference data. You will soon get a feeling for the field.

In the meanwhile, don't neglect the help-wanted advertisements in the newspaper. Frequently, companies seeking part-time or even free-lance help in your area will use classified help-wanted advertising to find candidates for such assignments.

Later, in discussing marketing, you will see some other ways to search out possibilities, but there is at least one other thing you should do: read the help-wanted display advertising of the major newspapers (these advertisements appear in business or financial sections of the newspaper). You will get some ideas from reading these, too. The *Wall Street Journal*, especially the Tuesday and Wednesday editions, the *New York Times* Sunday edition, the *Washington Post*, and a few other major newspapers are good vehicles for this.

## AN ITERATIVE PROCESS

There are at least three variables you are dealing with:

Your locality and local facilities and characteristics.

The things you are equipped to do and wish to do.

The kinds of companies who can use your services.

With this many variables, the process of working out a plan is un-avoidably an iterative one. You will do some preliminary research to form some early ideas about the kinds of services you can offer and what kinds of companies would be interested (would find the services useful); then you'll begin to search out the companies and you will talk to some people. Each step will probably modify some of your earlier ideas and cause you to repeat an earlier step. Don't be dismayed by this: it's to be expected in this kind of undertaking. Proceed in full expectation of making changes as you go. Maintain a deliberate maximum flexibility and you will eventually evolve a pattern of services all your own. This, of itself, is a decided advantage in this kind of enterprise for it makes your service an exclusive and unique one so that prospects cannot do much in the way of comparison shopping. However, that brings up another point worth considering carefully. Do you want your services to be standardized or customized services? Let us discuss this and consider the pros and cons of each approach.

## STANDARD VERSUS CUSTOM SERVICES

As one example of standardized services, there is a service offered by several Washington-area entrepreneurs and by a Washington-based small business association that will order *bid sets* (government solicitation packages) for subscriber companies. In this service the vendor keeps in touch with government procurement needs and bidding opportunities and selects items for subscriber companies, ordering the solicitation package sent directly to the subscriber. The vendor charges each subscriber two kinds of fees usually: a first fee for the work of setting up the account and establishing the watch over procurement in behalf of the subscriber, and a fee for each solicitation package ordered. (At least one such service has charged subscribers a $50 "initiation" fee and a $15 charge per solicitation ordered.)

This is a standard service, regardless of the subscriber's size and type of enterprise or interests. Large companies generally get more solicitations than do small ones, and some types of companies get more than do others because of the nature of government procurement.

Some vendors offer other services related to these such as a service of helping subscribers apply and qualify for inclusion on federal supply schedules, which means becoming approved sources for certain types of supply, at standardized prices.

Some of the reps offer custom services rather than predefined, standard services, which casts their work more in the nature of a consulting service. This enables the rep to adapt to each client's individual situation and needs, and charge according to the effort (time and expense) rather than on some predefined scale.

As in most things, there are trade-offs, pros and cons, in each case. The standardized service enables you to be more efficient since you provide the same basic service for all and can organize efficiently. It also is a bar to signing up some clients, although they become subscribers, in this case, whose needs do not match the standard services you offer. The custom service generally requires higher fees because each service is individually planned and designed and, therefore, is relatively less efficiently performed than is a routine service. The custom service is much harder to sell, normally, than is a set of standardized services, and that is another consideration.

You can hybridize your service, offering certain standard services, and yet accommodating clients who need custom services. This may seem to be an ideal solution, but it has drawbacks too, in that it complicates your marketing severely for one, and it is often difficult to manage a service of this mixed type if you want to remain a small or independent venture. It also offers at least one important advantage: the standardized services will provide the business base (reasonably reliable income and cash flow) while the consulting or custom services offer opportunities to make greater profits.

Let us go on now to the next chapter, the one on marketing, and get a better idea of the marketing problems and how they are best solved.

# Chapter Twelve

## Marketing

*If marketing is not the most important function of any business enterprise, it is nevertheless an absolutely indispensable one, for nothing else matters if you don't have customers.*

### JUST WHAT IS "MARKETING"?

In general terms, *marketing* refers to selling whatever it is you have to sell: finding customers, getting orders, winning contracts, acquiring clients. However you express it, it simply means doing whatever it is you must do to sell your goods and/or services.

However, if marketing is selling your goods and services, what do we mean by *selling* or the *sales* function? Obviously, there must be some difference or we would not use both terms.

There is, in fact, a profound difference, and the need to make the distinction is not merely of academic interest. It is important to understand the difference if you are to market and sell effectively.

There are several ways to explain the difference or to distinguish one function from the other in a few words. None of these will give you all the information you ought to have, but they will help to orient you so that you can make good use of the information. Here, for example, are a few thumbnail definitions:

1. Selling is the final function of marketing, the culmination of the entire marketing effort.
2. Selling is getting orders; marketing is deciding what orders to pursue and get.
3. Marketing is deciding what to sell and how to sell it; selling is carrying out the marketing plan.

Each of these is a true statement—as far as it goes. None of these tells the entire story. Here are a few observations that explain why none of these handy little definitions is properly definitive.

The failure of sales effort, the failure to produce an adequate volume of business, that is, is probably the number one cause of business failure in our economy. And probably the number one cause of sales failure is marketing failure: the preparation for selling was faulty.

Take note that this disease can affect the largest corporations as well as the small companies. Robert Hall, Korvette's, and W. T. Grant are no longer with us, as large as they were, and even giant Chrysler Corporation was saved from bankruptcy only by the intervention of the federal government. All of these suffered from marketing failures. They failed to do that which made adequate sales volume possible. In each case, in fact, they failed to recognize what was happening in the marketplace and to accommodate their marketing efforts to the changes taking place.

There are other enterprises, most of which we do not even hear about, which are stillborn because even the intitial marketing is inadequate. Their failure is much more to the point of this discussion because we are primarily interested here in launching new enterprises and bringing about success.

In fact, marketing includes deciding what to sell, to whom to sell, how to reach the customer-prospects with your offers, and how to present the offer. Sales effort takes over at that point and does what was planned in the marketing function.

If that happens to sound suspiciously like marketing includes virtually all the basic business planning and business concepts, it is not by coincidence. Marketing, carried out properly, does consider and embrace virtually all aspects of the venture, if it is to be successful, and you will soon see why this is true, although it is likely that you begin to see this already. Throughout the discussions that follow, bear in mind that the two major requirements of marketing are to decide what to sell and to whom to sell it. Does that sound like a simple proposition? Let us explore it and see.

## WHAT BUSINESS ARE YOU IN?

A major problem a great many people face in addressing the marketing function is that they don't know what business they are in. Of course, they think that they know very well what business they are in. For example, when I asked a group at one of my little seminars what businesses they were in, each of them explained what they sold. (And, of course, all looked at me with a somewhat puzzled look that I would cross-examine them on such a fundamental matter as knowing what they were selling.)

They simply bore out the point I was making: each could tell me what they sold, but none even gave a thought to what their customers were buying, or even wondered if the two (what they sold and what the customers bought) were the same.

One young woman explained to me, for example, that she was in the word-processing business. She served customers' needs for word processing, and handled such chores for legal, scientific, and other documents. Her specialty was the quick-response service (alluded to earlier in these pages), however, and by far the majority of her clients came to her in desperate need of getting the work done "yesterday."

What she was selling was her time and her machine's time, as a labor charge, but what the client was buying was rescue service. The woman was, at least as far as those kinds of clients were concerned, in the rescue business: she made the impossible possible.

Why is that important? What difference does it make what the client thinks he or she is buying, as long as the seller makes the sales and gets paid?

One reason it's important is that it helps you in doing certain things (in marketing and sales, especially) to know "what business you are in." The simple fact is that you can sell only what customers will buy—a fairly obvious truth, I would think—so it is necessary to know what they will buy, if you are to market efficiently.

For that reason, the questions *What will you sell?* and *To whom will you sell it?* are really a single question, translated as *What business are you in?* The two questions are not easily separated, although each must be considered because each strongly affects the other. Instead of considering the question of what you will sell, which is probably what most budding entrepreneurs address first in contemplating a business venture, try considering some other questions:

What do people need, within the range of the things I can do?

What kinds or classes of prospects (people) can I reach with an offer?

What matches can I make between the answers to the two questions?

Look around you at some of today's problems in both the business/career and personal lives of people. With so many women with small children back in the work force today, Louann Chaudier saw the need for a day care directory. She had a clear fix on the prospective customer and the problem or need she could address with a product she could prepare. Her customers are not buying books; they're buying a service, a solution to the baby-sitting problem so they can go out to work every day.

In that sense, every business is a service business. That is, every business can (and should be) defined in terms of what it does for the customer, the service it renders. That is the way to discover what business you are in or should be entering.

Consider the products you yourself buy and why you buy them, what service each provides for you. In fact, let us look at a list of needs and problems and what you buy to satisfy the need or solve the problem:

| | |
|---|---|
| Headaches | Aspirin, other headache remedy |
| Transportation | Gasoline for your car, bus, taxi, train, airplane |
| Job | Resume writing, newspaper, employment agency, books |
| Recreation | Movies, beach, cruise, evening at the tavern |

These needs and the suggested efforts to satisfy them are rather obvious. Most people with a headache will take some kind of headache remedy. The question remains, however: *Which* remedy? Aspirin? (If so, the famous, advertised brand or some other, less-expensive brand?) Some one of the many nostrums?

Therein lies the heart of marketing, and especially of its critical functions of advertising and selling. How does one prove that one brand of aspirin is better than another brand of aspirin (when, scientifically, they are the same chemicals)?

Take the need for transportation as another case in point. Because between the growth of the trucking industry and the airline industry the railroad industry became almost moribund, the U.S. Government stepped in with Amtrak, designed to restore prosperity to the railroads or, at least, to preserve some vestige of railroads in the United States. The failure of the railroads to understand what business they were in has long since been the classic example of shortsightedness in business. Even today, and despite the wealth of government aid and the many problems of airline travel, passenger traffic on the railroads runs far below capacity. In fact, if you study railroad advertising as an example of how railroad executives regard what they offer the public, you can only conclude that they still do not know what business they are in.

The evidence for this is that they try to emulate the airlines by laying their chief stress on deluxe new cars, good food service, comfort, fast trains, and so forth. They are saying, "Me too," and *me too* has never been an effective sales argument or marketing philosophy. *Me too* is a confession of weakness, a sure sign of a bankrupt imagination. *Me too* is an open admission of being second-best, and that is hardly a good argument for selling what you offer. Why would anyone settle for second-best?

## THE TWO BASIC SALES/MARKETING PROBLEMS

There are two basic situations facing you as a marketer or prospective marketer:

1.  Marketing a new product, which means giving prospects a reason to want to own the product at all or competing with the prospect's desire to spend the dollars on something else.
2.  Marketing your own brand product or service against others that are at least nominally the same as or equal to competitive brands or services.

In the first case, the marketing problem is to inspire a desire—perceived need—for a new *kind* of product or service and competing with other kinds of products or services for the customer's dollars. (Example: Selling the new videocassette recorders to people who might prefer to use the money to buy a new TV or apply it to a new car.)

The second case is the more typical case of selling against a similar but competitive product such as a TV receiver. Here the customer does not need to have help in perceiving a want for the product (presumably, the customer wants to buy a new TV) but rather must be made to focus that want as a want for the TV you wish to sell. Here, then, you are competing against the same kind of product. To put it more pointedly, you are competing to satisfy the same need or want: a want for new and better TV.

Each is a different kind of marketing problem, and each must be approached with full recognition of what kind of problem it is. But let us deal first with the more common problem of selling against direct competition, not necessarily selling a similar product or service, but selling a product or service that is addressed to the same need or problem. Note that because it is an important point. It means that when you sell your own brand of aspirin you are not competing only against other name brands of aspirin, but you are competing with all headache remedies.

Therefore, although airline travel and railroad travel are markedly different from each other in a number of ways, they do compete with each other as alternative ways of traveling from one place to another. If Amtrak is to sell effectively against the competition of air travel, *me too* won't do it, but not only because *me too* is a confession of weakness and an ineffective argument. It is also a violation of every sound principle of competitive advertising and selling. It attacks the competition where the competition is strong and neglects to attack the competition where the competition is weak. Let us examine this briefly as an object lesson in how to make a competitive analysis.

| | Airlines | | Trains |
|---|---|---|---|
| STRENGTHS | Fast travel between cities, comfortable, on-board service, good terminal (airport) facilities in major cities | STRENGTHS | Convenient terminals, generally easy to reach, in town, served by public transportation, arrival in town at destinations, relatively inexpensive |
| WEAKNESSES | Remote locations, difficult to reach, difficult (on arrival) to get to specific destination, expensive | WEAKNESSES | Relatively slow, many stops, food service usually less effective, little on-board service |

That is a rather rough and hasty analysis, of course, and could be developed in far greater detail. It makes its major point, which is that the chief advantage of railroad travel happens to be the chief weakness of airline travel, just as the reverse is true: the chief strength of airline travel happens to be the chief weakness of train travel.

The principle is the same as it is in military affairs. Never attack the other side where they are strong and you are weak, but always where they are weak and you are strong. (Not too difficult to grasp!) In this case, it is no great trick to point out that the advantage of train travel is an end to all the many modes of getting to one's final destination such as buses, limousines, taxis, and rental cars, as well as airplanes, by being delivered downtown. There is a cost advantage, too, enhanced by the fact that little or no additional transportation cost is required when traveling by train.

## WANTS AND NEEDS

The original meaning of the word *want* was to be without, and is often still so used in British usage. In our usage the word means *desire*. However, for purposes of marketing, *want* and *need* are the synonyms. The classic admonition to "find a need and fill it" might as well be stated "find a want and satisfy it" as a formula for business success. In fact, most of us are quick enough to rationalize our wants into needs. If we take it into our heads to decide that we want a new car or a new pair of shoes, we find it easy enough to devise arguments to prove that the want reflects a true need, a must. As far as the discussions here are concerned, the words are usually interchangeable.

Perhaps you have perceived by now that although you may be selling the same product or service to everyone with whom you do business, not everyone who buys from you is buying the same service. In the train–airline situation, for example, some train passengers choose that mode of travel because of a fear of flying. Train travel represents a sense of comfort and security. Other train passengers prefer the leisurely atmosphere of a train where one can read a book, stroll around a bit, or sit in a club car. Some dislike the hustle and bustle of getting to and from airports, often being compelled to fight to get a taxi, and often spending more time in a taxi or limo on the ground than in the airplane between cities. Some object to the cost of air travel and all the related costs of traveling by air, and seek the savings possible by using trains for travel.

It isn't the same motivation for all. But how then do we devise a marketing strategy and sales appeal if we can't appeal to all prospects in the same way? The answer is not a simple one, although the problem is common to a great many marketing efforts, perhaps even to most marketing. The answer lies in what some people call *segmentation* of the market. This simply means that we recognize that we have various groups of prospects and we need a different main appeal for each group or segment of the market. In the case of the airline–railroad problem, we need to develop marketing strategies and appeals for at least these market segments:

Those who are afraid to fly.

Those who want or need to minimize their expenses.

Those who simply prefer the relaxed and leisurely railroad-car atmosphere.

Those who hate the problems of getting to and from airports.

Those who fit into more than one of the above classes.

As you can see, wants and market segments relate closely to each other. That is, the market segments are most usefully defined in terms of wants, although some use other methods such as demographics. This is simply the statistics of our society. A statistician addicted to demographic methodology might decide to determine how many people over 60 travel more or less regularly, how many of that class prefer air travel to train travel and vice versa, and otherwise try to determine whether age differences relate to travel preferences. Logic might suggest that since people over 60 are more likely to be retired than younger ones, they have the time to travel by train, are probably on retirement budgets and watching their nickels carefully, and are probably a bit timid about traveling at 30,000 feet in the sky. That would suggest that a sales appeal for train travel would do well if directed at the senior-citizen class. However, it would take much effort, time, and expense to verify these assumptions and they might easily be entirely wrong. Or, a very good possibility, the research might produce inconclusive results, leaving the researcher no wiser at the end than at the beginning.

Demographics can be most useful when you happen to know for a fact what the characteristics of the typical customer are: age, occupation, income level, education, area of the country, or whatever else you can add to the profile. Once you know that (if you ever do) you can use demographic information to help you find the best advertising media and messages. Until you have such diagnostic data, demographics is not a great deal of help.

The more useful way to identify market segments is the way we just did for travelers, by identifying their wants. Determine what motivates buyers—their wants or what services or results they seek—and you can begin to fashion your marketing and sales strategies. (Later we discuss testing and demographics may become a useful and interesting subject.)

## WANTS VERSUS OFFERS

If you pay close attention to how beer is sold in TV commercials, you will soon realize that the commercials do not sell beer at all. What do they sell? Most of the time they sell fun: good times at the tavern and on the beach, or out with the boys fishing. They also sell the macho image, with prattle about gusto and images of brawny laboring men and outdoors types. There is also the focus on "light" beer, which means a slightly smaller alcohol content and thus fewer calories, a recognition of the fact that many men and women are diet conscious today.

Yes, brewers are today selling beer to women as well as to men, so we don't see as much of the macho as we once did, but we see both men and women in the taverns and on the beaches.

Brewers are, therefore, segmenting the market into three wants:

1.  The want to have fun.
2.  The want to be manly.
3.  The want to feel good about drinking beer while also dieting.

Again, some of the people fit into more than one segment, but overall these segments capture or at least address most of the beer-drinking population and those who are likely to be enticed to try beer.

You might wonder why the brewers don't simply explain why their beer is better than the other fellow's beer, and leave it to the audience (prospects) to do the sensible thing and buy their beer. The main reason is: logic, reason, is a poor motivator. Most people act out of emotion, rather than out of rational analysis. They are more likely to buy "Old Country" beer because they associate it with good times or because some hairy-chested movie star has urged them to drink a man's drink than because they think it actually tastes better or is made of higher-grade ingredients than "Horsecollar" beer. There are some other reasons, too (the chief one is that it is all but impossible to prove that one beer is actually better or even much different than another), but they are of relatively little importance here.

All products are sold that way, through emotional appeal. (Perhaps you are already objecting silently that you have seen evidence to the contrary, arguments for superior quality. Patience; we discuss that too presently.) We all like to believe that we are rational creatures and do not act out of anything but cool-headed analysis and solid reasoning. Fortunately, that is just not true. (If it were, a great many companies, perhaps whole industries, would collapse.)

Therefore, we come to an interesting question. Can we always translate our sales appeal into an emotional drive or want of some sort? The answer to that is simply that we must be able to do so, if we are to succeed. The offer we must make to prospects is not to sell him our beer or whatever we sell, but to have fun, solve problems, be loved, be comfortable, gain prestige, avoid disaster, get ahead in the world, avoid embarrassment.

Consider other TV commercials. The "ring around the collar" is a good one. The appeal there? To avoid embarrassment. The advertiser is threatening the women who watch the commercial, even the men who wear the shirts, to some extent, but principally the women. The message is to use the product and be spared the embarrassment of "ring around the collar."

The two main motivators, some of my publishers have assured me, are fear and greed, and research into advertising tends to prove that they are right. How is insurance sold? With visions of disasters, burnt-out homes, smashed-up automobiles and properties, untimely deaths, and other such calamities. Security equipment such as burglar and fire alarms is sold the same way, through fear.

Greed doesn't do badly as a motivator, either. That book, *How to Prosper in the Coming Bad Years,* made the best-seller lists for many weeks. Could that have been because it had *both* fear and greed in the title?

We humans are all insecure to some degree and in some areas. We all feel need for love, success, prestige, money, recognition, and sundry other boosters of the ego and other gratifiers. We all want to believe those glowing promises of great things that will come to us as a result of buying whatever it is that we are being offered. Therefore, the offer is not the product or service we sell, but the result we promise. Pay close attention to that because it is at the very heart of marketing and marketing strategy. It is what "knowing what business you are in" is all about, because you must offer the prospect what the prospect wants to buy. Never forget that the prospect *always* wants to buy love, security, comfort, prestige, success, pleasure, freedom from disaster, and all other such benefits. Find the emotional offer that fits what the customer-prospect wants to buy and is a reasonable offer in terms of the product or service you sell.

For example, if you are selling an accounting service, it is not reasonable to promise the prospect that your service will bring great wealth and fame; there is no way that you could make that promise a convincing one. You can, however, probably promise better profitability (within reason), surfacing information to help the client plan better, and a sounder footing for the business: a *reasonable* prospect of greater success. That's quite enough if you can back it up with persuasive evidence.

## THE OFFER AS A PROMISE

From this perspective, what you are selling—always—is a promise, expressed or implied. Whether the promise is an attractive or appealing one (a motivating one, to be most direct) is one thing; whether the promise is believable is another thing, but equally important. The prospect is motivated by the promise, if it addresses the prospect's self-interest, "strikes a nerve," that is, but will not usually act until you have presented some kind of evidence that you can and will deliver on the promise. If the prospect buys what you offer, the results you promise are likely to come about.

This is where the logic and reason enter the picture, *after* the promise that appeals to the emotions. Everyone would like to believe that the purchase will bring riches, happiness, prestige, security, career advancement, love, an easier life, or whatever you have promised; few are naive enough or trusting enough to accept the word of a stranger that it will happen. The prospect must have some kind of evidence. Remember that the evidence you offer is not offered to prove the superiority of your product or service; it is offered to back up the promise, to "prove" that your product or service will deliver.

That is an important point, and far too often marketers lose sight of it in their enthusiasm to laud their offering. If you offer emergency word processing, for example, your basic offer may well be *rescue service: we'll help you meet your deadlines.* The explanations that follow that promise must support the promise by showing how you manage the feat (e.g., evening and weekend work), perhaps proof in the form of testimonials from others you have served, and even evidence of your reliability by making money-back guarantees. Don't go off into rapturous explanations of the marvelous quality of your system, your peerless accuracy, and so forth. These are corollary arguments and have no direct bearing on the basic promise that represents your offer. If you want to include this kind of information or claim, add it later, after you have provided the evidence that backs your promise. (In many cases, however, adding such information is harmful, rather than helpful, because it dilutes the basic message and lessens its overall impact by distracting the customer's attention from the main message.)

Remember, then, that an offer is not what you sell, but what a customer buys or wants to buy. An offer is always a promise of some desirable result, whatever your product or service will do for the prospect. An offer is always an appeal to the emotions, never to the logical mind. Offer appeals to wants and fears, or both.

Remember, however, that the greater the promise, the more persuasive must be the evidence you supply to prove your case. If you promise prospects something that will increase their income 20 or 30 percent, that's not too hard for most people to accept, and a reasonable argument will probably prove your point to most people. If you promise to double their income, however, that will take a bit more convincing. If you promise to make them absolutely wealthy, as many advertisements do, that takes a great deal of evidence, much as most prospects would like to believe the promise. Therefore, you must keep in mind what you can offer as evidence when you decide what to promise: what you can really accomplish and can demonstrate an ability to accomplish.

## THE EYE OF THE BEHOLDER

Just as beauty is said to be in the eye of the beholder, so is evidence or proof of your promises in the eye of the beholder. Evidence and proof are whatever the prospect will accept as evidence or proof. You must sell to the prospect's perceptions, not to your own. What you regard as evidence may not be so regarded by the prospective customer. That's part of knowing what business you are in: you must sell to the customer's perceptions.

The natural question now is: How can I know what the prospect's perceptions are? It is in quest of the answer to that question that testing is done by enlightened marketers. Testing is the only way to know for sure. Typical research produces projections which may or may not be accurate forecasts of how the population at large will react, but only testing can provide reliable data as to how the population does react. The essential difference is that typical research into records and, quite often, questionnaire surveys extrapolates the results. Testing actually conducts the marketing under controlled conditions and measures what people actually do, rather than what they or recorded data say they will do.

Testing, therefore, is the most reliable way of determining what the customer's perceptions are. What you need to know about, in terms of customer or prospect perceptions, is what they perceive as their needs or wants if you are doing general market testing, or what their reaction is to your offer if you are testing an actual venture. (Later, we discuss how to conduct tests.)

## ADVERTISING

Advertising takes many forms, each with its own name so that we sometimes tend to lose sight of the fact that it is all advertising. Among the earliest methods were the many kinds of signs used to huckster products, and to this day you can see a few weatherbeaten signs lauding Mail Pouch Tobacco and a few other products on the sides of farmers' barns on narrow country roads, although the classic Burma Shave signs have apparently vanished completely.

There is still a great deal of print advertising used: in newspapers, magazines, and other periodicals. In fact, print advertising was the backbone of the advertising industry, and is still a major element of it despite the inroads of radio advertising a few years ago and the huge advertising budgets for TV commercials today. (Major advertising agencies have complete studios to audition talent for TV commercials and to develop the commercials.)

There is also, however, a huge market in direct-mail or direct-response marketing and advertising. That "junk mail" that appears in your mailbox is representative of this. Not all direct-mail advertising consists of gaudy envelopes, catalogues, multicolored brochures, and expensive *broadsides* (big, foldout circulars); included in your unsolicited mail are also occasional dignified letters urging you to call the writer for information on insurance, suggesting investments, and otherwise pursuing a more dignified, *soft sell*, approach.

There are pros and cons to all these advertising and marketing methods, but probably the one you will find most appropriate and useful is that of direct mail, although you may want to use print advertising on a limited scale. The major problem with print advertising is its cost, which is generally prohibitive for small ventures except on a limited basis. Aside from this, direct mail offers a number of other advantages which we consider here.

The drawbacks to print advertising in magazines are: (1) unless you are a rated account, you have to pay in advance when you place your order. Typically, your copy won't run for two or three months (you usually have to order that far ahead for magazine advertising), which means that your money is tied up in payment for a service you won't get for a number of weeks, giving the publisher interest-free use of your money in the meanwhile; (2) testing is difficult because of that long lead time for placing and running your copy; (3) unless you are a large-volume advertiser, you have little control over position and other factors in placing your copy in the publication. In addition, waiting two or three months for results, even if your copy works very well, may be prohibitive for you as a small entrepreneur. Moreover, in a periodical you are paying for all the circulation, even though only a small percentage of the readers are good prospects for you. Even with newspapers, where the lead time is short, the situation is not a great deal better.

The main virtue of marketing by print advertising is that it is easy. There is little to do except write and insert your copy. Direct mail, on the other hand, is quite the opposite. It is a great deal of work (unless you hire a direct-mail or addressing service to do it for you), but it has many virtues. It is relatively inexpensive; that is, you can control costs closely by deciding how large or small a mailing to do, and you can *rifle-shot* your messages to carefully selected targets, rather than *buck-shotting* your message to thousands of people who could not possibly be good prospects for you. In testing, direct mail has the enormous advantage of speed. Instead of waiting two or three months (and sometimes even longer) to get measurable results on which to base a go-ahead or further tests, you can get results in a few weeks and you can even run several tests simultaneously at affordable cost.

## COSTS

In print advertising, your main cost is the insertion cost, the charge for the space. In direct mail, you have two main costs, printing and postage, if the labor is your own, but you have the third cost of labor if you use hired help or contract your mailings out.

If you mail on a limited basis (a few hundred or, at most, a thousand or so pieces), first-class postage is probably the only practical way for you to go. However, if you mail heavily (many thousands of pieces), bulk mail will save you nearly one-half of your postage cost (as compared with first-class postage). You should talk to your local postmaster about this or write the U.S. Postal Service at L'Enfant Plaza, Washington, DC 20024, and request the booklet they have available that explains bulk mail services.

## MAILING LISTS

One cost of direct mail, for many people, is the cost of the mailing list(s). There are many companies in the business of compiling and renting out (renting, not selling) their mailing lists, and you can order lists from these companies arranged in a variety of classifications. For example, I recently had occasion to search out some classes of prospects for a direct-mail campaign—those offering technical and professional services—and from only one source and in only a few minutes I found the following mailing lists were available:

| | |
|---|---|
| Accountants | 167,000 names (in about 15 subcategories) |
| Administrative engineers | 150,000 |
| Financial analysts | 13,000 |
| Economists | 14,500 |
| Business/industrial consultants | 55,000 |
| Management consultants | 17,500 |
| General consultants | 100,000 |
| Consulting engineers | 18,200 |
| Industrial consultants | 1,480 |
| Insurance consultants | 12,200 |

| | |
|---|---|
| Investment advisors | 9,800 |
| Marketing consultants | 1,900 |
| Real estate consultants | 8,200 |

You can generally get these lists in lots of 1000 names each, although some list brokers will not rent less than 3000 or 5000 names at a time, arranged geographically (by zip codes and, usually, in zip-code/alpha-betical order), or by any of several other parameters. (Most of these lists are in computer files and can be printed out in any of a variety of ways or formats.) Typical rental fees are from about $35 per 1000 names to $75 per 1000 names.

There are other ways to get mailing lists, including compiling your own, as suggested in the previous chapter, from advertising in newspapers and by inserting small inquiry advertisements designed especially to produce inquiries and thus identify prospects for your services or products. You can also turn to various directories, many of which you will find in your public library.

Whether you want to use direct mail heavily is primarily determined by what you wish to sell. If you are selling your personal services in some form, you probably want to confine your marketing to your local area. (There are exceptions to this such as writing resumés for customers all over the country, using the mails as the medium of exchange.) If you are selling a product, it is likely that you will want to sell it all over the United States (may, in fact, be compelled to sell nationally, to make the venture viable) and will, therefore, be actually doing business by mail instead of merely using the mails as an advertising medium.

## SOME ADVERTISING IS FREE

Perhaps you've heard the term *PR*, which means public relations. Actually, public relations is a euphemism for *publicity*, and PR specialists, whether they are individuals or firms (there are some very large PR firms), are charged primarily with getting favorable publicity for clients. For *publicity* you can read *free advertising*, although it is not entirely free. For the large corporation or public figure, in fact, PR may be more expensive than advertising would be, but it will do for the client what paid advertising cannot do because the public will tend to believe the publicity, whereas they will disbelieve the advertising. For the small business, publicity is usually free or nearly free advertising, however, and has sometimes been the main key to success for the new venture.

There are several media for publicity. There are, for one, all the news media: newspapers, radio, TV, newsletters, and other news periodicals. There are other print media such as columns and *new product* features in periodicals. Anything that gets your name and product mentioned favorably in any medium that reaches prospective buyers is publicity for you.

Still another (and largely neglected) medium is your own mouth and those of others who speak publicly before groups of interested listeners. You should make it your business to speak publicly as much as possible: at conventions, seminars, conferences, business meetings, and anywhere else you can draw some attention to yourself and what you do. Seek out trade and professional associations, business clubs (Rotary, Lions, and others), chambers of commerce, and offer your services as a speaker. Make your talk relevant to what you do. If you are into word processing and offer WP services, make up a little speech that explains word processing and what it can do: the problems it helps solve and the benefits it brings a user. If you are selling a directory of some sort or an information service, talk about that. Remember that you are there to sell, although it must not be a blatant commercial but must be a soft sell, a disguised commercial. But selling it is, if it is worth doing, so consider the sales message: benefits to the user.

## WRITE YOUR OWN INTRODUCTION

When you speak before a group, you are generally introduced by someone. You will find that if you trust the individual who introduces you to extract from some general information the relevant things to say about you, it will not happen. Your purpose in making a speech is, of course, to market your services: to get some useful publicity and to let people know what you do and what you offer to do for them.

That being the case, it is necessary to take steps to ensure that you are properly presented, and the only way to ensure that is to write your own introduction.

In fact, you will actually be doing your host a favor by doing this since introducing you is something of a chore if you are a stranger to your introducer. Many introducers expect you to write your own introduction, so you won't be making any waves by doing so.

Of course, you must show some restraint, and not make yourself out to be the greatest person of the last 2000 years. At the same time, you cannot afford false modesty either, if you are going to accomplish your purpose. The way to avoid both going overboard and being overly modest is to avoid the adjectives and adverbs and stick to the nouns and verbs. That is, forget all hype and simply report facts, but select the facts carefully. If you do so, you will come across as suitably impressive without any hyperbole at all. Simply report your own credentials (experience, when, where, how, why), what you do now and offer to do (e.g., self-employed computer consultant, helping managers select and install efficient systems), and what you are going to talk about. Keep rewriting your introduction as you use it, and you will soon have one that satisfies you completely and does the job for you. You will soon learn how to make objective reporting even more effective than the most enthusiastic hype.

## GET OTHERS TO WORK FOR YOU TOO

Write up your information too, and offer it to other speakers to use with the proviso that they quote you. (Be sure to put a copyright notice on the material you send and explain that you grant permission to use it with attribution to you as the source.)

Send that information also to magazines and newspapers as free information, either as free articles (make that point clear in your cover letters) or as news releases (which we discuss shortly). Be sure to send your material also to syndicated columnists. Quite often you can get such a columnist to use the information or at least part of it. (In one case, such a notice picked up by a syndicated columnist produced over 3000 stamped and self-addressed envelopes from readers who wanted more information.)

## NEWS RELEASES

Probably the most widely used tool of PR is the news release, also called press release and publicity release (see Figure 5.1). Just as you might prepare such materials for others as a service, you might do the same for yourself—write releases to publicize your own venture. However, there are definite right and wrong ways to write releases as there are right and wrong ways for all things.

First of all, the word *news*, as used in *news release*, is used rather carelessly. Some releases do contain news; many do not. If releases are the favorite and most widely used tools of PR, they are also the most widely *mis*used and *ab*used tools of PR, and they are also probably the most widely *un*used tools of PR. Some overwhelmingly great proportion of all releases wind up in the "circular files" of editorial offices all over the world.

To write a release that will do its job and find publication elsewhere, you must write it as though it were a prime marketing tool—for it is. You are trying to sell it to an editor, and the editor will buy it only if it offers something worthwhile in terms of benefit or result. What any editor wants is to offer information that is useful and interesting to the readers.

Take that release of Figure 5.1, as an example. It would probably be of extremely little interest or use to the general public, but would probably be of great interest to a columnist writing on related subjects, to editors of certain specialized magazines, and possibly to a financial editor of a publication because these writers and editors make it their business to bring news of new products to their readers. Therefore, writing a release is not different actually from writing other copy; it is still intended to induce someone else to "buy" what you are offering. And you must consider the potential interest from the other party's viewpoint, of course, not from your own.

## PROMOTIONAL NEWSLETTERS

One way to get your message into print and before your prospect's eyes is to print and publish it in your own newsletter. A great many of the newsletters published in the United States are not published as profit centers at all, but are published as PR to promote products and services. Many are free of charge (you may have been the recipient of some of these) whereas others are published at some nominal charge such as $5 per year.

The newsletter, if handled well, is an especially effective promotional tool and one that is relatively inexpensive. In fact, it may well be the least expensive way to advertise and promote your enterprise, if you use it instead of, not in addition to, all the brochures, calendars, memo pads, and other promotional giveaways. It is almost surely the most effective way to promote many kinds of enterprises.

The chief factors to bear in mind, in addition to what has been said earlier in reference to newsletter publishing, are these:

1.  Remember that it is a promotional device intended to produce sales, but is not an advertising brochure. It claims to be a newsletter, so provide enough useful editorial matter to persuade the recipient to read and keep the newsletter for future reference.

2.  Try to include some material that the recipient will want to keep for permanent reference.

3.  Have three holes drilled along the edge to suggest saving the newsletter in a standard ring binder.

4.  Don't go overboard and make the thing a burden. Keep it small (two or four pages is ample) and publish infrequently, not more than four times a year. Time enough later to step it up, if you want to.

5.   Remember that the objective is to get the newsletter into as many hands as possible, so keep the subscription fee as small as possible. Best of all, print a price on it, perhaps $18 per year, but give it away free. Get yourself a second-class mail permit and send out as many as you can.

6.   Find other ways to distribute copies such as leaving them on literature tables at meetings, seminars, and conferences, offering them to inquirers who respond to small advertisements and/or notices you persuade editors and columnists to run for you, supplying them to speakers, offering free subscriptions to members of relevant associations, and otherwise exploiting all opportunities to get copies into people's hands. (Note that some of these methods involve no cost to you, not even postage, other than the printing cost.)

7.   Use the routing box (see Figure 10.1) on your newsletter, especially if copies are going out to multidepartment companies.

8.   Despite the fact that you must not be too blatant in your advertising in this piece (in fact, you won't qualify for a second-class mailing permit if you are too openly commercial in your advertising), you must not lose sight of your purpose in publishing it. Be sure that the reader has ample opportunity to learn of your offers and to express interest in buying or at least learning more about what you offer.

## THE FOLLOW-UP

One cardinal principle of sales and marketing is that you do not sit back and wait for customers to take the initiative that will lead to a sale. Quite the contrary, a great many prospects who can be sold easily if you pursue them will never get around to calling you if you wait for them to exercise initiative. Another, equally relevant, principle is that prospects cool off rapidly when you do not follow up and pursue the sale.

The essence of this is that sending out the newsletter in the maximum number of copies possible is a great first step, but it is a first step. There is more to do if you are to extract the greatest possible benefit from the gambit, for the newsletter is most fruitful when used as a gambit.

If you do nothing at all but publish a respectable newsletter and get it distributed in ample quantity, you will get at least some inquiries from readers. You will follow these up promptly and do everything you can to convert these inquiries into orders or contracts. You can also do things that will greatly increase the number of inquiries. Let us digress, for a moment, to consider something quite basic about sales and marketing.

Some kinds of sales, generally small sales, at retail levels are made spontaneously and often on impulse. There are certain kinds of sales, usually those of *big tag* items, which are by nature not *one-call sales*. Instead, they require intensive effort and often several calls before the sale is consummated. These tend to be the same kinds of sales that are almost always made through the seller's initiative and persistence, and practically never without that effort.

Another fact of life about such sales is that even before a serious sales effort can be made, there must be an effort to produce sales *leads*, the names of people or organizations who are good prospects for those sales. A great many of those magazine advertisements that include a tear-out, postage-paid card to send in for more information are designed to carry out that first step of finding good prospects, developing good sales leads.

You can use your newsletter in that manner too. You can use any or all of the following techniques to stimulate your newsletter in producing leads to be followed up:

1.  Run a little questionnaire promising to publish the results, which would presumably be of use to readers, but are really intended to help you identify readers who are good prospects for whatever you sell.

2.  Enclose a return card or return envelope with your newsletter which is a request from the reader for more information, and represents, again, an interested prospect.

3.  Offer some kind of free report to anyone who requests it on a

company letterhead (you can ask for an *SASE*, self-addressed, stamped envelope, and save the postage costs); the subject should be such as to attract the interest of and draw inquiries from good prospects.

4.  You can offer information by telephone to anyone who wishes to call (you may be surprised at how many people who wouldn't trouble to even send back an addressed, postage-paid card don't mind responding by telephone, even long-distance and at their expense).

Follow-up to inquiries ought to be as prompt as possible, not only because prospects generally cool off pretty rapidly, but because they are as well impressed by a prompt response as they are adversely impressed by a laggard response. The prompt response, of itself, suggests that you are a live wire and mean business.

## TRADE SHOWS AND CONVENTIONS

Many entrepreneurs find that exhibit booths at trade shows, conventions, and other such events are good marketing methods for them. Especially, such exhibits are useful for developing sales leads, and if you have ever filled out cards or signed guest registers at such exhibits and booths, you probably experienced some of the follow-up with literature and calls.

However, some people run such booths for direct profit, making a charge for services or selling things at their booths. One example found rather commonly at such events is the computer-printed T-shirt, in which a camera takes a picture of the customer which is digitized by a small computer, and then reproduced on a printer as a graphic printout on a T-shirt, shopping bag, or other such item.

Others do computer-generated horoscopes (astrological readings) for visitors which they print out on a form and for which they make a charge.

This idea can be extended to many possible applications. A word-processing system, for example, might be used to generate a resume, a brochure, or other product of general interest. You might devise some interesting and different resume format, perhaps a brochure, instead of an 8½ × 11-inch sheet, and print up a master copy for the customer, or perhaps print out a dozen copies. You might give mini-seminars or lectures with demonstrations on home computers and what one can do with them and charge some admission price. Or if it is impractical to do it that way, as it sometimes is at shows, you might give free seminars/lectures/demonstrations (very brief ones, for just long enough to gather a good crowd), and then sell your self-published book or booklet on the subject. Perhaps, as a variant, you might run actual classes, giving each attendee an opportunity for some actual hands-on experience.

Any of these or related ideas can be used either way: as an income-producing effort on its own or as a means for winning new customers, or both ways. Sometimes you can do both, charging a small fee for the immediate session or product, but offering to make that refundable (i.e., to be credited) when signing up for the full program. That makes the initial session or booklet free to those who sign with you, but protects you against dead loss to idle curiosity-seekers, of whom you will find an abundance.

## TALK SHOW INTERVIEWS

Radio and TV use up material at an alarming rate, and producers are always looking for interesting guests to interview on talk shows. Some of these shows simply have the host interview the guest, whereas others take spontaneous telephone calls from listeners and ask the guest to answer the questions.

For TV shows you normally have to be in the studio, but for radio and, occasionally, for TV too, many guests are interviewed entirely by telephone.

You arrange to be invited to guest on one of these shows in very much the same way you pursue other publicity. You need to prepare some kind of mailing piece, perhaps a two-page letter, in which you present the following things:

1.  Your photo, what you want to offer the audience, and some information about yourself: brief bio, credentials, personal data of interest.
2.  An explanation of your availability and what you propose to do.

Your letter might be along the lines suggested in Figures 12.1 and 12.2. These are based on a hypothetical case which is not likely to coincide with your own. For example, you might be able to discuss a book you have written, an information service, a pen-pal service, or something else of general interest. If you are not offering a product or service that lends itself directly to such presentation as talk show interviewing, you might offer a somewhat related subject that is of interest.

---

Dear Producer:

Here is an opportunity to entertain and instruct your listeners at the same time in that most popular modern subject, owning and using a personal computer.

As an instructor in the subject—I conduct seminars at the local adult-education classes in Blackbird Community College and hold private classes in my own facility—I am especially well qualified to offer useful information and to handle all questions from listeners who call in during the interview.

We can conduct this entire session by telephone, or I can be in the studio with the show's host, if you prefer.

Cordially,


Mary Maxwell

---

**Figure 12.1.**   Cover letter seeking talk show interviews.

> | PHOTOGRAPH | THE JOY OF USING A PERSONAL COMPUTER |
> Personal computers are not just for playing games, although they are useful for that. In fact, the most popular use made of personal computers is for word processing, although many people use personal computers for managing household budgets, storing names and addresses, keeping memoranda for birthdays and holidays, managing stock portfolios, receiving special information from subscription databases, helping the kids with homework, taking special courses, starting an at-home business with a computer, joining a computer pen-pal club, or many other possible uses. We can also take questions and answer them spontaneously.
>
> MARY MAXWELL    1726 Hardship Lane    Vamos, NM    (505) 555-9989

Figure 12.2.    Brochure describing proposed subject for interview.

For example, suppose that you offer accounting services to small companies as your main venture. It is possible that talk show producers might not consider the subject of accounting services interesting to more than a small proportion of their audience. However, you can offer to discuss something of much greater interest, and still get your main message across that you are in the business of doing computerized accounting for small business. To do this, you can tackle any subject related to personal computers and their use, such as the following examples:

Household budgeting (by personal computer).

How to select the right computer for your needs.

Is it difficult to learn how to use a personal computer?

Do personal computers help kids with school work?

What kinds of things can you do with a computer?

How to start an at-home business with a personal computer.

As you can see, this is only a partial list of possible topics that are sure to interest a great many listeners or viewers.

You do not have to list only one topic. You might select several topics and offer the producer a choice. Incidentally, the individual to whom to send your offer is not the talk show host, but the talk show producer. Even if the host wants to bring a specific guest on board, the arrangements always go through the producer.

You must, of course, determine what shows there are that are suitable candidates. If what you offer is such that you want customers only in your immediate area, you will want to address your offer to local shows only. If you work on a national scale, you will have to trot over to the public library and enlist the librarian's help in locating directories (they do exist) of TV and radio stations, the shows they run, and the producers of the various shows. (You can address the show by title, but it is usually much more effective to address the producer by name and refer to the show, since some producers produce more than one show.)

As in all direct mail, don't get discouraged if your first mail-out does not ring the bell. Reminder mail-outs, following the first one, will often produce far better results did than the first one. In fact, in some cases, it takes several mailings to do the job.

## SOME MISCELLANEOUS OPPORTUNITIES

For the small, work-at-home entrepreneur there are a number of other opportunities to do some advertising and win some business at little or no expense other than a little of your time.

Today, most of the thousands of supermarkets that form the core of busy shopping centers have large bulletin boards on which are displayed advertising brochures of many kinds. There is a section of the board devoted to slots for little yellow cards you can use to sell a bicycle, announce a baby-sitting service, or announce a desire to buy an air conditioner. If whatever it is you want to sell is of interest to the general public, one of these little cards posted in as many supermarkets as you can reach will bring you some business. (I once ordered my business cards from a dealer whose brochure I found in one of these bulletin boards.)

Most public libraries have a literature table or rack or even a bulletin board, in many cases. Try posting your notices in some of these, as well.

The same may be said for many other public places: town halls, recreation centers, community centers, and other such establishments.

Some chambers of commerce publish directories of businesses in their areas of interest. You may be able to get yourself listed in one or more of these.

Newsletter editors are always seeking items of interest to their readers. Hunt up those you think relevant (newsletters that reach the kinds of people you believe are good prospects for you), send them your notices of available services or products, and/or offer to write brief articles for them without charge.

## BARTER

That latter item, writing brief articles without charge, invokes a new image: barter. Because of the high income tax burden of modern times, a great many people have resorted to barter, trading goods and services for other goods and services rather than for money. In some quarters, barter has always existed and one of these is advertising in some periodicals, especially the smaller ones that circulate among small mail-order dealers. Most of those who write columns in those little periodicals do so in exchange for advertising space. If what you wish to sell fits into this format, you may wish to try your hand at this, if those who read these little periodicals are good prospects for you.

As a rule, the larger publications, those slick-paper magazines (which are called *slicks* by writers, in fact), do not barter their advertising space, although they do go in for P.O. and P.I. advertising far more than they wish anyone to know. (Those are advertisements for which they get paid so much for each order or inquiry received, rather than for the space used as they would normally.) However, as one prominent author has observed, everything is negotiable, and it is entirely possible that you may be able to arrange to barter an article or column for advertising space in a prominent publication.

## WRITING BIDS AND PROPOSALS

One important element in any enterprise that is based on signing individual contracts with customers is the proposal. Ordinarily, when a customer seeks a supplier to undertake custom work or almost any project that constitutes a large effort and a substantial budget, the customer is going to ask for bids or proposals.

The two are not the same and it is necessary to understand the difference. Nor, in fact, does everyone have the same idea in mind when referring to proposals. Here is the essential difference.

A bid is generally a statement of price alone, although usually accompanied by a list of specifications to clarify precisely what the price will buy, and a statement of terms and conditions, especially what the seller or bidder expects the buyer to do.

A proposal includes the information generally found in a bid, but also discusses the project, explains the bidder's rationale in planning the project, presents the bidder's credentials, and otherwise works to sell the project.

In the commercial world a great many people submit bids when asked to submit proposals because they do not understand the difference. That is, they submit paper that explains what they will do, what it will cost, and what is expected of the customer, but the paper makes no effort to persuade the customer and is evidently based on the assumption that the customer will accept the lowest bid without regard to other considerations.

The fact is that if the customer wishes to make an award to the lowest bidder, he need merely ask for bids; there is no need and no point to asking for proposals.

The government, on the other hand, especially the federal government (as distinct from state and local governments, who also do a great deal of purchasing), presents a set of rules to prospective proposers when requesting proposals. They make it clear that being the lowest bidder is absolutely no guarantee of being the winner and that other considerations are important, too, perhaps even more important than price. In general, the federal government wants the proposer to offer the following in a proposal:

1. Analysis and discussion of the requirement to show a true understanding of the government's need.
2. Analysis and discussion that explains the proposer's rationale in choosing the path proposed, explanations to help the customer understand why the proposer considers this plan the best one.
3. Specifics of the planned project: people, hours, tasks, products, schedules.
4. Qualifications of the staff (resumés).
5. Qualifications of the equipment (if equipment is to be delivered): specifications.
6. Qualifications of the proposer, as an organization: resources, experience, references, other.
7. Management discussions: how the project is to be managed successfully.

This is more than most commercial customers demand in a proposal. Yet, it proves most helpful to include all of this when submitting a proposal to anyone, even to a typical commercial account, because all of this helps to *sell* the job and a proposal ought to be a sales presentation. It is, therefore, necessary to plan a proposal as you plan any sales presentation or advertising matter. Consider first what business you are in: What does the customer really want as a result of the project? The accuracy with which you determine that want and the effectiveness with which you persuade the customer that you can and will satisfy that want well is the chief determinant of whether you will be the winner in the contest for the contract (for almost invariably you are only one of several, maybe many) submitting proposals in bidding for the contract.

## PROPOSAL REQUESTS ARE OPPORTUNITIES

Oddly enough (at least in my own view), a great many entrepreneurs groan when they are confronted with an *RFP* (request for proposal). They tend to regard this as a barrier to surmount or at least as a burden to bear. In fact, there are those who rarely agree to write proposals but prefer to drop out of the contest if they must write a proposal to compete.

To those who write good proposals, proposals that win contracts, a request for a proposal is not an obstacle; it's an opportunity. The customer who sends you an RFP is inviting you to sell him! If a proposal is a sales presentation—as it is—an RFP is an invitation to make that sales presentation. Not only do you have a solid sales lead here, but you have a sales lead that says, "I am definitely going to buy. I am going to buy from whomever does the most effective job of selling me."

The request for proposals is the customer's way of shopping around. By reading all the proposals submitted, the customer can compare the plans, the rationales, the promised results, and the qualifications of the various bidders as well as the prices. The customer wants to buy the service and/or goods as cheaply as possible, but only as is consistent with his idea of necessary quality, performance, dependability, and other considerations. The customer is looking to the proposers not only to argue the merits of their own offerings, but also to help him or her, the customer, gain a suitable education in whatever is involved in satisfying the requirement. Therefore, the proposal to sell the customer must usually also "educate" the customer by explaining the rationale. Never assume that the customer can easily see the merits of your proposed plan of action. The customer may or may not be as expert as you at whatever work is entailed, and so may or may not perceive the merits of what you offer. You can only assume that it is necessary to explain yourself in detail, to explain *why* your plan or product is superior.


## BUT WHEN THE CUSTOMER DOES NOT ASK FOR PROPOSALS

Although in many businesses (such as those involving customer services in substantial volume) proposal requests are almost obligatory, there are many exceptions, and these especially in the case of relatively small-volume services and projects. That is, there are many cases where the customer does not ask for proposals, but merely inquires as a kind of shopping around for a supplier of some kind of service, or perhaps even asks for quotations, prices only, that is. What then?

What this means, usually, is that the customer is interested in price only, and seeks the lowest bidder. Perhaps the customer has some consciousness of quality and other considerations than price alone, but hasn't really given it a great deal of thought. That is, the fact that a customer appears to be seeking a low bidder does not necessarily mean that the customer cannot be persuaded to give consideration to other factors than price alone. (It may well be that the customer has had no experience with proposals, and isn't aware of the process of selecting a supplier through the proposal process.)

If a proposal request is an invitation to make a sales presentation and thus represents an opportunity, it would make good sense to do everything possible to create such opportunities when they do not already exist. A few entrepreneurs do realize this and they, therefore, take positive steps to induce the customer to accept a proposal and use that as a basis to judge where, how, and to whom to award the contract (or purchase order, for that matter).

There are two situations which prevail in this respect. In the first, a supplier submits an unsolicited proposal because the supplier believes that the customer will benefit by something the supplier has to offer. The proposal is, therefore, somewhat in the nature of a specialized, custom-written brochure that attempts to persuade the customer to become interested in buying what the unsolicited proposal offers.

In the alternative situation, the supplier wisely proposes to respond to the customer's inquiry with a proposal (usually a *letter proposal*, which is a letter of a few pages, but includes all the functional elements of any proposal). In short, when a prospect inquires, even casually, about what you have to offer, what your charges are, what your availability is at the moment, and/or other particulars of what you can do, be cautious about your answers. Instead of making direct answers, try to lead the exchange into a proposal situation.

You kill the sale if you supply immediate and direct answers to such questions as, "What does your service cost?" or, "What would it cost me to have you handle my accounting every month?" Obviously, the customer is not thinking beyond price, and is apparently assuming that everyone who does what you do provides services equal to each other in quality, accuracy, promptness, dependability, and so forth. Unless you are so low in price that you are confident of winning all jobs on that basis, furnishing the price asked for, or answering even other questions of the same nature, is instant death for the sale almost invariably. (It is, in fact, a cardinal rule to withhold price discussions until you have had a chance to make the sales presentation.)

The way to handle this is to respond with some such thing as, "It's difficult to give you a sensible answer without knowing more about what you need. In fact, it would be totally unfair to you to give you a short answer like that. If I knew more about your need, and could study your problem, I would probably be able to show you better and less expensive ways to do things. Why not tell me a little bit about your problem, and let me give you a brief proposal that will explain everything to you as a result of my study.

"There is no charge for this—it's part of marketing expense—so you have nothing to lose, of course, and a great deal to gain, even if you buy from somebody else. You are not obligated to me in any way."

Then prepare that little letter proposal, and you'll have a good chance of winning the job.

## A BASIC PRINCIPLE ABOUT HEADLINES AND TITLES

A number of prominent advertising executives have agreed that headlines and titles (which are almost the same thing) have a special importance. Their consensus is that if you don't sell it in the headline (title), you will probably not sell it at all, no matter how good the rest of your copy is. (It is likely that few readers will read the copy, if the headline fails to grab them.) Conversely, they say, if you do an effective job in the headline, the rest of the copy can be relatively weak and still succeed.

Perhaps that's something of an overstatement, but it's true enough that most people won't read beyond the headline if the headline does not capture their interest. They will judge what the thing is all about by whatever the headline (title) says or does not say. Here are a few book titles that told the whole story in a single headline and helped the books to their successes. The titles serve very well as advertising headlines, do they not?

HOW I RAISED MYSELF FROM FAILURE TO SUCCESS IN SELLING

HOW TO FORM YOUR OWN CORPORATION WITHOUT A LAWYER FOR UNDER $50

UP YOUR OWN ORGANIZATION!

HOW TO SUCCEED AS AN INDEPENDENT CONSULTANT

HOW TO PROSPER IN THE COMING BAD YEARS

And here are a few famous advertising headlines that worked for long periods of time (some of them for many years) without change:

DO YOU MAKE THESE MISTAKES IN ENGLISH?

THEY LAUGHED WHEN I SAT DOWN AT THE PIANO, BUT WHEN I STARTED TO PLAY—

TO PEOPLE WHO WANT TO WRITE—BUT CAN'T GET STARTED

# HOW TO WRITE THE HEADLINE (OR TITLE)

In my seminars on proposal writing, I usually ask my attendees when they write or should write the introduction. There is generally a surprised silence for a few moments while all consider whether I have become brain-damaged suddenly to ask such an absurd question. Obviously, the first instinctive reaction is, an introduction comes first. Then I can see lights dawning in almost every face before me as they suddenly realize that an introduction is written last, after you know what you are introducing!

The same philosophy applies to writing headlines and titles. If you are going to try to tell the story in a few words, you must first know what the story is.

Sometimes my publisher wants to discuss titles with me when we have our first serious discussion of the proposed book on which we have reached agreement. Again, I always suggest deferring that discussion until the book is completed, making do with a *working title* in the meanwhile. For no matter how thoroughly I plan and outline the book in advance, in the actual writing I find flaws in the plans and must make adjustments. By the time I have exhausted myself mentally with the labors of the book, I can come up with a list of candidate titles, of which I will have favorites and my editor will have favorites, from which we will finally reach agreement. (Only once, so far, has one of my books emerged from the press with the same title I used as a working title.)

I must confess that, in fact, I always write an introduction first. It is a straw introduction, a psychological crutch for me, because somehow I am psychologically unable to start with the second chapter. Therefore, I write an introduction which I plan to discard later when I have finished the rest of the material, and come back to write the real introduction.

I do the same thing when writing advertising copy, news releases, or other material. I conjure up a working title or headline and use it until I am satisfied with the copy. I then return to the headline and discard it as a preliminary to having the "real" headline "stand up."

If I have written that body copy well, whether it is a brochure, a sales letter, or anything else, my notion of what I am offering—what my promise is—should spring out at me and inspire me to write the headline. For the first duty of the headline is to state or at least strongly suggest to the reader what the promised benefit is. Let us look at those titles and headlines cited a few paragraphs ago and see what they promise:

HOW I RAISED MYSELF FROM FAILURE TO SUCCESS IN SELLING.   Truly a classic, now in its nth edition. The promise is clear enough: *You will learn, from my example, how to succeed at selling, even if you are now a failure at it.*

HOW TO FORM YOUR OWN CORPORATION WITHOUT A LAWYER FOR UNDER $50.   This, too, has become a classic and has been through numerous editions. Here, the message is explicit: *You can be a corporation for less than $50, and you can do it yourself.*

UP YOUR OWN ORGANIZATION!   Another multiedition classic with the message (playing on the Robert Townsend book, *Up the Organization!*): *Here's how to start your own company.*

HOW TO SUCCEED AS AN INDEPENDENT CONSULTANT.   A relative newcomer, but through four printings in less than a year. The message is plainly enough this: *You can be self-employed in that glamorous profession of consulting and be successful at it.*

HOW TO PROSPER IN THE COMING BAD YEARS.   A runaway best-seller, this title says: *Here's how to not only avoid disaster, when the tragedy strikes, but actually benefit from it.*

DO YOU MAKE THESE MISTAKES IN ENGLISH?   This one ran for 40 years successfully because it said: *Here's how to avoid future embarrassment from using faulty English.*

THEY LAUGHED WHEN I SAT DOWN AT THE PIANO, BUT WHEN I STARTED TO PLAY—.   A classic headline that ran for many years. It said: *You can be the life of the party, and wipe the grins off the faces of all the people who ever put you down.*

TO PEOPLE WHO WANT TO WRITE—BUT CAN'T GET STARTED.   This one made a plain enough promise: *We'll help you get started and succeed as a writer.*

In each of these cases, it was after the writer analyzed what he had to offer the prospective customer and what he could and would do for the customer (what beneficial result he could promise) that he was able to begin studying how to express it in a headline.

The headline must do more, however, than express the promise, either implicitly or explicitly. It must also be something of an attention-getter and have a little "pizzazz" in it. The problem with this, however, is that too many copy writers get carried away with their own cleverness and begin to write "cute" headlines and copy. In the process they tend to focus entirely on being clever and they appear to then forget their mission completely. For example, one writer of magazine copy for a motel chain urges readers to "turn in" at the chain's establishments, an obvious play on *turn in*, with reference to driving, and *turn in*, as an idiom for *go to sleep*. This may or may not draw attention and amused chuckles (although many people do not like puns) but it doesn't *sell*.

Study examples of advertising and you'll find this to be the case distressingly often. Achieving some pizzazz, something that draws attention to your headline, is always second to making an appeal to the reader's interest. The objective is to do both, but if it is not possible to do both, by all means make selling the sole objective and save your cleverness for other occasions.

A really good headline—and body copy too—does not wear out soon. In a writer's magazine I read regularly, one advertisement that appears each month without change (and has been so appearing for years) has the simple headline: WE'RE LOOKING FOR PEOPLE TO WRITE CHILDREN'S BOOKS. Nothing clever about it; just a clear statement with the clear implication that here is a route to success, which the body copy elaborates on immediately. There are many other examples of successful advertisements with headlines that are not clever but do the job.

It's a mistake, generally, to believe that advertising copy and head-lines must sparkle with originality and wit. These are assets if you can bring them into play and, obviously, the headlines and copy should not use trite and hackneyed terms. The procedure for writing effective copy is to first decide what the major promise is to be and then draft copy to present the promise, explain it if it needs explanation (some promises do), and offer the evidence and bona fides.

Typically, that first rough draft will be wordy, far beyond the need. But that's desirable, in a rough draft. It's far better to get it all down in writing—everything you can think of that appears relevant—so that you can then decide what is most important, most impressive, most persuasive, and/or most of anything else you are striving for, but do get it all down in the first draft. (If you wanted to find the two largest eggs in a dozen eggs, you would have to examine the entire dozen, would you not?)

This first draft need not be in any particular order. Just sit down and write out all the thoughts you have about what you sell: characteristics, effects, arguments for buying, evidence that it will do what you say it will do, and anything else that comes to mind.

In the second step, focus on the benefits: select all the benefits you believe the product or service can bring the buyer.

In a third step, decide which is the most important benefit, impor-tant to the prospective buyer, that is. That "most important" ought to translate as "most motivating" or "most likely to persuade the prospect to buy."

Finally, having made that decision, find the set of words that best presents that promise and rough draft your headline (or title).

Now you can begin to write the body copy, expanding on the head-line, explaining it, and proving its truth. Remember that the headline is itself a promise, a promise to provide more information in the body copy, and if the headline misleads or betrays the reader, it is likely to produce the adverse effect that a sense of betrayal is bound to produce.

For example, have you ever read a headline that featured the word

FREE in connection with something or other, and then found by reading the body copy that the item offered was not free at all, and the headline was grossly misleading? Or that the headline was designed solely to draw attention and had virtually nothing to do with whatever the body copy was offering?

Be sure that your headline at least implies the basic promise, and tells it completely, if at all possible. Then be sure that the body copy picks up promptly where the headline ends.

Obviously, if you know in advance exactly what the promise is to be—if, in fact, you have designed your offer especially to satisfy a perceived need—you won't need to go through some of the steps suggested here, and it is not suggested that the procedure outlined must be followed slavishly.

# Chapter Thirteen

## Fees and Prices

There is no simple rule of thumb, nor even a complex formula for determining what fees and prices to charge. The question certainly merits its own chapter.

## BASIC ACCOUNTING PRINCIPLES ARE A STARTING POINT

In Chapter 4 we discussed some basics of accounting and analyzing the various costs of running a business enterprise. That was for the purpose of helping you devise a service to help small businesses with their accounting and bookkeeping chores. However, all the information provided there is equally appropriate to your own enterprise if you are to charge fees and prices that enable you to conduct your venture successfully. It might be appropriate, therefore, to go back and review that material preliminary to discussing your fees and prices.

## HOW TO BASE FEES AND PRICES

Typically, that word *fee* is used to refer to the payment for professional services. It covers services only and is based on a flat rate, either one for each occasion or one based on some unit of time. For example, a physician is likely to charge a fee for each visit or treatment, whereas a lawyer is more likely to charge a fee for each hour of time and a consultant tends to charge a fee by the day.

This is not to say that fees have no relationship to costs, or that one necessarily charges the same fee on all occasions. Whether you choose to have some flexibility and maintain more than one fee schedule, or adjust your fees to each individual case, is entirely up to you. One can make good arguments pro and con, as the following demonstrates.

### Arguments for Fixed Fees

Some professionals maintain that it is unprofessional and undignified (perhaps even unethical) to have a variable fee for various clients or circumstances. Moreover, it leads to bargaining over fees in each case, which is even more undignified and unprofessional.

### Arguments for Variable Fees

Just as volume buyers of any commodity get special discounts, so do those clients who retain a professional for lengthy contracts or on a semi-permanent or retainer basis get discounts from the regular fee schedule. If you study direct costs versus indirect costs in the case of lengthy assignments and/or annual retainers or semi-permanent contracts, you can't help but recognize that your overhead rate is much lower because you do far less marketing when you have some of these kinds of contracts or assignments. Thus even from the purely fiscal or financial point of view, it appears to make good sense to offer special rates to such clients.

There is also the consideration that perhaps your enterprise is such that you do not regard yourself as a professional or believe that fees are the proper basis for charging clients. (Perhaps you call them *customers*, rather than *clients*, for the same reason.) That is, perhaps you have some unit of supply on which to base a price (e.g., price per page) or perhaps you get your contracts by bidding, which means offering a fixed price for the whole job.

All of this concerns *how* you base your charges, but there is another concern: *what* to charge. That involves some other considerations and rationales.

## HOW MUCH SHOULD YOU CHARGE?

Recently, an acquaintance who took a managerial position with a large corporation remarked to me that he never realized before that the prices charged a customer had so little to do with costs. He was saying this to express shock that the prices charged customers for goods and services often were or seemed to be many times the cost of those goods or services. For example, one item that costs his employer approximately $375 is sold for $695, whereas another item that costs $320 sells for $1272.

Aside from the naiveté about business that this gentleman's shock reveals, it reveals also some ignorance or at least misunderstanding of costs and prices. We discussed the subject briefly in Chapter 4 where we explored the business of helping others keep their books, but we did not probe deeply into some of the matters. Let us do so now, but let us first understand that there are certain general considerations that enter into arriving at prices:

1.  The direct cost of the goods or service.
2.  The indirect costs such as overhead, amortization, depreciation, taxes, and others that must be added to direct costs before setting a selling price.
3.  The market: what competitive goods and services bring generally, and what potential buyers are willing to pay or consider a fair price.

Direct costs are easy to determine. If you are selling something at retail that you bought at wholesale, the direct cost is whatever you had to pay for the item. If a service is involved, the direct cost is whatever labor costs you encountered in providing the service. (Even if you do the work yourself, you have a direct labor cost in the form of whatever salary or wages you pay yourself.)

Indirect costs are far more complex. They include advertising, fringe benefits, insurance, taxes, rent, heat, light, telephone, and just about everything else that is not a direct cost, but is part of what it takes to remain in business and deliver the goods or service you sell. That is far from all of it: there is also the matter of recapturing the costs of capital equipment and original investment or venture capital, and that requires some special discussion.

## INDIRECT COSTS

It's easy enough to understand the general indirect costs of heat, light, rent, taxes, insurance, and other such necessities of business. But there are other indirect costs that many who are not well experienced in business find a little more difficult to understand, yet they are every bit as important and as real (as costs) as are those more common ones.

One of these is capital equipment that must be depreciated. When you buy something that has a useful life of more than one year such as a desk, a filing cabinet, a computer, a modem, a printer, or just about anything else in the way of long-lived equipment and fixtures, you must *capitalize* it. That means, simply, that you cannot deduct the entire cost in the year you bought it, but must take part of the cost each year for several years, on the premise that it is depreciating each year.

There are no absolute rules or guidelines for this, although there are general practices, and there are rough guidelines as to what the IRS will and will not accept. Basically, furniture and fixtures can be depreciated over an expected useful life of about 10 years. Mechanical equipment (and computers may be included here) do not normally have an equivalent life expectancy, and may usually be depreciated over five years.

This means that you write off or deduct, as expense, one tenth or one fifth of the purchase price each year until you have written off the entire cost. You may go on using the equipment or furniture after that, but you can no longer deduct any part of its purchase or acquisition cost. If the item has required service or repairs of any kind, that is additional deductible cost, and can be taken off as a legitimate business expense.

There is another, similar kind of indirect expense in some businesses, in items which are capital assets when purchased, but must be amortized. And amortization is quite similar to depreciation. Yet it is different. In fact, amortization is almost a direct cost that has to be written off over some lengthy period, in some situations.

Depreciation is writing off a capital cost on a year-by-year basis at some fixed annual percentage. Amortization is writing off such a cost as part of the selling price of the product or service, without direct regard to time.

If you paid someone to write a software program or bought the rights to a program for several thousand dollars, you would have to recover that investment as part of your selling cost. To do that, you have the constraints of the maximum selling price you are likely to be able to command for the program, the number of copies you can reasonably expect to sell, and the period of time over which the program will be a viable offering, that is, before it is too out of date to attract buyers. (That latter period is known as its shelf life.)

If you had $5000 invested in that item, for example, and you thought it would have a shelf life of three years, during which time you expected to be able to sell 500 copies, you would have to recover at least $10 of that cost in each sale. That is, you would count that $10 as part of your indirect cost.

In general, it's a wise idea to try to recover the original investment cost over one-half the estimated shelf life of the item. If you think that it is difficult to do so, perhaps the whole idea is not a wise one and ought to be studied carefully.

Another example of amortization is tooling. When a manufacturer spends the money to make the dies and tools necessary to manufacturing an item, that cost must be amortized in very much the same way, by spreading it over the expected sales on a per-unit basis.

In any case, this is another cost that must be recovered and, therefore, reflected in the selling price. However, do not make the mistake of assuming that if you yourself have developed the product or designed the service, it does not represent a cost to be amortized. You should have decided what your own time is worth and should, therefore, have placed a value on the item, even if you have not actually paid yourself for the work but owe the money to yourself. You should regard that as a business debt to be paid when it is possible to pay it.

## RECOVERING LOSSES OR WRITE-OFFS

There is one other kind of cost you often experience in business which is a special kind of indirect cost: it is that of recovering losses encountered in other efforts, efforts which are usually written off as losses.

For example, suppose you invested a sum of money in developing a special software program or set of programs, and then invested still more money in marketing them. Over time, you managed to sell a few at a nominal profit, but because you did not succeed in selling nearly as many as you expected to sell, you are actually losing money on the proposition.

Or suppose, for whatever reason, that you have experienced a loss of some kind, a not unusual occurrence in business. At some point, that point at which you perceive the effort as a failure or casualty loss, you must decide to write the thing off and turn your efforts to more promising propositions.

You now have a loss on your books, a loss that you must somehow recover (and recover from). There is no direct way to recover it, of course; the money is gone. However, there is an indirect way: you can and should make that loss a part of your indirect burden, your overhead. It is something that you ought to try to recover indirectly, from profits on more successful ventures. The only way to do that is to spread the loss over your other ventures by adding the loss to your general overhead costs.

In short, you treat that loss as a typical cost of doing business, for occasional losses are a typical cost of doing business. Rare is the business that never makes a mistake or has a plan go astray. It would be contrary to all experience to expect to guess right on each and every venture or contract. Yes, even if you offer everyone the same custom services on a contract or project basis, you would have to be some kind of unusual genius to never err and overrun a project, which means sustaining a loss of some kind.

This does not mean that you should be careless about your ventures, but it does mean that you should try to recover all losses.

## THE "MARKET"

There is a market for everything, a value set by buyers. Sellers may name prices, but the prices named by sellers do not mean anything if buyers do not pay those prices. If you ask $25 for something for which you cannot find buyers who will pay more than $20, the value of that something is $20, not $25.

Conversely, if buyers are willing to pay $25 for the item and you sell it at $20, you are selling it below the market, selling it for less, that is, than its value or what you can get for it.

There is nothing wrong with selling below the market, if you choose to do so and do so consciously and deliberately. Nor is it wrong to ask a price which is above the market if you choose to do so. But to do either of these out of ignorance is a poor business practice.

There are occasions when you can get a price that is above the market, either because you are doing an outstanding marketing job or because you have given your goods or service something that adds value, makes it more valuable in the buyer's opinion, that is. It is not at all unusual for one seller to charge several times what another seller charges for an apparently similar article or service. IBM, for example, generally gets a greater price for their goods than do their competitors for what appear to be similar items. As long as the buyers are willing to pay more for the IBM product, that product has greater value and the seller is entitled to get that price.

This is why my acquaintance, referred to earlier, got the impression that asking prices bear little or no relationship to costs. In one sense they do not, when there happens to be such a vigorous market that it—the market demand—pushes the asking price up. Remember that it is always the buyers who establish the value of anything in the market, the buyers who *make the market*, as some put it. (Advertising, publicity, and other influences can also make the market, since the term refers to anything that creates demand and/or sets the price.) At the same time, remember that many of the underlying costs are hidden in the sense that they are not readily apparent, but may reflect high overhead costs, amortization, loss recovery, and other such real costs.

Setting your fee or price is, therefore, a matter of making an accurate determination of all your real costs, direct and indirect, and deciding how much of this must be recovered in your fee or selling price.

## COST/PRICE ANALYSIS

The example of recovering an investment cost through amortization reflects, in principle at least, the general method for identifying all costs on a per-unit basis and setting the per-unit price so as to recover all those costs and still produce some slight profit. This is one of the prime uses of your accounting records. Even when your venture consists of buying at wholesale and selling at retail, it is not possible to arrive at an exact cost per unit because you have to allocate indirect costs so that each sale carries its fair burden for recovering those costs.

In practice, in many businesses prices are set by external forces such as a manufacturer's list or whatever the market happens to be for that item or service, and the entrepreneur must manage somehow to survive with that price, to cover all overhead and profit while living with the prices imposed by external influences.

However it's done, you must arrive at some overhead or indirect *rate* as well as some profit percentage and direct cost to set the selling price. (Or, if the price is set for you, as explained, a variant of this process tells you what your maximum indirect or burden rate can be if you are to turn a profit.)

Burden rates, as some refer to indirect costs, are usually articulated as some fixed percentage of direct costs. For example, if your accounting records tell you that out of every $1000 of sales, $560 is the direct cost and $430 is the total of indirect costs, your burden rate is 430/560 = .77 = 77%. Therefore, if you price what you sell by adding 77% of the direct cost to each item or service you sell, you should manage to turn a little profit. (Actually, the figure is 76.78571%, but 77% is close enough for practical purposes.) That leaves you only $10 as your net profit on sales, which is only 1% of gross sales or 1.78% of direct cost, which is a bit slim for a profit margin. Therefore, you should either raise your prices a bit, reduce your overhead burden a bit, or both, if possible.

Of course, burden rates are not static. They do change, and in modern times they tend mostly to rise, so that it is necessary to watch this closely and to raise your selling prices accordingly.

## DETERMINING THE BURDEN RATE

When you start an enterprise you have no history, no records, on which to base burden rates. At this point in a venture, you must estimate your costs of doing business and base your overhead burden on that estimate. However, this is not as much guesswork as you might think. There are many costs you can calculate in advance: rent, heat, advertising, insurance, telephone, and others which are more or less fixed.

If you work in your own home, the IRS will allow you to write off that portion of your home dedicated to your business. That is, if you have a room or two rooms that you set aside as offices and work space and do not "live" in these rooms, you can charge your business rent for these. You cannot charge rent for your living room because you do not use that directly for business, or, at least, it is not dedicated to business.

Using some realistic formula, you can also charge off some portion of your heat, light, telephone, trash removal, water, and other household bills. If the government challenges these, it will most likely be on the basis of how accurate the allocation is. It is then a matter of your judgment versus theirs and, surprisingly enough, they won't fight you too hard if you are simply a few inches off in your estimating (or so it has been my own experience).

You can apply the same reasoning to your automobile expenses if you use your vehicle for business purposes. Probably the best basis for doing this is to charge yourself mileage at some per-mile rate.

Keep records, the more detailed the better. The biggest headache you'll have in tax matters is not having records. Even memoranda, petty cash slips, notations of taxi fares, and restaurant meals (when entertaining a customer or prospect) that you have made out yourself are usually accepted without demur, as long as the costs appear reasonable. But make up the paperwork as you go and have all of it ready to show if and when it becomes necessary. You will not often be challenged seriously if you have the records, and if the figures are not unreasonable.

Keep checking the books you set up to see what is happening to your burden rate. Keep comparing direct costs with indirect costs and selling prices to determine whether you are making a profit. It is quite easy for even a very small business to become unprofitable and remain so for a period of time without discovering it. So you must deliberately and consciously check. Accounting information is management information, and the quality of the information determines the quality of the management. More than one business is done in by operating at a loss for a long time before the proprietor discovers it, but it is not always possible to save the day by that time. You need "early warning systems" to survive in a small business and that means checking almost daily on how you are doing.


## ACCOUNTING SYSTEMS

It will probably pay you to set up your books on your microcomputer since you have one already. However, do not make the mistake of employing a complex, highly sophisticated system. Such systems are designed for larger businesses and not only are unnecessary for you, but can work against your best interests by being confusing, rather than enlightening. Choose the simplest system you can find, one that gives you the feedback you want on a continuous basis. Essentially, these are the basic figures you want on an up-to-date basis.

## All Direct Costs, Broken Down Into Labor, Material, Other

1. For last week (or month)
2. For year to date
3. For current week (or month)

## All Indirect Costs, Broken Down by Categories

1. For last week (or month)
2. For year to date
3. For current week (or month)

## All Sales Receipts/Income

1. For last week (or month)
2. For year to date
3. For current week (or month)

With these kinds of figures you can easily calculate overhead for year, on a month-by-month basis, or currently. You can also perceive the trend of sales receipts or income, and you can detect an unreasonable increase in any given expense. Even that is not the end: you can determine many other things by making the right analyses and correlations.

If you track advertising and marketing costs against sales receipts, you can soon determine whether your advertising and related marketing costs are having an effect on sales, producing sales, that is. You can relate sales volume against the overhead rate. (An increasing sales volume ought to reduce the overhead rate since indirect costs ought never to mount as rapidly as sales receipts do when sales are increasing.)

In practice, even simple accounting systems for small enterprises tend to be somewhat more sophisticated than this, although not very much so. Also, the complexity of an accounting system varies with the complexity of the enterprise. If you are engaged in a very simple enterprise such as word processing, you don't need a very complex system of accounts and records. If you are selling a variety of products, either hardware or software, you need accounts that enable you to judge how each item is doing so that items that do not sell well do not pull down the winners in your inventory, nor do those strong sellers support weak items that should properly be dropped and discontinued. If you sell 50 items, therefore, the books become a bit more complex as you determine whether it is worthwhile to continue carrying the slower-moving ones. (Of course, if you offer a variety of services, the same philosophy applies because it may be wiser to discontinue some of your services and concentrate your efforts on those that move more briskly.)

There is a cliché which is nonetheless true and worth taking notice of in this connection. It says that in far too many organizations, 90 percent of the total sales volume is produced by only 10 percent of the sales effort (or items sold), whereas the remaining 10 percent of the sales is produced by the remaining 90 percent of the sales effort (or items sold). The point is clear enough. Drop the slow movers or efforts that produce sparse results and concentrate on the better items or efforts.

This is, of course, marketing, rather than fees, prices, and accounting, but it is the duty of the accounting functions to point out to management where that 10 percent and 90 percent lie so that management can take the appropriate actions. Although in a small enterprise you would have a pretty good idea, even without looking at the books, of which items or services move best and which slowest, the odds are that you will completely underestimate the great disproportion between them. You must look at the actual records to get a full appreciation of what is happening so that you can make the right decisions.

## TYPICAL FEE STRUCTURES

If you operate a professional service along the lines of a consultant or similar technical expert, it is likely that you will find it most appropriate to charge a daily or hourly fee as such individuals generally do. Here there is not a great deal to guide you because the range of fees that others charge varies so enormously. There are at least a few such specialists who claim to be able to charge as much as $5000 a day successfully, that is, to be able to persuade clients to pay that much for their counsel and guidance. However, it is not too likely that these figures are helpful here in guiding you. More typical for such specialists are daily fees of from $300 to $750, with most in the midrange of approximately $500.

That works out to about $60 to $70 per hour if you wish to charge by the hour as lawyers generally do, and the typical hourly fees for lawyers range about $75 to $100 per hour.

Now it may occur to you that $500 a day is a huge amount of money for your personal services. However, you must consider your overhead, and you do have overhead even if you work from your own home and have no employees and little capital equipment or furniture. Here's why.

You should be paying yourself a regular salary or owing it to yourself, if there are times when you cannot actually pay yourself. Nevertheless, your time is worth money, and you must consider your business as something separate and apart from yourself personally. Therefore, you would no more work free of charge for that business than you would work free of charge for anyone else. To put this into other words, your own salary is not profit; it is cost, a cost of doing business. When you are performing a service for which you are billing a client, that labor cost you represent is a direct cost. When you are not employed at something you can bill—not on billable time—you are on overhead. Your salary goes on, but it is now a cost to your company. If you are working on your books, it is administrative time; if you are calling on customer prospects or mailing out brochures, it is marketing time; if you are doing nothing, reading the newspaper, it is idle time. All of these are indirect, overhead, costs. All are costs that must be recovered in your fees and prices.

If you manage to get only one day's work each week and command $400 a day, that is $400 total. From that must come everything else, all the indirect costs. Thus the daily rate really doesn't mean very much unless you get enough days' work each month.

That is a problem for many who offer specialized services. Such work is often a feast-or-famine kind of business. Those who are most successful in operating such an enterprise often do so by having a few other strings to their bow, other income-producing activities such as the newsletter discussed earlier, lecturing for fees, producing seminars, writing articles and books, selling books, or any of several other things to supplement their main activity. One man who started out to establish himself as a professional consultant self-published his own little book on the subject, and now spends most of his time publishing and selling a small library of over a dozen books on the subject. Another runs a newsletter and retails a number of books related to consulting and consultants. Another fills his otherwise idle hours with as many seminars as he can find time to produce.

It is possible to diversify in another way, by doing nothing but consulting but offering a variety of consulting services. There are some who do that. There are also a few others who make an enterprise out of services for other technical or professional specialists such as networking parties and referral services.

## SEMINARS AND TRAINING

There are at least two different ways to produce and present seminars and/or training sessions. You can announce such a session, open to anyone who wishes to attend, and charge a registration or admission fee. You can also do such sessions on a custom, to-order basis for organizations such as companies, universities, associations, and/or others. In fact, some seminar producers will retain you to make the seminar presentations which they produce. Here are the pros and cons of the two basic situations.

## Producing Your Own Seminars

This is the most profitable way to present seminars since you get all the receipts and the costs are not that great. If you can fill a room (20 to 50 people, as a rough rule of thumb) you can make a good day's pay.

The problem is that it is not just a day's work. You will spend a good bit of time mailing announcements out, making up materials, talking on the telephone, getting brochures and letters printed, making arrangements, and otherwise preparing.

Then there is risk. You have to make commitments without knowing how many people you will attract.

Typically, for a full day's seminar, fees vary from as little as $75 to as much as $300. Your range ought to be somewhere between these extremes if you are going to hand out a manual, conduct the session at a motel meeting room, serve coffee, and put on a professional presentation. You may have to pay speakers, too, although many people conduct all-day seminars alone.

If you want to reduce the risk while you feel your way with this, you may wish to put on mini-seminars of a couple hours in your own home for a limited audience of perhaps 10 or 15 people at a suitably smaller fee, or you may wish to make the program one of several two-hour sessions once or twice a week.

Getting attendees is the most expensive and most difficult part. If you are appealing to companies to send employees to a program that helps them do their jobs more effectively, you can probably get mailing lists and sell attendance by means of direct mail. If you are appealing to individuals, however, it is difficult to get mailing lists unless you first run inquiry advertising in the newspapers and/or by local radio, so you may be compelled to resort to display advertising in your local newspaper, a rather expensive proposition.

## Producing Custom or Contract Seminars

Frequently, companies who have a number of employees to be trained will retain a seminar leader to present his or her seminar as an in-house production. In this situation you use your own regular materials and program, but the customer provides all the facilities. Companies are not the only ones who might retain you for this. There are others.

One other is the local university or college putting on adult-education courses or seminars. If you have a prepared program, you can approach these institutions; quite often they will hire you on the spot.

There are associations who will hire you, too, especially when they have conventions and are making up programs. The situation is quite similar to that of producing a seminar for a company.

Finally, there are those who produce seminars as a full-time business, and who are often looking for people and programs to add to their offerings. These people will charge attendees, but as far as you are concerned, you will work for a flat fee (although some may ask you to work on a percentage) and the producer will handle all the arrangements.

The minimum you should ask for such a session is your normal day's consulting fee, although normally you should be able to do better than that. In any case, that ought to be your minimum fee. There are many associations and companies who are convinced that a full-day seminar costing them less than a $1000 cannot be very good, and you may do your cause more harm than good by being too modest in what you ask for. Pricing low is not always helpful, and this is one case where it often is not.

In any case, don't be too hasty in quoting a price. There are some customers who are seeking truly custom programs conceived, designed, written, and presented for them on a custom basis. Although some people refer to a seminar as a training seminar and think of it as a training session, that word *training* may very well have far deeper meaning to others. Therefore, instead of a few hundred or even a thousand dollars for presenting an all-day seminar, you may have the opportunity of earning several thousand dollars if you make sure that you know exactly what the client wants before you talk prices. It's true that many company clients want off-the-shelf training materials so that they will not have to spend a great deal of money, but there are many others who believe that they must have programs designed for them, and who are not unwilling to spend some money to get the programs developed and presented.

Today the market is ripe for such programs. Many companies are today buying personal computers for their executives and even middle management people because they believe that it is in the company's interest to do so. It is probably a good time to explore the training possibilities this trend promises.

# Chapter Fourteen

## Reference Data

An assortment of miscellaneous information that will probably
prove useful at one time or another.

## OTHER BOOKS

The pages you have been reading do not contain all the possible wisdom
or knowledge of how to use your computer to earn money, or of the
various business ventures you can enter in which your computer will
be a valuable asset. The following lists of books are offered with whatever comments seem appropriate to help you find more details about
whatever venture(s) you find attractive. This is not, however, a complete
list, but is only a starter list. Check with your local librarian to find
other titles of interest.

*Home Computers Can Make You Rich*, Joe Weisbecker, Hayden Book Company.
This is a little paperback of a little over 100 pages that tends to ventures in writing
articles and books about computers and software programs for computers with some
technical coverage and not a great deal of depth in any subject.

*Making Money With Your Microcomputer*, Robert J. Traister & Rich Ingram, Tab
Books. This is a small hardcover (about 150 pages) that has a great many useful ideas,

although none are explored in any real depth but are likely to provoke your own imagination.

*The $100 Billion Market*, Herman Holtz, AMACOM. This is a hardcover book of well over 250 pages which describes and explains the federal government markets in great detail with ample how-to-do-it guidance for the neophyte in that market.

*Mail Order Moonlighting*, Cecil C. Hoge, Sr., Ten Speed Press paperback, 400 pages. An exhaustive exploration and how-to of mail order by a thoroughly experienced pro in the field.

*Mail Order Magic*, Herman Holtz, McGraw-Hill Book Co., hardcover and paperback, 200 + pages. Intended for the small business owner who can and should expand his or her marketing by the mail-order route. It does not, therefore, deal with business how-to per se, but only with mail-order/direct-response how-to.

*Handbook of Home Business Ideas and Plans*, the staff of the *Mother Earth News*, paperback. This has nearly 400 pages of ideas, many illustrated by case histories with lots of food for thought.

*How to Succeed as an Independent Consultant*, Herman Holtz, John Wiley & Sons, hardcover, nearly 400 pages. This explores the entire subject, including some covered in these pages. Useful if you plan to sell professional services, lecture, run seminars, or publish a newsletter.

*Writer's Market*, the staff of *Writer's Digest* magazine, published annually in hardcover, 1984 edition over 900 pages (grows each year). This is a must if you plan to write for sale to publishers as part of your plan. It is also helpful in finding prospects if you are into computer typesetting, which has become a home business with the advent of some of the modern typesetters.

*Profit From Your Money-Making Ideas*, Herman Holtz, AMACOM, hardcover, 350 + pages. This book discusses the acquisition/conception of basic business ideas and their development into full-fledged enterprises along with much other business lore.

*You, Inc.*, Peter Weaver, Doubleday, hardcover and softcover. A both informative and inspirational book by a journalist who found more than one road to success as an independent entrepreneur/professional.

*The Publish-It-Yourself Handbook*, a collection of articles and chapters, edited by Bill Henderson, the Pushcart Press. This book has been recommended by many as must reading for those who would self-publish.

*How to Form Your Own Corporation Without a Lawyer for Under $50*, Ted Nicholas, Enterprise Publishing, paperback. The original classic on the subject, this book has had imitators, but none better than the original. It is practical and includes all necessary forms.

*My First 65 Years in Advertising*, Maxwell Sackheim, Tab Books, paperback. The title is wry, but the author is delightful and obviously deserves the title "Dean of Mail Order Advertising," which has been conferred upon him. It is first-class guidance in writing copy, from the master.

## USEFUL PERIODICALS

There are a great many periodicals of interest to anyone working at home with a microcomputer. Some of these address that specific interest directly, whereas other address it indirectly, but all relate to small business enterprises, mostly those based at home, and mostly those requiring little or no capital to start. Following, in no particular order, is a starter list.

*Cottage Computing*, Home Business News, 12221 Beaver Pike, Jackson, OH 45640. This home-made number, in 7 × 10-inch format, produced (obviously) on a word processor, is a monthly journal dedicated to the computer-based cottage industry entrepreneur. I found it on an especially well-stocked newsstand, but you are more likely to have to order it directly from the publisher.

*Software Market Letter*, POB 813, Vienna, VA 22180. This is available only to members of the National Association of Freelance Programmers, but if you are a freelance programmer and care to join the association, the newsletter offers help in finding markets and providing other useful information.

*The Information Age Letter*, Jerry Buchanan, POB 2038, Vancouver, WA 98688. This is a new arrival (at this writing) that offers to help those entrepreneurs in the information business function effectively on small advertising and promotion budgets and get free advertising.

*Micro Money*®, HOW Publishing Co., POB 218, Washington, IL 61571. This newsletter is dedicated to ideas, plans, tips, and guidance in making money with your personal computer.

*Home Business News*, 12221-C Beaver Pike, Jackson, OH 45640. This is a monthly tabloid with many articles and ideas for computer-based money-making ventures.

*Micro Moonlighter*, 4121 Buckthorn Street, Lewisville, TX 75028. This is a monthly newsletter on computer-based money-making ideas and plans.

*Sideline Business*, JG Press, Box 351, Emmaus, PA 18049. This is a monthly newsletter about moonlight business ventures.

*In Business* is a bimonthly magazine by the same publisher as that of *Sideline*

*Business,* aimed at small businesses, and always carries some coverage of computers and business.

*Towers Club, USA,* POB 2038, Vancouver, WA 98668. This is a monthly newsletter designed for small self-publishers.

*Profit Seminar,* H. K. Simon Co., 1280 Saw Mill River Road, Yonkers, NY 10710. This is a monthly newsletter of ideas for various kinds of small businesses.

## ADVERTISING MEDIA

There are many publications that accept classified advertising, although in some of the slick-paper magazines the classified advertising section is so small as to represent virtually zero readership. If you wish to advertise in classified, display, or display-classified columns and reach a large readership, you are best advised to turn to publications with large classified advertising and mail-order sections. (Their sections are large because the advertising in them brings results.)

Some of these are general-interest publications such as the *National Enquirer,* whereas others are specialized such as *Income Opportunities.* Which ones are of greatest value to you depends on who you are trying to reach, and the best way to judge that is to study the advertisements in a sample copy of any publication you contemplate using.

All of the following carry substantial advertising sections for all the classes of advertising mentioned. (Addresses are given only for those not commonly found on newsstands.)

*Popular Mechanics*

*Popular Science*

*National Enquirer*

*The Star*

*Army Times, Navy Times, Air Force Times, Federal Times* (Army Times Publishing Company, 475 School Street, SW, Washington, DC 20024)

*Grit*

*Capper's Weekly*

*Mechanix Illustrated*

*Money Making Opportunities* (13263 Ventura Blvd., Studio City, CA 91604)

## MAILING LISTS, SPECIAL (COMPUTER RELATED)

Following are some special mailing lists of people who are owners of computers and/or otherwise with special interests related to computers. After that are listed several mailing-list brokers who offer general mailing lists in various categories.

15,000 users of TRS-80 computers: Southern Software Co., 217 West Bassett Street, Rocky Mount, NC 27801.

2,000 computer retail dealers, 700 software publishers, 500 computer clubs/user groups: National Directory Co, POB C, Syracuse, NY 13214.

10,000 TRS-80 owners, 600 TRS-80 software vendors and writers, 1,200 computer retailers, 130 computer magazine publishers, 600 Apple software suppliers and writers, 500 computer clubs, 1500 Pet owners, 1500 Apple owners, 2000 VIC owners: Computermat, POB 1664, Lake Havasu City, AZ 86403.

425,000 micro owners, various classifications/subcategories, offers free catalogue: Irv Brechner Targeted Marketing, POB 453, Livingston, NJ 07039.

2,500 retail stores/distributors: Computer Intelligence, 3344 N. Torrey Pine Ct., La Jolla, CA 92037.


## MAILING-LIST BROKERS, GENERAL

Edith Roman Associates, Inc., 875 Avenue of the Americas, New York, NY 10001.

National Direct Marketing, 206 West State Street, Rockford, IL 61101.

Dunhill International List Co., 2430 West Oakland Park Blvd., Fort Lauderdale, FL 33311.

Ed Burnett Consultants, Inc., 2 Park Avenue, New York, NY 10016.

Dependable Lists, Inc., 1825 K Street, NW, Washington, DC 20036.
R. L. Polk and Co., 5640 Nicholson Lane, Rockville, MD 20852.
List Services Corporation, POB 2014, Ridgefield, CT 06877.
Dun's Marketing Services, 3 Century Drive, Parsippany, NJ 07054.
American List Counsel, Inc., 88 Orchard Rd., Princeton, NJ 08540.

## PROPOSALS

The subject of proposals came up and was discussed in the main text
in earlier chapters. However, for your reference, in the event you do
have to prepare proposals, be aware that there are, in general, two
different types of proposals: the informal letter proposal and the formal
proposal. The informal or letter proposal is generally used for small
procurements or to respond to a prospect's request for information about
what you offer to do. It generally is just what is claimed for it: a letter
of a few pages which offers to do some kind of work, explains the work,
and specifies the price.

The formal proposal is a separate document, usually bound in some
manner, that generally includes all or most of the following elements:

Front and back covers.
Front matter:
    Title page
    Foreword or preface
    Abstract or executive summary
    Table of contents
    List of illustrations
Chapters or sections:
    Introduction: background of information submitted, general qual-
    ifications of proposer, general summary of requirements to which
    proposal responds

Discussion: Expansion, elaboration of understanding of customer's needs, exploration of pros and cons of various considerations/approaches, selected approach and rationale for it, selling of approach

Proposed program: Specific commitments proposed: staff, tasks, schedules, descriptions of items to be delivered (products or services), other specific details

Qualifications: Proposer's experience, track record, references, resources, anything else needed to demonstrate ability to handle job

Appendices: Details that may be of interest but which customer may not wish to read as part of proposal per se

The formal proposal may be corner- or side-stitched (stapled), or bound in some other way, but should normally be bound. However, for the at-home entrepreneur printed covers may be unreasonably costly, and a perfectly acceptable method is the use of any of the inexpensive report covers you can buy in any well-stocked office supplies or stationer's store. These usually have clasps for binding the pages the way a three-ring binder does, and many have a cutout window so that you can type the title of the proposal on the title page in a position where it can be read through that cutout window of the cover. (Some proposers use a three-ring binder as proposal covers and binding, although this is a bit more expensive.)

Many clients, and especially the government, want the price submitted in a separate document, so that the evaluation of the technical proposal will not be influenced by price, but will be based entirely on the merits of the proposed program or project. Therefore, unless the customer specifically requests that the price be included (ask, if there is any doubt), do not state your price in the proposal, but submit it as a separate statement in another, sealed envelope.

## GUIDELINES FOR WRITING COPY

The general principles of marketing and advertising apply to all copy-writing: proposals, brochures, advertisements, sales letters, radio and TV commercials, and anything else that you offer as persuasive presentations. In a proposal, for example, every chapter title and every paragraph title or sidehead is a headline or ought to be regarded as such. Therefore, whereas the proposal format outline just presented uses such generic chapter titles as "Introduction" and "Discussion," in the actual case you will make your proposal far more powerful and persuasive by using more dynamic titles based on headline-writing principles. Following are some suggestions, some drawn from actual case histories, but all reflecting coverage and the hypothetical Acme Industries:

> For "Introduction": A New Broom Sweeps Clean, About the Offerer, The Perfect Tool for the Job, A Perfect Match, Acme Industries Can Do the Job
>
> For "Discussion": How to Get There From Here, A Certain Route to Certain Success, The Necessary Do's and Don'ts, The Critical Examination
>
> For "Proposed Program": What We Will Deliver; Guaranteed Results; Where, What, and When; Acme Industries Pledges; The Proof of the Pudding
>
> For "Qualifications": Acme Industries' Powerful Credentials, Here Is Why You Can Depend On Us, Acme Industries' Peerless Track Record, Putting a Winner on the Job

The same philosophy applies to writing sales letters, news releases, newsletter stories, and anything else intended to persuade. Headlines can never be cryptic if they are to do the job. They must be clear and explain the reason for reading on.

Don't be misled about this matter of using headlines freely. A great many sales letters, for example, begin with a date and a salutation, such as "Dear Friend" or "Dear Consumer." It is not necessary that a sales

**Figure 14.1.** Sample of a sales letter using a headline.

letter resemble formal correspondence that closely, and the "Dear Friend" kind of opening is a definite turn-off for many readers who find it to have a phony ring. An easy way around the problem is to eliminate the date and the salutation, and simply begin the letter with an introductory headline which can be simply typed in capitals, or may be typeset, as in Figure 14.1.

You can use your regular business letterhead, or you can design one especially for this use, whichever you find more suitable.

The same philosophy applies to news releases. Not all releases begin with headlines, and some PR specialists believe that it's not a good idea to use headlines. However, they are commonly used (as in Figure 5.1, for example), so obviously not everyone agrees with that philosophy. The idea is to tell the editor in that second or two that it takes to read the headline what the story (release) is all about. The busy editor who might not take the time to read the release is far more likely to take the second or two necessary to scan the headline.

Figure 14.1 is the first page of what was a two-page sales letter originally, selling a lengthy folio on consulting, as a profession. The second page went on to urge the reader to action and to provide an order blank. One way this sales letter is much different from others you may see is that it has none of those circles, underlines, and penciled comments many copy writers believe are helpful and even mandatory in sales letters. They may be right, but I have found that such things are unnecessary gimmicks when the copy is strong enough. If the offer is appealing enough and the sales arguments motivating enough, all the little visual tricks are unnecessary in my opinion.

## HEADLINING AND GRAPHICS

You can probably find a shop in your area that can supply you with headlines for your copy if you choose to use typeset headlines with typed copy. Most areas have typesetters today and those shops are usually able to supply headline copy of almost any size in a physical form ready for pasting down.

You may prefer to have someone else make up your copy for the printer. In that case you can turn the whole job over to the typesetter or graphic arts shop. You can usually find such firms in the Yellow Pages but your printer may also be able to recommend someone.

You may want to use decalcomania type such as you can get on sheets in most well-stocked stationers and retailers handling artists'

**Figure 14.2.**    Portion of decal type font and clip art sheet.

supplies. In fact, you can get more than type fonts in decal sheets; you can get decals of a wide variety of graphic symbols, boxes for making up charts, lines, borders, and other such items. Moreover, not all these are actually decals either, but are sometimes available printed on transparent tape, which has a self-adhesive backing, and is all but invisible when pressed down on art board or paper. Figures 14.2 and 14.3 illustrate a few of these items including *clip art*, which is artwork ready to be pasted down and available to use without copyright restraints on its usage.

**Figure 14.3.** More clip art and samples of boxes available to use in charts.

In sum, it is easily possible today for anyone to make up camera-ready copy, even with headlines and simple art, by using these simple aids. It takes a little practice, but the skills are easy to acquire because there are so many types of artists' aids that you can try them all and select those you find easiest to use.

You can also find a wide variety of templates available in any well-stocked artists' supply emporium, and these are also useful in preparing final copy for printing. Professional artists use templates themselves because they are time savers.

## DO'S AND DON'TS CHECKLIST FOR PERSUASIVE COPY

( )　Have you explained your offer immediately (preferably in the title or headline)?

( )　Have you made that offer a promise of some beneficial result stemming from doing what you urge?

( )　Have you made the initial offer an *emotional* appeal?

( )　Have you tried to be cute and clever or have you focused effort sharply on making your offer crystal clear?

( )　Have you followed up the promise (offer) by providing evidence that you can and will make good on your promise if the prospect does what you urge?

( )　Have you instructed the prospect in what you want: "Fill in the enclosed order form," "Call me at the number given below," and so on?

( )　If you are using inquiry advertising, does your copy offer some inducement to the reader to make inquiry?

( )　Is the size of your advertisement or the package of literature you are mailing appropriate to the size of the sale or order you are asking for?

## AUDIOTAPE TUTORIALS

*How to Start a Word Processing Service* is the title of two tapes on the subject, an interview with Barbara Elman who developed a successful home business in word processing. For information, write Home Enterprises Unlimited, 677 Canyon Crest Drive, Sierra Madre, CA 91024. Other audiocassette tapes from this same source include these: *How to Start a Business with Your Computer* (2 tapes), *How to Start and Manage a Computer Consulting Practice* (2 tapes), *How to Start a Home Typing Service*, and *Now is the Time to Start Your Own Business*. This firm also offers a double-sided 11 × 17-inch chart titled "101 Ways to Make $$ with Your Personal Computer" and "50 Resources for Succeeding in Business with Your Computer."

## GLOSSARY OF EDITORIAL, PUBLICATIONS, AND PRINTING TERMS

If you are in word processing or any other service that supports clients in publications work of any kind, you should know the jargon used in the publications and printing trades. Even if you are not in a related trade, it is likely that you will want to do some work to support your own marketing that will bring you into contact with printers and publications people, that is, in connection with creating your own brochures, promotional newsletters, sales letters, news releases, or other such material. In any event, you should know the jargon of the trade. The following glossary ought to help.

| | |
|---|---|
| Bleed | Printing that runs to edge of sheet and "bleeds" off |
| Blow-up | Photographic enlargement |
| Burn | Process of making metal plate from negative |
| Camera-ready | Reproducible material, material ready for plate-making; applied to both final pages and to material |

|  | that may be pasted up on final pages without other preparation except trimming or sizing |
|---|---|
| Coated paper | Printing paper coated with materials that make it dense (such as clay) for high-quality publication; also paper used for typing to make camera-ready because typing on such paper is sharp and clear |
| Comprehensive | Detailed layout drawing showing exactly where all copy will fit on final page; actually stands for *comprehensive layout* |
| Copy fitting | Process of making all copy fit together to make up pages by editorial and physical functions |
| Crop marks | Marks showing printer or camera operator what portion of photo is to be reproduced (see Figure 14.4) |
| Em dash | Dash of same length as capital "M" of font in use; generally double hyphen, when using typewritten copy |
| Font | Entire family of typeface, including upper and lower case characters and symbols; may also include boldface, italics, and even small capital fonts |
| Format | Design of publication; applies to both editorial style and to physical design and style |
| Forms | Preprinted forms used for some publications with imprinted guide lines for layout and final composition or makeup |
| Goldenrod | Yellow paper form on which negatives are mounted prior to platemaking |
| Halftone | Photograph or other continuous-tone material (e.g., wash drawing) broken into dot pattern by photographing through screen; also applied to printed pictures reproduced by process |
| Headliner | Machine that creates headlines in large type, using photographic process |
| Justification | Arranging copy so that right-hand edge of each line |

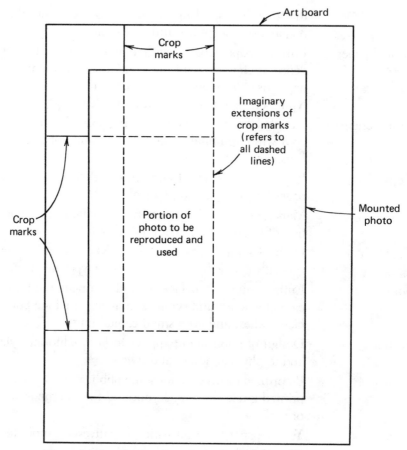

**Figure 14.4.** Photograph mounted and cropped for reproduction.

of type aligns with the one above and below it; is then called justified or right justified

Layout

Pattern or sketch showing how copy will be arranged; may be rough (for preliminary layout) or comprehensive (for final, detailed layout)

| | |
|---|---|
| Line copy | Type, line drawings, and other copy not requiring halftone screens to plate and print |
| Logo | Symbol or device characteristic of organization or individual; abbreviation of logotype |
| Make-ready | Installing plate on press and making all adjustments for printing from the plate; most printers charge for each make-ready |

## SEMINAR TIPS AND REMINDERS

Seminars are a popular activity today, and the seminar offerings continue to grow steadily as the need for special training in special subjects continues to grow. Following are some general guidelines to help you plan and conduct such sessions.

### Seminar Topics

These should be specialized subjects or aspects of subjects and information not readily available elsewhere or by other means. Demand for information and hands-on experience is great today for virtually any computer subject, but is especially great in word-processing areas due to the popularity of its use. Be sure to select a topic that offers direct benefit to attendee if directed to individuals personally, or to employer if directed to companies or other organizations. Examples of such topics are how-to sessions in office automation, selecting the right software, using personal computers in decision-making, inventory control, and project management.

### Fees

If you run a seminar in-house for an organization (i.e., on a custom basis), be aware that many organizations are accustomed to paying at least $1000 minimum for such a session, even if it is less than a full day, if they are paying a flat fee. (This does not include your expenses if you have to travel out of town to deliver this.) Some presenters charge a minimum plus so much per head in attendance; others charge only per-head fees, but set a minimum nevertheless. Typical per-head fees are on the order of $25 to $50, although some charge even more. If you run *open registration* seminars (anyone may attend), registration for a full day runs $200 to $300, double and triple that figure for two- and three-day sessions. However, despite this, many self-employed entrepreneurs offer seminars at fees well below these because they do their own presentation and keep costs down.

## Costs for Open-Registration Seminars

A hotel meeting room for 30 to 50 people tends to run anywhere from a low of about $40 to a high of $100, depending on the hotel, the location, the day of the week, and the season. (All of these are variable factors and you must call around and get quotes to be sure about this cost.) Newspaper advertising, if you use this medium to solicit registrations, varies widely according to the newspaper's circulation rates, but is normally charged by the column-inch, and may run as little as $10 per column-inch on small newspapers to as much as over $100 per column-inch on major metropolitan dailies. However, even here there are variants other than circulation: position (place in paper the copy runs) and day of insertion are other variables. If you choose to use direct mail, you have the postage and printing costs, and possibly also cost of mailing-list rentals to consider. However, don't overlook publicity possibilities such as press releases, for example, in promoting your seminar.

## Making Presentations

If you are new to public speaking and nervous about it, have the room arranged with a table instead of a lectern at the head, and speak sitting down. You will feel more at ease doing this, won't worry about what to do with your hands, and feel somewhat shielded by the barrier of the table. If the idea of doing this offends you, be sure to speak from behind a lectern of some sort; you will get some of the same sense of comfort. Also use various aids so that you do not feel that all eyes are on you all the time: posters, transparencies, slides, chalkboard, models, and/or demonstrations. Make eye contact with individuals in the audience, and do not focus on any single individual (despite some bad advice some give to do just this) but make eye contact with many people in the audience. Smile frequently, and try to *appear* to be completely at ease, no matter how you actually feel. Don't try to be Bob Hope, on the other hand; comedy is much more difficult than you might imagine, and it's easy to offend someone unintentionally, so it's dangerous too. If you must tell funny stories, make yourself the victim and the butt of the stories. You will not only avoid offending individuals, but you will make a positive impression of being a secure and well-balanced personality.

## Registration Tips

Some seminar producers announce registration fees and accept registration fees at the door. It is much better if you can persuade attendees to register in advance, for at least two reasons: you get a pretty good idea in advance of how many attendees you will have, and you have the use of the money, relieving your own cash-flow burden. To do this, caution prospects about limited seating and the need for early registration, and offer an inducement by making registration at the door a bit more expensive. Arrange to accept Master Charge and Visa (see your local Visa and Master Charge card-issuing banks for details of how to do this, for it's quite simple) to increase response.

## Miscellaneous Tips

If you are using direct mail to solicit seminar attendance, allow six to eight weeks for responses, especially if you are soliciting organizations to send employees. Include a registration form of some kind for respondents to send back. If you are mailing to business organizations, you probably will not benefit from enclosing a return envelope, but it is a definite help when soliciting individuals.

# Index

**315**